SOUTHERN CROSS
CRIME

SOUTHERN CROSS CRIME

THE POCKET ESSENTIAL GUIDE TO THE CRIME FICTION, FILM & TV OF AUSTRALIA AND NEW ZEALAND

CRAIG SISTERSON

Oldcastle Books

Oldcastle Books
First published in 2020 by Oldcastle Books,
Harpenden, UK
oldcastlebooks.co.uk
Editor: Nick Rennison

The following interviews are published with kind permission of the original publishers. Peter Corris –
"The Godfather of Australian Crime", *Good Reading*, 2011, Paul Thomas – "Out of Exile", *New Zealand
Listener*, 2012, Paul Cleave – "Christchurch's Dark Prince of the Pen", *Latitude*, 2010, Michael Robotham –
"Digging Up the Bones", *New Zealand Listener*, 2014, Liam McIlvanney – "Shocking secrets and lies",
Canvas magazine in the *Weekend Herald*, 2009, Jane Harper – "After the Dry", *Mystery Scene*, 2018

ISBN
978-0-85730-400-1 (print)
978-0-85730-401-8 (ebook)

2 4 6 8 10 9 7 5 3

Typeset by Avocet Typeset, Bideford, Devon, EX39 2BP
Printed and bound in Great Britain by **Severn, Gloucester**

For more information about Australian and New Zealand crime writing
follow @cross_crime

'Out where the river broke
The bloodwood and the desert oak
Holden wrecks and boiling diesels
Steam in forty-five degrees'

Midnight Oil, 'Beds Are Burning'

'Out here on the edge,
The empire is fading by the day …
… There's a woman with her hands
    trembling, *haere mai,*
And she sings with a mountain's
    memory, *haere mai,*
There's a cloud the full length of
    these isles,
Just playing chase with the sun,
And it's black and it's white and it's
    wild,
All the colours are one.'

Dave Dobbyn, 'Welcome Home'

Contents

Contents

Digging Up The Bodies

Michael Robotham

Thus far, I have killed more than forty people in my career. The exact number is verifiable, if I were to dig up the bodies or look back over my notes. I haven't hidden my crimes. The details are written down in black and white, stored on bookshelves and e-readers across the world, documented in two dozen languages.

It might seem like a large body count, but I've been at this for a long time. I have shot, stabbed, suffocated, smothered, speared, squashed, drowned, poisoned and run-down my enemies and friends; good people and bad. On top of this have been numerous kidnappings, suicides, robberies and sex crimes.

I am a serial offender, killing for company and entertainment, feeding readers who like their crimes to be dark and twisty, with motives that are grand, or base, then never, ever (hopefully) boring.

Crime is in my blood. My great great great (I can't count any higher) grandfather, George Robotham, was transported to Van Diemen's Land (Tasmania) in 1827 after he robbed a cottage and stole a watch. He was only seventeen. Ten years later, he married an English girl, Anne Harris, who was also seventeen when she was transported for stealing a shawl. They had nine children and neither saw England again.

People have often made fun of Australia's convict ancestry, most notably New Zealanders. It's like when the Aussie customs officer asked a Kiwi if he had any criminal convictions and was told, 'Why? Is it still necessary?' **An oldie but a goodie.** Equally, it could be argued that we Aussies don't miss importing our thieves and petty criminals from England, because now we get them from New Zealand. **Touché.**

The rivalry is alive and well, and not just on the sporting field, but when push comes to shove (I'm not talking rugby) Aussies and Kiwis have far more in common than we'll ever readily admit. One of these things is that we punch way above our weight when it comes to crime fiction.

This book is evidence of that fact; a long overdue guide to the very best in Australian and New Zealand crime fiction, film and TV drama, put together by one of the world's most knowledgeable and respected reviewers and interviewers, Craig Sisterson. The word 'essential' is in the title for good reason because few people know as much as Craig does about crime writing in Australasia or have devoted so much of their lives to their passion for stories that thrill, frighten, puzzle and surprise us.

All the usual suspects are within these pages, including the giants upon whose shoulders I have stood, such as Ngaio Marsh, Arthur Upfield and Fergus Hume. These pioneers laid the groundwork for those who followed – the next generation of writers like Peter Corris, Marele Day, Peter Temple, Paul Thomas, Vanda Symon and Paul Cleave, who showed Aussie and Kiwi readers that we didn't have to look to America or Britain to find our whodunits and whydunits; our cosy crime reads and our thrillers.

When my first crime novel was published in 2004, the bestseller lists in Australia and New Zealand were dominated by Dan Brown, Patricia Cornwall, John Grisham, Michael Crichton and James Patterson. There wasn't a single Aussie or Kiwi crime writer who got within cooee of the top fifty books, let alone the Top Ten. Now our lists are dominated by the likes of Liane Moriarty and Jane Harper, along with a growing list of equally brilliant young crime writers.

What has changed? I think we've grown up and no longer see ourselves as upstart younger siblings, who have to copy what has been successful overseas. Australia and New Zealand have our own unique landscapes and language, the dry humour and disrespect for authority. We have our own stories to tell, full of characters we recognise, set in places we know. Novels that explore the individualism of the outsider, as well as mateship, gender, race and justice.

Readers around the world are beginning to crave what we are

offering: a unique sense of place and distinctive voices. We are not Nordic Noir, or Tartan Noir, or Emerald Noir. We are Outback Noir and Yeah Noir.

Our protagonists are a mixed bunch of whisky-soaked private eyes, ex-strippers, political fixers, hitmen, paramedics, pathologists, psychologists, detectives and outback policemen. The broken and the unbreakable. Heroes and anti-heroes.

If you want to know us better – this can be your guide. Follow the directions carefully and you will enter a world of suspense, tension, murder and intrigue, where you will be required to expose the lies, interrogate witnesses and interpret the evidence.

These aren't just mysteries. They are laden with information about who we are; our politics, laws, police, and criminal underworld. And they will help us explore the dark side of our psyches. That's why we love crime stories, because deep down, in places we don't like to talk about, we wonder what it would be like to pull that trigger; or fear that someone we know might be lying beneath that white sheet.

You want bodies? Start digging.

Author's Note and Introduction

Gidday and *kia ora*, thanks for dropping by. What you're holding in your hands, or perusing onscreen, is something that several mates have told me is the inevitable result of my lifelong passion for mystery writing. Or more particularly the result of the last dozen years or so during which, among a rollercoaster of other adventures, shifts, and life changes, I've loitered around the crime scene on three continents as a feature writer, critic, awards judge, panel chair, event organiser, festival co-founder, and just general all-around nuisance.

Looking back, it's been a crazy, random ride, full of memorable moments, unexpected opportunities, and hundreds of brilliant people. This mystery-loving kid from small-town New Zealand has been warmly welcomed by the crime writing community at home and abroad. I've got to wield a fiery torch while wearing a kilt and standing alongside Val McDermid, Denise Mina, and Liam McIlvanney as hundreds of mystery fans marched through historic Stirling. I've descended into the bowels of a medieval church in Dublin with John Connolly and Paul Cleave to tap fingers with an 800-year-old mummy. I've tried to keep my voice steady while speaking in Māori before elders and international guests as we opened the first-ever New Zealand crime and thriller writing festival on a Rotorua *marae*.

It all started with two libraries 7,000 miles apart, a legal magazine, and someone else not getting their article in by deadline, but that's a story for another day. The key thing I want to say is that I feel amazingly lucky and very grateful to have become so involved in the crime writing tribe. There are too many people to thank – a sampling are listed in the acknowledgements. This reader's guide is one way for me to pay all that forward.

Southern Cross Crime is designed to sit alongside my learned friend (sorry, once a lawyer...) Barry Forshaw's excellent series of Pocket Essential guides to various slices of the international crime and thriller fiction pie. I'm here to bring the pavlova to Barry's buffet.

Feel free to skip ahead and dive right in. The water's warm and we have more than 300 Australian and New Zealand authors, television shows, and films for you to hang out with.

We've cleared out the crocs and things are reasonably signposted. But for those who are interested in a bit more background and context to *Southern Cross Crime*, read on.

The current state of antipodean crime writing

How ya goin' mate? It wasn't until I started travelling extensively in my 20s that I realised this common greeting Downunder wasn't quite so typical elsewhere. I got some confused looks from new pals in America. But if we were to ask Australian and New Zealand crime writing just how it was going, the answer would be clear. Pretty good, mate, not too shabby.

Oh yeah, we do understatement a lot too. Antipodean crime is flying high internationally in recent years, arguably higher than it ever has in terms of a deep, wide pool of authors and books set Downunder catching the eye of publishers, awards judges, and hordes of readers.

We've always had some terrific crime writers in Australia and New Zealand, dating back 150 years (see below), but there certainly seems to be 'something in the water' lately.

The global success of *The Dry*, a sublime Outback mystery that won the CWA Gold Dagger in 2017, among many other awards, has certainly helped turn the eyes of northern hemisphere readers and publishers more and more towards lands 'down under'.

Just as Ian Rankin and Val McDermid opened the sluices for Tartan Noir, and Henning Mankell and Stieg Larsson did the same for Scandi Crime, Jane Harper has become the crest of an increasingly powerful Downunder crime wave. Shortly before I typed these words, Canberra author Chris Hammer won the 2019 CWA John

Creasey (New Blood) Dagger for his brilliant debut *Scrublands*. One of his fellow shortlistees was Vanda Symon, for the first in her terrific Sam Shephard series, *Overkill*. Dunedin author Liam McIlvanney was shortlisted for the Historical Dagger for *The Quaker*, which had already won Scotland's crime writing prize and been shortlisted for other major awards in the United Kingdom and New Zealand.

The year before, Harper's fellow Melbourne author Emma Viskic had her excellent debut about a deaf private investigator, *Resurrection Bay*, shortlisted for both the Gold Dagger and the New Blood Dagger, and Stella Duffy's brilliant literary tag-team with a Queen of the Golden Age, *Money in the Morgue*, had been shortlisted for the Historical Dagger.

International bestseller status and overseas awards recognition are rolling in thick and fast for antipodean crime writers, whether they're setting their tales at home or abroad. Beyond the UK, several other authors have won or been shortlisted for major American mystery writing prizes like the Edgar Awards and Barry Awards, and German and French prizes. Hit TV dramas and films have also sprung from the keyboards of Aussie and Kiwi storytellers.

For those of us who've been reviewing and writing about Australian and New Zealand crime writing for a while, it's terrific to see overseas crime lovers jumping aboard. While there's a bit of an 'about bloody time' feeling, given there have been some superb crime writers operating Downunder for many years before this recent 'wave', it's also true that there's been a surge in the numbers of people writing crime in Australia and New Zealand.

Entries for the Ned Kelly, Ngaio Marsh, and Davitt Awards have leapt significantly in recent years. Dozens of fresh voices are joining the Downunder crime tribe each year – a blend of first-time authors and storytellers from other spheres embracing their darker side. Crime (writing) is on the rise, and it's bloody awesome. Our gang is growing.

While global recognition may be growing fast, antipodean noir is not a sudden trend or 'overnight success'. The currents beneath this crime wave surging from the south run strong and deep; in fact, they can be traced back to the earliest days of the detective fiction genre.

Craig Sisterson

A murderous history

'What was the bestselling detective novel of the nineteenth century?' is a good pub quiz question that may even stump many teams at the annual Theakston Old Peculier Crime Writing Festival quiz run by Mark Billingham and Val McDermid. Several years ago, I too would have guessed something like *A Study in Scarlet*, the first Sherlock Holmes novel, or thought I was clever by mentioning *The Moonstone* by Wilkie Collins.

Wrong, and wrong again.

The answer is, in fact, *The Mystery of a Hansom Cab* (1886), a still-very-readable tale set on the streets of 'Marvellous Melbourne', a city booming because of a gold rush and full of wealth and poverty rubbing up against each other. It was penned by theatre-loving Kiwi Fergus Hume who'd moved there from Dunedin hoping to become a playwright. Hume self-published the novel as a calling card, only to sell the copyright and then see his novel take off in the United Kingdom and United States, becoming the first-ever global blockbuster.

'The success of *Hansom Cab* helped consolidate the emerging publishing genre of detective fiction, as well as drawing attention to the potential of antipodean writers,' says Dr Lucy Sussex, a 'literary archaeologist' I first spoke to a few years ago when she published *Blockbuster!: Fergus Hume and the Mystery of a Hansom Cab*. It was more a biography of a book and its astounding success than about the author himself. 'Hume understood that the setting, boomtown Melbourne, was as important as a character to crime fiction.'

As groundbreaking as Hume was on a global scale, he wasn't the first antipodean crime writer. Sussex has long championed the importance of Mary Fortune, a trailblazing pioneer who began writing from remote goldfields and could be considered not only the mother of Australian crime writing, but the mother of the police procedural in a global sense. Under the pseudonyms Waif Wander and WW, Fortune penned more than 500 stories from the viewpoint of a police detective for the popular *Australian Journal* between 1865 and 1908.

Fortune's use of a police narrator, her focus on realism, reliance on police procedure and 'almost forensic depiction of violence'

15

predated and anticipated much of the more famous detective fiction that began emerging later in the nineteenth century, notes Sussex.

When Sisters in Crime Australia decided to establish their own crime writing awards on their tenth anniversary in 2001, specifically to celebrate female Australian crime novelists, they also honoured another rather forgotten but groundbreaking ancestor. 'Ellen Davitt – who wrote one of the first crime novels ever published anywhere – by man or woman – was the natural fit for our own awards,' says National Co-Convenor Lindy Cameron.

A few decades after Fortune, Davitt, and Hume were plying their trade, another theatre-loving Kiwi swept to global fame. From her home in the Cashmere Hills of Christchurch, an apartment in London, and on long steamship rides between New Zealand and Great Britain, Ngaio Marsh wrote 32 novels starring gentleman detective Inspector Roderick Alleyn, becoming one of the world's bestselling authors of the mid twentieth century, earning a Grand Master Award from the Mystery Writers of America, and being acclaimed as one of the Queens of Crime.

While millions of mystery lovers around the world have read Dame Ngaio, fewer realise she wasn't British like her fellow Queens of Crime (Agatha Christie, Margery Allingham, Dorothy Sayers), her detective, and most of her settings, but a 'colonial' from Christchurch.

Dame Ngaio stood out from her contemporaries and peers in several ways. Perhaps her love of theatre gave rise to her sharper dialogue and deeper characterisation. The *Encyclopaedia Britannica* credited Marsh with helping 'raise the detective story to the level of a respectable literary genre by writing books that combine an elegant literary style with deftly observed characters and credible social settings.' Her murder mysteries were massively popular. In 1949, one million copies were released on a single day. The only other authors to get that treatment were Christie, HG Wells, and George Bernard Shaw.

While the Mystery Writers of America bestowed its Grand Master Award for lifetime achievement on Ngaio Marsh in 1978 – making her the first author from outside North America or Europe to receive such an honour – she wasn't the first antipodean author to earn an Edgar. In fact, the very first Edgar Award for Best Novel in 1954 went to Adelaide author Charlotte Jay for *Beat Not the Bones*, a psychological thriller set in New Guinea.

Four years later, *The Bushman Who Came Back* was shortlisted for the same prize. That was the 22nd of 29 mystery novels Arthur Upfield wrote starring Aboriginal detective and noted tracker Napoleon 'Bony' Bonaparte of the Queensland Police. Upfield began the series in 1929, during two decades he spent travelling through the Outback and learning about Aboriginal culture after he had served at Gallipoli and on the Western Front during the Great War. The books inspired a television series in the 1970s, after Upfield's death, as well as a telemovie and spinoff series in the early 1990s.

While the early days of Australian and New Zealand mystery writing saw the likes of Fortune, Hume, and Marsh excel with antipodean spins on European traditions, the latter part of the twentieth century bled into the new millennium on more American influences.

In 1980, Peter Corris melded the hardboiled genre of Chandler and Hammett with distinctly Australian settings, characters, and voice in *The Dying Trade*, the first of more than 50 books starring Cliff Hardy. Upfield's final Bony novel had been published in 1966, and publishers had lectured Corris that local readers didn't want local mysteries, but he persevered, becoming the Godfather of modern Australian crime writing.

'My enthusiasm for Sydney, tempered by all the things I know are wrong about it – the corruption, crime, political chicanery – all makes for interesting texture,' Corris told me back in 2011. ''You can't just have action and character for a crime novel. There has to be backdrop, context to the story, and Sydney provides that for me in spades.'

Corris, who passed away in August 2018, broke new ground and opened doors for many Australian crime writers who are included among the pages of *Southern Cross Crime*, including encouraging the likes of Peter Temple and Michael Robotham (the first antipodeans to win the CWA Gold Dagger) early on in their crime writing careers.

About *Southern Cross Crime*

Putting together this reader's guide to Australian and New Zealand crime writing, I had to set myself some parameters, for space constraints as much as anything. There are some fascinating stories about the early pioneers and the long history of antipodean crime writing. For those interested, I'd recommend you check out the books of Dr Lucy Sussex and Professor Stephen Knight, as well as *Ngaio Marsh: Her Life in Crime* by Joanne Drayton.

But for our purposes here, both in order to complement the fine works of Barry Forshaw in this Pocket Essentials series and to corral the contenders for inclusion while exploring the recent surge in global recognition and local numbers, I've focused on the 'modern era'. I've chosen the establishment of the Australian Crime Writers Association and inaugural Ned Kelly Awards in 1996 as our starting point, giving us a pleasant quarter-century time span.

Perhaps fittingly, the first-ever Ned Kelly Award for Best Novel (named for the infamous Australian outlaw whose gang created suits of armour to wear in shootouts with police) was shared between Barry Maitland, an Australian author, and Paul Thomas, a New Zealander.

Our neighbouring countries – which share a frontier spirit, laidback attitude, and sense of humour that's a little different to elsewhere, while having some stark differences in landscape, weather, and wildlife – have produced a range of fascinating crime writers over the years. I hope to give you a great taste of that within the pages of this pocket guide.

Within *Southern Cross Crime* you'll find a diverse array of more than 300 Australian and New Zealand crime writers, television shows, and films. I've endeavoured to be as inclusive and wide-ranging as possible, covering the hugely popular bestsellers and highly regarded award-winners some of you may recognise, as well as plenty of hidden gems and lesser known authors, both fresh voices and those from the earlier days of our modern era.

I've also gone my own way a bit (sorry Barry), by including some historical crime written during this modern era alongside contemporary tales, and some examples of crime and mystery writing for younger readers. I fell in love with mystery fiction by reading the Hardy Boys and Enid Blyton tales as well as Sherlock Holmes and Hercule Poirot as a youngster.

Anyone who encourages kids to develop a love of reading, who opens those early doors to a whole world of learning and stories and imagination and possibility, is a rock star in my books. So, there's no way I was going to write a book that didn't include some of them.

In Section Three there are extended interviews with a baker's dozen of leading Australian and New Zealand crime writing figures; some brand-new interviews conducted specifically for *Southern Cross Crime*, and some from different points over the past decade.

It's been an absolute privilege (and slog) putting this readers' guide together. The hardest part has been – despite including more than 300 storytellers and screen stories – leaving out others that readers and viewers would enjoy. So please consider *Southern Cross Crime* a comprehensive overview of the modern antipodean crime and thriller writing scene, but not the definitive final word. Come in, join the party, I hope you enjoy having a look around.

A note on locating authors in *Southern Cross Crime*

In order to bring some shape to this survey of modern Australian and New Zealand crime writing, you'll see that I've divided things into sections, using a bit of a cocktail of geography, content, and intended readership. I'm usually more for inclusion than division, but hopefully these headings will provide some guidance for you to find things you may be particularly interested in, whether it be rural noir or mysteries for younger readers.

Of course, being the headstrong, multi-talented bunch they are, many Aussie and Kiwi crime writers resist pigeonholing, and spread their wings across multiple locations and styles. Authors living in one place write books set elsewhere: should they be placed with their hometown or their detectives? I've tended to lean to the latter. Rather than burdening you with footnotes and intricate cross-referencing that my old law professors would have loved but you might hate, I've tried to keep things relatively clean and simple.

With one exception, there's one entry for each author in the main section of this book. I've aimed for common sense in terms of where I placed them, but some were 50:50 calls. If you want to find a particular author, the speediest way is to use the index at the back.

Section One:
The novels and the authors

Mean Streets – Big City Crime

Sydney

While clinical psychologist **LEAH GIARRATANO** harnesses her expertise in psychopathology and trauma counselling in her four crime novels, she doesn't go as far as some crime writers whose main characters seem akin to author avatars, sharing the same profession. Instead, Giarratano's series centres on ambitious Sydney detective Jill Jackson, who survived a traumatic childhood. In the third book *Black Ice*, Jill has shed her cop persona and is experiencing Sydney's drug scene up close: working undercover in a dingy flat, befriending addicts, and aiming to take down one of Sydney's most violent drug kingpins. But when Jill's sister Cassie, a model dating a high-profile lawyer, overdoses and is hospitalised, plans fray. Cassie's boyfriend is connected to the drug trade and being targeted by a vengeful ex, further complicating matters. Giarratano guides readers into a gritty world where addicts high and low will do anything for a fix, and amoral suppliers harvest profits from others' suffering. Taut writing and memorable, authentic characters elevate a troubling tale that will make readers think about the lives behind the headlines.

* * *

For all the middle-aged aspiring crime writers out there who are worried they've left it too late, **BARRY MAITLAND** is an inspiration on two fronts: first, he's a superb storyteller worth studying as well as reading for enjoyment; second, he's had a fruitful career (16 novels and counting) since publishing his debut partway through his sixth decade. Following a dozen books starring Detectives Brock and Kolla and set in his childhood home of London (the second of which, *The Malcontenta*, was co-winner of the inaugural Ned Kelly Award), Maitland launched a new series set in the land he's called home for most of his adult life. *Crucifixion Creek* introduced maverick Aboriginal detective Harry Belltree, who carts plenty of baggage from his military service and the car crash that killed his parents and blinded his wife. When a Sydney journalist uncovers a link between three peculiar incidents – a meth-addled biker gunning down a woman during a siege, an elderly couple committing suicide, a tradesman being stabbed – Harry has to turn to the soldier inside himself as much as the cop. Maitland keeps the tension crackling with gripping action, characterisation, and setting, leaving readers wanting more of Harry Belltree. Thankfully, *Ash Island* and *Slaughter Park* followed.

* * *

Nowadays known for its exquisite Vietnamese cuisine, a generation ago the western Sydney suburb of Cabramatta was considered a 'war zone' by police, an open-air heroin market sparked by American servicemen and fought over in gang shootouts. **PM NEWTON** plunges readers into that maelstrom via Detective Nhu 'Ned' Kelly, a part-Vietnamese cop who stars in a very fine duology. In *Beams Falling*, the follow-up to Newton's award-winning debut *The Old School*, Nhu's body and mind are torn by past events. She's seen as a hero by her bosses but not all her colleagues, and while struggling to recover is made the token Asian officer on a task force investigating Cabramatta's immigrant population as part of the War on Drugs. Politics and personalities clash as teen killers roam the streets, but Nhu has an elderly kingpin in her sights, for personal vengeance. Newton, who was a Sydney detective herself, delivers a confronting tale brimming with veracity that spares few from suffering. A crime novel that's as much about corruption, trauma, and healing as solving a mystery.

* * *

While the smash-hit HBO adaptation starring Nicole Kidman and Reese Witherspoon takes place in coastal California, **LIANE MORIARTY**'s novel *Big Little Lies* is set in Pirriwee, a fictional suburb in Sydney's ritzy Northern Beaches. It's an area known for its wealth and overwhelming 'whiteness' in an ethnically diverse and multicultural city. *Big Little Lies* is a captivating book that explores some disturbing issues (bullying, domestic violence, rape) beneath its chick-lit veneer. Opening with a shocking death at a school trivia evening, Moriarty then backtracks and takes readers through all that led up to the deadly night. Madeline, Celeste, and Jane are three kindergarten mothers, all with secrets and stresses, meeting at the school gate. It's a world of competitive parenting, schoolyard scandals, and factions forming over children's actions and accusations. Adult secrets, big and small, fester throughout an unusual murder mystery that's not just a whodunnit, but a who-died? Moriarty melds humour and gossipy characters with sharp observations about parenting and the complexities of family life, crafting a clever tale that deepens and darkens as it unfolds.

* * *

From Rebus's battered black Saab to Inspector Morse's burgundy Jaguar (a Lancia in Colin Dexter's original books), several famed fictional detectives have their favourite cars. Billy Lime, the anti-hero of **MARK HOLLANDS**' delightfully caper-style novel *Amplify*, leans more *Magnum PI* or *Miami Vice* in his means of transport. The music promoter is notorious for racing around Sydney streets in his bright-green Lamborghini. When a legendary singer is poisoned ahead of a lucrative world tour, and a biker gang has stashed $100 million in cocaine in the band's freighted equipment, Lime's world implodes. *Amplify* takes readers backstage for an unvarnished look at the world of rock music and events promotion. A compelling debut that veers over-the-top on occasions, it's a fresh and rip-roaring tale peppered with dark deeds and leavened by a fun, almost tongue-in-cheek vibe. Full of crazy characters, humour, and high-stakes action; Hollands does a fine job conducting the fray.

* * *

Long before the current, global 'domestic noir' boom, Sydney journalist and academic **BUNTY AVIESON** traversed such territory in her 2001 novel *Apartment 255*, an acute psychological thriller which went on to scoop two Ned Kelly Awards. It's the story of best friends Sarah and Ginny, who've known each other since their school days. Sarah is cheerful, Ginny is shy; Sarah is protective of Ginny. Things begin to go awry when Sarah meets Tom, moves into a stunning apartment with him, and starts planning a marriage. Ginny wanted Tom for herself; she wants Sarah's life, and starts stalking the couple. And worse. Sarah may be protective of Ginny, but perhaps she needs protection from her. A chilling tale of envy and obsession swirling around striking and indelible characters. Avieson followed *Apartment 255* with two further psychological thrillers, *The Affair* and *The Wrong Door*.

* * *

There's a rich tradition of campus mysteries in crime fiction, dating back to Golden Age queen Dorothy Sayers' *Gaudy Night* set among Oxford's spires in the 1930s. **CATH FERLA** offered a fresh spin on the pressures faced by students and teachers, and secrets cloistered within educational institutions, in her evocative debut *Ghost Girls*. When a Chinese student at a Sydney language school leaps to her death, only for it to be revealed that she'd stolen someone's identity, new teacher Sophie Sandilands is driven to investigate. The trail leads her deep into the city's Chinatown, a place of rich flavours and hidden networks that leaps off the page thanks to Ferla's assured and sensory writing. There's a pulsing authenticity throughout, from the scratching at the underbelly of Sydney and the exploitation of foreign students wanting to learn English to the times the tale flashes back to mainland China, where the author has lived and taught. An evocative and insightful first bow.

* * *

Long before Peter Temple, Michael Robotham, and Jane Harper were scooping CWA Gold Daggers and raising the flag for Australian crime writing on the global stage, a strong foundation was laid by the great **PETER CORRIS**. The prolific Sydney author singlehandedly kick-started the modern era Downunder in 1980 when he broke through after much publisher rejection with *The Dying Trade*. That tale was a distinctly Aussie version of the American hardboiled tales that Corris loved, with a distinctly Aussie hero: boxer and soldier and law school dropout turned private eye Cliff Hardy. By the time the Ned Kelly Awards were launched in the mid-1990s, Corris had already published 18 Cliff Hardy books. He was one of the early recipients of the Lifetime Achievement Award from the Australian Crime Writing Association, in 1999, and would go on to write dozens more. 'The Demon Dog of American Crime Fiction', James Ellroy, called Corris a true original and praised his 'forceful, hard-driven, compassionate' portrayals of Australian crime. In *The Black Prince*, the 22nd in the series, Corris delivers a pacy, engaging tale while exploring issues of sport and ethnicity in Australia as Hardy is called to investigate the disappearance of a star athlete, the son of the West Indian owner of Hardy's gym. The Sydney private eye finds himself traversing rural New South Wales, a remote Aboriginal settlement in Far North Queensland, and the corrupt world of underground, illegal boxing. In the more recent *Follow the Money*, Hardy is aging and in a slump: he's lost his private eye license and his entire life savings – embezzled by a dodgy financial adviser, who later wound up dead. But then Hardy's unofficially 'hired' by a slick lawyer to find out whether the embezzler faked his own death, an assignment that has the budding granddad entwined with ethnic gangs and Sydney's gritty underbelly. Sadly, Corris passed away in 2018, but he remains a giant on whose shoulders many have stood.

* * *

One of the pillars of the early years of Australian crime's modern era, **MARELE DAY** made her name with a quartet of novels that subverted the masculine tropes of hardboiled private eye fiction. Her Claudia Valentine mysteries explored the seedier side of Sydney in the late 1980s to early 1990s, scooping a prestigious Shamus Award in the United States. In the last 25 years Day has largely focused on other types of storytelling, although she briefly revisited Valentine in 2000 with *Mavis Levack, PI*. A book of short stories centred on the nosy neighbour from Valentine's first appearance, who desperately wants to be an investigator herself, Day's swansong-so-far to crime fiction is cosier, more light-hearted, and amusing.

* * *

Given that crime fiction deals with the darkest of dark deeds, it's no surprise that a decent seasoning of humour is also often part of the genre. From gallows to guffaws, many authors seek to balance out the bleakness. Former Sydney City councillor **CS BOAG** steers hard into the laughs in his Mister Rainbow series, tongue-in-cheek modern noirs featuring a shabby, retro private eye who lives (illegally) on a boat in Sydney Harbour. Careening around the city's dives, backstreets, and shady areas as he staggers towards solutions in tales full of quips, slang, and asides, Mister Rainbow is surrounded by an intriguing cast of characters. In *The Case of a Death of a Ladies' Man* a neck tattoo helps identify a headless corpse in a Kings Cross alley as a much-hated member of Sydney's underworld, but something fishier may be afoot. A clever, knowing spin on pulp tales from the past, Mister Rainbow's adventures bring the zing.

* * *

What would you do if you were falsely accused of a horrifying crime, your family turned against you, and no one was looking for the real culprit? That's the scenario facing David Kingsgrove, a single gay man in his 30s, in **NIGEL BARTLETT**'s hard-hitting *King of the Road*. David's 11-year-old nephew Adam regularly visits him on weekends but vanishes one day after heading out of David's door to play with a neighbour. Police and family suspicion turn towards the gay uncle, a fixation David knows will only worsen given someone has downloaded child pornography onto his computer. A virus, or is he being set up? Veering towards panic-stricken, and only believed by ex-cop and personal trainer Matty, David goes on the run, knowing that only makes him look even guiltier and will spark a police manhunt. Bartlett crafts a riveting, thought-provoking tale about a good man pushed beyond his limits into a dangerous place where he risks losing himself while trying to find his nephew.

* * *

Known as 'Australia's first lady of crime', **GABRIELLE LORD** broke through in 1980 with *Fortress*, loosely based on the infamous Faraday School incident in Australia where a rural teacher and her students were kidnapped and held for ransom. *Fortress* was later adapted into an award-winning HBO telemovie. While Lord's thriller career began in the backblocks, she subsequently built her legacy on character-centred tales set in and around Sydney's eastern suburbs. Lord's two series starring private eye Gemma Lincoln and forensic scientist Jack McCain contributed greatly to her receiving the Ned Kelly Lifetime Achievement Award in 2012. In *Death Delights*, former detective McCain reluctantly helps a detective mate investigate some grisly killings, while also following an anonymous tip about his own missing daughter. Links between crimes new and old spotlight the dysfunction within McCain's own family. Lord blends police procedural, forensic elements, family drama and Australian sensibilities into a compelling tale that kick-started a fine series as well as making her the first female winner of the Ned Kelly Award for Best Novel. In more recent years Lord has focused on thrilling younger readers with her Conspiracy 365 and 48 Hours series.

* * *

There are few characters in Australian storytelling that epitomise the concept of 'larrikin' more than **ROBERT G BARRETT**'s long-running protagonist Les Norton. For those unfamiliar, larrikin is an antipodean term for a boisterous young (usually) bloke who blends a disregard for authority or propriety with an underlying good heart. A mischievous, uncouth maverick, Norton could be the poster child. He's a strapping meat worker from rural Queensland who shifts to

Sydney in the 1980s, plays rugby league and works as a bouncer for underground casinos while getting himself into all sorts of scrapes. Norton starred in 20 books over 25 years before Barrett's death in 2012. (He was also belatedly brought to screen in 2019, with some of the roughest edges sanded off to reflect modern times.) Barrett firmly sets his phasers to fun in his series of pulp tales that are full of action, comedy, and crime. Delivered in distinctly Australian vernacular and full of irreverence and 'old school' attitudes, novels like *Guns 'N' Rose*, *The Wind and the Monkey*, and *High Noon in Nimbin* showed that Barrett and Norton remained an unforgettable duo even after the 1980s had long since passed.

* * *

Stroll into any second-hand bookshop around the world and you're likely to find dozens and dozens of detectives – on the shelves, that is, not standing behind the counter. But in **LENNY BARTULIN**'s endearing trilogy of Jack Susko mysteries, it's a bookseller who becomes an accidental sleuth. Following on from *Death by the Book*, Susko returned in *The Black Russian,* cash-strapped and in danger of losing his beloved bookshop. While visiting an art gallery in Sydney's eastern suburbs to raise money by selling an old art catalogue, he interrupts a robbery, losing a valuable Ian Fleming first edition in the process. When the gallery owner offers to pay to keep things quiet, then reneges, Susko ends up bumbling and wisecracking his way through his own investigation, and into all sorts of danger. In Bartulin's adroit hands, Sydney provides a vivid and evocative backdrop to Susko's misadventures. Clever and exciting storytelling with a through-line of fun; *De Luxe* capped the trilogy.

* * *

When **EMMA DARCY** turned to crime as the millennium turned, it was fitting that the heroine of her first mystery, *Who Killed Angelique?*, was a romance novelist turned amateur sleuth. For Darcy herself, like the fictional KC Gordon, had previously penned dozens of romances under her pseudonym (which began as wife-and-husband writing team Wendy and Frank Brennan in the 1980s – before Frank passed away in 1995 – and collectively sold more than 60 million romance novels). In *Who Killed Angelique?* KC Gordon is sparked into sleuth-mode when her old school friend, an international model, is gunned down before she can reveal the 'dirt' she told KC she had to share. Darcy leans cosy rather than gritty in her crime debut, delivering a victim whom many may want dead, an engaging heroine, and plenty of suspects and red herrings while switching perspectives among those involved. KC Gordon continued her sleuthing side-gig in *Who Killed Bianca?* and *Who Killed Camilla?*

* * *

Forced to leave a 20-year career policing the Newtown, Kings Cross, and Bondi areas of Sydney after she was diagnosed with chronic post-traumatic stress disorder, **KAREN M DAVIS** decided to 'write what she knew'. She first chronicled the highs and lows of her police experiences as therapy, then channelled her inside knowledge into a crime fiction series. Detective Lexie Rogers first appears in *Sinister Intent* as a freshly minted Bondi detective who has returned to duty after eight years patrolling Sydney's notorious Kings Cross district and surviving a brutal attack. In the third in the series, *Fatal Mistake*, Rogers goes deep undercover as a drug distributor to infiltrate and expose a huge drugs ring in her city. Davis shows storytelling chops to match her authentic detail. Crisp writing conveys an exciting page-turner which illustrates the thrills and dangers of undercover work, the nature of organised crime, and the pressures and trauma faced by modern-day police officers.

* * *

When the Australian Crime Writers Association inaugurated its Ned Kelly Awards to reward excellence in the growing local genre in 1996, it named Sydneysider **JON CLEARY** as its first-ever recipient of the prestigious Lifetime Achievement Award. It was an apt choice. Cleary began writing for newspapers and working on his first novel, about an army deserter accused of murder, while stationed in the

Middle East and the Pacific during the Second World War. He wrote more than 50 books over the next six decades, including 20 in his groundbreaking series starring Sydney homicide detective and family man Scobie Malone. In the years following his Lifetime Achievement honour, Cleary continued to write crime tales reflecting various aspects of modern Australia. In *A Different Turf*, Malone investigates a series of gay bashings and murders, shedding some prejudices. In *Bear Pit* a politician is murdered ahead of Sydney hosting the 2000 Summer Olympics, allowing Cleary to air issues he had with both the Olympics and the state of Australian politics. Fittingly, the 'grandfather of Australian crime' went out on top, with the final Scobie Malone novel, *Degrees of Connection* – about a murder case entwined with corporate crime and dodgy property developments – winning the 2004 Ned Kelly Award for Best Novel.

* * *

Sport is an intrinsic part of antipodean culture, and in Australia cricket is king. Some have even said that examining Australian cricket tells you a lot about Australian culture. **MALCOLM KNOX**, who was a renowned cricket correspondent then literary editor at the *Sydney Morning Herald*, tapped into that nexus in *Adult Book* (titled *A Private Man* in Australia). A respected Sydney doctor dies on the eve of a cricket test against South Africa; eldest son Davis is also a doctor and is suspicious. Middle son Chris is focused on playing in the test and salvaging his sporting career. Youngest son Hammett is a player in the porn industry, and shunned. Hypocritical, perhaps. A novel of grief and guilty secrets, blending sport, crime, and family drama. Knox brings a healthy verisimilitude to both the Sydney setting, from grimy red-light districts to wealthy suburbs, and moments of on-field action.

* * *

Crime fiction offers readers a huge range of private eyes, and 'Crocodile Dundee in female form' sounds pretty intriguing, eh? That's what **CLAIRE MCNAB** delivers in her five novels starring Los

Angeles-based Kylie Kendall, a gumshoe originally from the Outback. Delightfully entitled (*The Wombat Strategy*, *The Platypus Ploy* etc), they offer crime heavily laced with comedy, with Kendall the centrepiece of McNab's third lesbian crime series, spanning almost 30 books dating back to 1988 when the then-Sydney author (she later moved to LA herself, for love) broke new ground locally with her first Detective Carol Ashton book. Talented, intense, glamorous, and closeted, Ashton solves crimes in Sydney and beyond in a long-running and popular series (17 books) threaded with underlying social and political themes and relationship woes. In *Accidental Murder*, Ashton is stressed by a tricky case where a series of unconnected people have suffered what seem like accidental deaths. In 2012, McNab and Ashton, now a Chief Inspector, took readers on a final ride in *Lethal Care*, which involved two puzzling deaths: that of a media star undergoing controversial cancer treatment, and the police inspector who had originally been investigating the case.

* * *

Crime fiction is a far broader landscape nowadays than the crossword-puzzle mysteries and mean streets noir of days gone by, and Sydney professor **JOHN DALE** has roamed across that landscape. His oeuvre includes an intense, award-winning tale about a violent, ambisexual casino bouncer, a bestselling true crime biography, a futuristic thriller, and editing the excellent *Sydney Noir* collection of varied short stories. The latest of Dale's three crime novels, *Detective Work*, once again delves into issues of police corruption that have laced his earlier work. Young detective Dimitri Telegonus is paired with a senior detective who's a bit of a dinosaur and previously worked under a commanding officer found guilty of multiple corruption charges. Part of a new taskforce investigating unsolved crime, the duo is tasked with solving the historical disappearance of an escort, only for the long-time prime suspect to vanish. There's plenty of conflict between the detectives, and more broadly throughout this impressive novel. Dale does a good job reflecting the multicultural and increasingly stratified realities of modern-day Australia and tenders a fresh take on the common blueprint.

* * *

What would you do if you were a journalist who had an interview with famed chef Gordon Ramsay go so disastrously he threw you out of his house, topped only by another interview with deadly Australian gangster Chopper Read that became a yelling match? If you were **MARK DAPIN**, you'd seed those experiences into a short story, then propagate a novel. In *King of the Cross*, young Jewish journalist Anthony Klein has immigrated to Sydney from Britain and lives opposite the police station in the notorious Kings Cross inner-city suburb (shadowing Dapin's own journey). The underworld boss of the Cross, Jacob Mendoza, chooses to unload his extraordinary life story onto Klein: it's a confronting, slang-filled, sordid tale full of violence but also humour. Dapin's gritty novel told in sharp prose may be too much for those who lean cosy but it's a fresh and engaging take on local crime.

* * *

Back when I was at law school, we loved quoting rumpled lawyer Dennis Denuto from rollicking Australian comedy film *The Castle*, where he summed up a case with 'it's the constitution, it's *Mabo*, it's justice, it's law, it's the vibe'. Irreverent, yes, but also a nod to a key court decision that overturned the repugnant idea that Australia was *terra nullius* (empty land) before the arrival of Europeans, and recognised land rights of its indigenous peoples. I'm recalling that now as I think of groundbreaking crime writer **PHILIP MCLAREN**, not just because McLaren wrote some terrific thrillers entwined with race relations in the wake of *Mabo*, but because before the Kamilaroi tribe member came along the Australian crime fiction landscape was itself a pretty 'empty land' in terms of indigenous voices and perspectives. After an award-winning historical thriller, McLaren directed his considerable talents to contemporary Sydney crime in *Scream Black Murder*. Two Aboriginal detectives face scrutiny inside and outside the police department when they investigate the brutal murder of an Aboriginal couple in Redfern in a case that escalates into a hunt for a deranged killer targeting indigenous women. McLaren delivered a fine tale doused in social issues and a nuanced look at race relations. Later thrillers were set against the mining of sacred native land (*Lightning Mine*) and a deprived Aboriginal community in the Outback (*Utopia*).

* * *

After being made redundant from the public service, Canberra author **ALEX PALMER** turned to crime. Interested in the psychology of violence and its effects on both victims and those who constantly face violence in their jobs, Palmer wrote a trilogy of gritty crime tales starring detectives Paul Harrigan and Grace Riordan. In the first, *Blood Redemption*, the Sydney police duo face personal and professional demons while investigating a case where a son saw a teenage girl shoot his parents on a city backstreet. Things get even more personal for Harrigan when he discovers his own wheelchair-bound son has been emailing with the young killer. Palmer's engaging first bow was followed by *The Tattooed Man*, where Harrigan and Riordan are drawn into the murders of four dinner guests in a ritzy Sydney suburb, and *The Labyrinth of Drowning*, ignited by a body in the Sydney bushland.

* * *

Thirty years ago, **ALAN DUFF** took his first steps towards a reputation as the enfant terrible of Māori novelists with his searing portrayal of New Zealand's violent underbelly in *Once Were Warriors*. (His earlier attempt at a straight thriller was rejected by publishers; he burned the manuscript.) A harrowing tale of domestic violence and deprivation told with considerable literary panache, Duff's debut and the hard-hitting film it spawned earned him international acclaim. In the years since, along with his charity that has distributed more than 12 million books to children in the poorest schools, Duff continued to explore the intersection of violence, crime, and family relationships in several fine novels (including two sequels to *Once Were Warriors*). In the recent *Frederick's Coat*, Johno is a young Māori in Sydney with lawbreaking in his blood. After a stretch in prison he's left to raise his sensitive and increasingly odd son Danny. Can Johno stay on the straight and narrow and prevent calamity? Duff has penned a moving, beautiful tale about love and loss, choice and consequences, the ripples created from criminal acts and the struggle to break free.

* * *

In recent years **JEAN BEDFORD** has been co-founder and editor of acclaimed Sydney online magazine *The Newtown Review of Books.* But alongside her crowded resume of literary critic, awards judge, anthology editor, and university lecturer, Bedford wrote several crime novels herself in the latter part of the twentieth century. After an engaging trilogy starring wealthy Balmain widow turned private investigator Anna Southwood, Bedford delivered a darker thriller, *Now You See Me*, in 1997. That book, recently reprinted, tackles issues of child abuse and murder as journalist Noel Baker begins to suspect that a killer is targeting children in order to frame their abusive parents and carers. Worse, Baker's investigations start leading towards her own group of university friends. Bedford delivers a confronting and uncomfortable read that raises questions about how we treat victims. In 2019, Bedford edited *See You at the Toxteth*, a posthumous anthology of Cliff Hardy stories and columns on crime writing from her late husband Peter Corris, the godfather of Australian crime.

* * *

After turning to writing after fifteen years as a paramedic, **KATHERINE HOWELL** offered a fresh set-up to what became a terrific eight-book series. Rather than fictionalising her own first-hand experiences into her heroine, Howell has Sydney detective Ella Marconi as the spine, and different paramedics coming to the fore alongside Marconi in each tale. The life-and-death drama of first responders meshes with larger crimes in highly readable novels. In the award-winning third instalment, *Cold Justice*, paramedic Georgie Riley must revisit finding her classmate's body almost 20 years ago when political pressure reopens the case. Returning to work after time in a psychiatric unit,

Georgie's will be assessed by her childhood friend Freya, whom she hasn't spoken to since Freya left town a couple of days after the murder. Detective Marconi is also returning to work after sick leave, having been shot, and is assigned the cold case. Howell crafts a tense story that keeps readers guessing while learning plenty about the challenges of life as a paramedic. The series concluded with *Tell the Truth* in 2015, and Howell announced she'd gone back to healthcare, but readers can hope that – like a few other authors in this book – there may be a return in future.

* * *

The optimistic bubble of young love and holiday romance smacks up against the harsh realities of challenging families, violent secrets, and guilt and shame in Perth author **SARA FOSTER**'s sixth psychological thriller *You Don't Know Me*. Set in Sydney's Northern Beaches and Bangkok, it's an engrossing tale full of family drama alongside love and death. Noah Carruso is run down by running the family restaurant in Sydney, his tank further drained by memories of his first crush, his brother's girlfriend Lizzie, who vanished when he was a teenager. His brother left soon afterwards; the siblings have been estranged since. When Noah meets Alice Pryce while holidaying in Thailand, she reminds him of Lizzie and carries plenty of secrets of her own. Their burgeoning affair is challenged when both return to stressful situations in Australia: there's a new inquest into Lizzie's death, a tenacious journo stirring things up with a podcast, and Alice's father has been attacked in prison. Tom has also returned. Were the whispers about him being the prime suspect right all along? Foster shows a nice touch for clever plotting and pacing alongside nuanced character relationships.

* * *

In recent times **CATHY COLE** has been a well-travelled creative writing professor who has shepherded the careers of some leading Australian authors, but 20 years ago the Sydneysider was juggling her own crime novels alongside completing her doctorate. *Dry Dock* introduced private eye Nicola Sharpe, an Annie Lennox-lookalike happy to confront dodgy developers and slimy union officials in Balmain. As the blue-collar suburb gentrifies and long-time locals are squeezed out, Sharpe realises something's gone badly wrong when a local woman is stalked and a family friend who made waves about union fraud disappears. Cole sprinkles plenty of social commentary throughout an entertaining tale with its 'feisty chick' heroine, delivering a profound sense of place and an ache for the community lost. Sharpe returned in *Skin Deep*, which won the Readers' Choice Davitt Award.

* * *

Auckland

A doyen of New Zealand storytelling, **MAURICE GEE**'s resume ranges from fantasy and science fiction for younger readers through to realistic explorations of diverse lives, dysfunctional families, and local issues and settings in his adult fiction. While not generally considered a 'crime writer', Gee has a nuanced touch when depicting violence, and a few of his novels centre on the uncovering or impact of violent crime. As *In My Father's Den* and *Crime Story* predate this guide's remit, we'll look at 2009's *Access Road*. Rowan Pinker is the 78-year-old narrator (matching Gee's age at publication) of a brooding tale of family secrets. She lives a semi-contented life with her 'silly old git' of a husband in a ritzy suburb while regularly visiting brothers Roly and Lionel who've returned to their old family home in west Auckland. Visits that spark memories of a sinister childhood friend who may be the cause of Lionel's troubles. Gee crafts a slow-burn mystery in spare prose, masterfully evoking natural and human landscapes, unearthing the menace in the mundane, the evil in the everyday.

* * *

On the surface, it's an odd literary coupling: a millennial playwright with a knack for subversive comedy, and a Swedish-born baby boomer whose poignant novels traverse secrets, love, and friendship. But Thomas Sainsbury and Linda Olsson successfully colluded as **ADAM SARAFIS** to produce assured crime tale *Something is Rotten*, the first of a planned trilogy. After emailing a file, a budding writer takes a deadly tumble down the stairwell at the university library. His friend Jade, a sex worker, doesn't believe it was a suicide and beseeches mechanic Sam Hallberg, a former government adviser, to investigate. Meanwhile a journalist is delving into dirty politics relating to New Zealand's food exports to Europe. 'Sarafis' crafts an engaging crime read that's seasoned with thought-provoking themes including dealing with grief and tragedy, power imbalances in society, and the nexus between politics, big business, and the media. While the second instalment in the trilogy is yet to be published, hopefully we'll see more from Sarafis in future.

* * *

Blending supernatural elements into crime fiction can be dicey, with a risk of any paranormal gimmick overwhelming the crime story. Fortunately, **ANDREA JUTSON** avoided such pitfalls with her impressive debut *Senseless*. In a small park in Auckland a bludgeoned body is found by James Paxton. Double trouble: the police tab him as a suspect, and the dead man talks to him. James is a psychic, but a reluctant one who sees his 'gift' as a curse. He has no interest in fortune-telling or making a fortune from telling. Drawn into the hunt for a killer, his tightly-held world is upturned as he works with and gets in the way of Detective Andy Stirling, a non-believer. Jutson strikes a good balance, with James' abilities adding texture rather than obscuring the crime spine. An engaging read with good character interplay, strong threads of black humour, and an authentic evocation of the modern Auckland setting. A crime novel that's likely to be enjoyed by fans of television series like *Ghost Whisperer* and *Medium*. Paxton's misadventures then continued in *The Darkness Looking Back*, a fine sequel.

* * *

Back in the 1980s, tiny New Zealand became a world leader in the anti-nuclear movement when it broke from military ally the United States, declaring itself nuclear free and banning US nuclear warships and submarines from its waters. It was a defining political moment for a nation that has long punched far above its weight globally in the fields of sports and innovation. **THOMAS RYAN** harnesses that anti-nuclear backdrop for *The Mark of Halam*, the second thriller in his action-packed series starring former Special Forces soldier Jeff Bradley. Now focused on his winery, Bradley is dragged into the fray when a friend is nearly killed and a lethal terrorist infiltrates New Zealand ahead of an historic visit by a state-of-the-art US submarine. Ryan, who has been a soldier in war zones himself, embroiders his 'big threat' thriller with an engaging hero who's not invulnerable, memorable supporting characters, plenty of action, and a nice evocation of the physical and social geography of Auckland. Other Bradley thrillers take place in the Balkans, the Middle East, and Southeast Asia.

* * *

Kicking back with a glass of wine, a good book, and a handful of chocolatey delights sounds like a pretty appealing way to replenish the batteries, right? Waikato author **JULIE THOMAS** is best-known for her bestselling family sagas entwined with the Second World War, but in *Blood, Wine & Chocolate* she has some fun vacationing in the crime genre. Vinnie Whitney-Ross is a Waiheke Island winemaker married to his chocolatier sweetheart, but his blissful Kiwi lifestyle was bought with the betrayal of a childhood pal entangled in one of London's most psychotic gangland families. Vinnie himself was more nougat than hard nut and worries his new life will eventually be upended. Or just ended. Thomas adroitly contrasts Vinnie's gritty East End upbringing with his midlife rural idyll (though neither are immune from violence), building to an inevitable showdown. Quaffable thrills with moreish descriptions.

* * *

What do you get if you cross the formidability of Polynesian rugby players with the relentlessness and honour of Māori military instructors? For **PAUL THOMAS** that combination, twisted with undisciplined personal habits, resulted in Detective Tito Ihaka. First sighted a quarter century ago in groundbreaking tales that hauled Kiwi crime writing into a new era and saw Thomas described by critics as 'Elmore Leonard on acid', the hulking Māori copper is an unpinned grenade of a man who stormed from role player to series star over the course of an initial trilogy. In 2012, Ihaka returned to the fray after a long hiatus in *Death on Demand* (a rollicking tale which added a Ngaio Marsh Award to Thomas's earlier Ned Kelly Award for *Inside Dope*, the second in the series). Ihaka was now older, a shade wiser, but still a rhino in a china shop. *Fallout* is the latest – and hopefully not last – Ihaka novel. It sees the demoted detective ordered by his long-suffering mentor Finbar McGrail to turn a scrap of new information about a 1987 election night murder into a solved file. Meanwhile, a journalist proffers allegations that Ihaka's trade unionist father may not have died of natural causes years before, and Ihaka's former best mate – a disgraced detective – is hired by a PR rep for a shady millionaire to track the recent sighting of a political powerbroker who vanished in the late 1980s. Past collides with present in a tale brimming with wit, action, and crackling prose. There's a sense of fun among the dark deeds – as if the story like its hero wears a cavalier smirk – while Thomas expertly evokes a sense of both modern-day and 1980s New Zealand life. More please.

* * *

A deceptive distillation: a jaded anti-hero stumbles across a crime and doggedly pursues his own investigation through a troubled world to uncover the truth. So far, so hundreds of hardboiled mysteries. But in the talented hands of **CHAD TAYLOR**, that setup transforms into *Shirker*, a surreal, mesmerising neo-noir tale truly unlike any other. It's vivid, hallucinatory, brilliant, and marmite-y; readers are likely to love it, or hate it. Our dubiously reliable narrator Ellerslie Penrose lives in his office deep within Auckland's concrete jungle. The part-time financial analyst, full-time existentialist pockets the wallet of a dead man in a dumpster, then embarks on a bizarre quest through past and present, via brothels, antique dealers, and a matrix of oddballs. Taylor's Kiwi crime writing colleague Paul Thomas was famously described by critics as 'Elmore Leonard on acid'. If that's the case, then Taylor's storytelling is akin to Raymond Chandler having a pill party in a dilapidated Auckland villa with Sartre and du Maurier. Taylor continued to both embrace and upturn crime and thriller tropes in further novels including *Electric* and *Departure Lounge*.

* * *

I've never liked the saying 'those who can't do, teach' – a throwaway witticism by George Bernard Shaw – because, frankly, teachers are vital and have challenging jobs many couldn't do (think sports stars, where the greatest doers often fail if they later try coaching). But for former cop **SIMON WYATT** it certainly was a case of those who can't do, write. The young detective turned to fictional crime when he was struck by a life-threatening auto-immune disorder and penned his engaging debut *The Student Body* while recovering. When a schoolgirl's body is discovered in coastal bushland, pressure quickly ramps up on newly promoted Detective Sergeant Nick Knight and his CIB colleagues. The school, family, media, police bosses – all want answers, and fast. Wyatt guides readers through the realities of a murder enquiry, keeping the pages turning even as we witness the grunt work rather than TV-land glamour. Wyatt has a nice touch for the west Auckland setting, and builds to an action-packed finish. Hopefully the next DS Nick Knight book won't be too far away.

* * *

Literary knight Sir **JAMES MCNEISH** was an incisive and versatile storyteller, with a lengthy resume ranging across novels and plays, journalism and biography. McNeish bounced between New Zealand and Europe during his lifetime, and similarly shifted often in his subject matter, ranging from an early biography of an anti-Mafia campaigner in Italy to a fictionalised diary of an Olympic gold medallist, to a play about a 1970s politician who resigned after being accused by the

Prime Minister of engaging in homosexual activities (then illegal). In 2010, a few years before his death, McNeish published his first novel in more than a decade: the unusual courtroom drama *The Crime of Huey Dunstan*. A blind psychologist reflects on a baffling case where he was an expert witness for a young man accused of a brutal murder. There's no doubt Huey is the culprit, but what lay behind the crime? And what sort of crime was it, really? McNeish takes readers on a sedate but fascinating trail entwined with deep issues of law, justice and humanity.

* * *

A Kiwi doctor who spent her childhood in apartheid South Africa, **FIONA SUSSMAN** blended literary fiction and crime fiction in her outstanding second novel *The Last Time We Spoke*. The result was a harrowing tale that examined the ongoing impact of violent crime on all involved, rather than focusing on whodunit or how-catch-em. Carla Reid had a nice life on her family farm near Auckland, until one night her world collides with that of Ben Toroa, an illiterate teen caught up in gang life. A brutal home invasion tears both from their axis. A violent act, fodder for headlines, but what happens long after the media moves on? Readers witness Carla's stuttering recovery and Ben growing into adulthood in prison; a survivor and a perpetrator struggling with forever-altered lives. Sussman crafted a sublime story that burrowed into unspoken aspects of crime. Lyrically written yet confronting, provocative yet hopeful. Packed with a heart-wrenching array of authentic characters, *The Last Time We Spoke* is the kind of novel that sticks with readers long after it's finished.

* * *

In South African lawyer **CHRIS MARNEWICK**'s second novel former soldier Pierre de Villiers has, like Marnewick, moved across the world to Auckland. After being a supporting player in *Shepherds and Butchers*, a visceral exposé of the use of the death penalty during apartheid (made into a 2016 film starring Steve Coogan), de Villiers takes the lead in *The Soldier Who Said No*. Now an Auckland policeman, de Villiers catches crooks while trying to move on from fractured memories of his traumatic history. When the Prime Minister is nearly assassinated with an African weapon, de Villiers' past smashes into his present. Like its predecessor, *The Soldier Who Said No* asks huge moral questions, and pricks at uncomfortable topics such as the racism lying beneath the veneer of modern New Zealand. Viewing that through the jaded eyes of a man who fought for one of the world's most flagrantly racist regimes is unsettling. A tale that gets the mind whirring as well as the pages.

* * *

After working as a schoolteacher and a postie, and writing memoirs about both careers, **FREDA BREAM** turned to crime during her final years in a rest home, producing 13 mysteries starring amateur sleuth and Auckland clergyman Jabal Jarrett. Her penultimate tale, *Murder at the Microphone*, sees the amiable reverend entangled in a murder investigation at a radio station thanks to his gig on 'Faith for Today'. A well-known broadcaster announces his own murder live on air and is discovered with a knife in his back. With the Chief Inspector's blessing, Jarrett noses around in concert with the official investigation. The Reverend has a sharp eye and mind. Cosy in style, Bream delivers a pleasant read speckled with humour and a light touch, somewhat reminiscent of *Murder, She Wrote* in tone. Bream wrote in a straightforward manner, crafting a classically styled mystery with plenty of suspects, an interesting location, and a series of motives and red herrings to confound the issue.

* * *

A decade ago, there was plenty of speculation about the identity of **ALIX BOSCO**, a 'successful writer in other media' who wrote a terrific novel under a pseudonym and won the inaugural Ngaio Marsh Award. *Cut & Run* introduced social worker turned legal researcher Anna Markunas, who was easing herself back into work after a breakdown, her husband's suicide, and problems with her meth-addict son. When a rugby star who rose from a tough life is murdered in the arms of a socialite, it looks like a drug deal gone wrong. But as she investigates, Markunas doesn't believe the convenient confession of her firm's client, the star's former friend and teammate. Bosco sucks readers in with great storytelling, strong characters with plenty of complexity beyond their role (some of whom may be amalgams of real celebrities), and a strong sense of Auckland's diverse neighbourhoods. After the publication of *Slaughter Falls*, a fine sequel, Bosco 'came out' as former junior All Black Greg McGee, a screenwriter and famed playwright who'd feared some might not accept his troubled middle-aged heroine based on the blokey persona of her creator.

* * *

Some thrillers build to a bloody confrontation; **JULIAN NOVITZ**'s moody and unsettling tale *Little Sister* is sparked by one. We meet teenager Shane fleeing through the woods after taking a samurai sword to his girlfriend's father a few days before the Twin Towers fell. What follows is an intricate unravelling of personal relationships and family secrets as readers witness events through the slanted perspectives of Shane, his best friend Will, and his girlfriend Eileen, along with their English teacher Mr N. And what of Eileen's little sister who has provoked events even though Shane and Will have never met her? Is she stalking Eileen a decade later in Melbourne? Novitz expertly keeps readers off-kilter as his multiple narratives build; each convincing yet not wholly consistent. Dark themes beckon through an exquisitely murky atmosphere as we encounter fractured lives either side of a violent act.

* * *

The daughter of CK Stead, a writer compared by British newspapers to 'a cultural monument', **CHARLOTTE GRIMSHAW** grew from an Auckland childhood doused in books and literary friendships into a young adulthood of legal briefs and murder trials before finding her own way as a superb novelist with a fine touch for differing voices and the confluence of reality and fiction. Her 1999 debut,

Provocation, was semi-autobiographical and featured a law student who gets dangerously caught up with a shady older man and the violent clients he defends. An onyx tale, dark and glittering with sharp prose, it announced the arrival of a terrific new voice. In that book and several that followed Grimshaw has regularly tangoed with violent crime, suspense, and legal drama while eschewing the label 'crime writer'. (Perhaps due to the fact she broke through at a time when too many in the local literary world took a narrow or sneering view of the genre.) With crime-laced books like *Guilt*, *The Night Book*, and *Starlight Peninsula*, Grimshaw has shown immense talent for playing with structure, building suspense, and raising questions about power and morality while showcasing the interconnected lives of a variety of characters who call Auckland home.

* * *

Feeling helpless after witnessing a friend and an ex-boyfriend fall prey to meth addiction, **KELLY LYNDON** swerved from her prior romance writing to take readers into harrowing places in *Crystal Reign*. David and Chrissie Johnson have a happy marriage and great life with their three kids, until Chrissie tries methamphetamine at a friend's New Year's party. Swiftly addicted, her deterioration begins gradually before snowballing to attack every aspect of her and her family's life. When she vanishes, David is forced to confront the dangerous netherworld with which Chrissie has become entangled, especially when the police begin to suspect the loving husband and father may have killed his addict wife. Lyndon pulls no punches in a confronting tale about a drug that is ruining lives and tearing apart families across the country and the world. Well-researched and traumatically authentic, *Crystal Reign* is a compelling story that avoids stereotypes.

* * *

Prolific Auckland author **ANGUS MCLEAN** didn't have to look far for research material when he launched his Chase Investigations series a few years ago. Protagonist Dan Crowley was an ex-cop who'd set up a private eye shop with his wife Molly in Ellerslie, a local suburb famed for its historic racecourse. McLean is the pen name for a working copper who'd also been a private investigator and who wrote his pacy, action-packed crime tales in the gaps between his work and family life. In less than six years McLean has produced 15 novels and novellas, including nine in the Chase Investigations series and four in his 'Division' series focused on international terrorism. *Red Mist* is the sixth Chase Investigations book, but serves as a prequel, taking readers back to when Crowley was an Auckland street detective battling brutal gangs and internal politics. Easy reading and forthright crime tales infused with a strong sense of modern Auckland.

* * *

Malaysian-born Kiwi **JOHN LING** has said he taps into his 'exotic cultural background straddling East and West' to inform his storytelling. That was certainly on show in *The Blasphemer*, a socio-political thriller inspired by the death sentences issued by Islamic extremists against Bangladeshi author Taslima Nasreen (akin to the infamous fatwa on Salman Rushdie). In *The Blasphemer*, Abraham Khan, a moderate Muslim author, has lived in exile in Auckland for several years. After Khan and his wife are attacked, the Prime Minister takes a special interest and protection is beefed up. But is the new threat due to Khan's past writings, or something else? Ling furnished a fast-flowing novel seasoned with insights into the Islamic world (illustrating how it is far more complex and heterogeneous than media coverage focused on the Middle East may convey). Think high-octane beach read blended with engaging dissertation. Security expert Maya Raines is a tenacious heroine. Her adventures continued, along with Ling's exploration of Muslim sectarianism in Asia, in novels like *Rebellion* and *Vengeance*.

* * *

Two British detectives whose jobs assaulted their mental health move to New Zealand for a fresh start: one a character, the other his creator. **IAN AUSTIN** had a deep well of personal experience to draw from for *The Agency*, having been nearly beaten to death while a British policeman, and worked undercover, as a detective, and as a national trainer in surveillance during his service. In his second crime novel, Dan Calder is an ex-British cop who brought plenty of baggage with him when starting afresh and as far away from his old life as possible in New Zealand. While new friends and the possibility of new love bring some sunshine, Calder stumbles upon a deadly business which preys upon people who are ill, terminally or mentally, and may have links to an unsolved case in the UK. Calder may have ditched his warrant card, but he's still a cop at heart. Austin creates a clever tweak on cop tales, while providing a lot of background detail and ensuring readers don't overlook plot points by repeating them from multiple character views. Calder's adventures continued in *The Second Grave* and *Frozen Summer*.

* * *

It was no surprise when leading overseas crime writers and critics consistently praised **NATHAN BLACKWELL**'s superb debut *The Sound of Her Voice*, for its gritty authenticity and storytelling power. Blackwell is the pseudonym of a former undercover cop and Auckland detective who'd turned to the page to process some of what he'd experienced, and he brought readers chillingly into law enforcement realities in ways psychological as well as procedural. Detective Matt Buchanan is plunged back into his early years as a cop when the body of a long-dead woman is unearthed on a beautiful beach. Is this tied to an old case that risks putting Buchanan over the edge? Unusually, *The Sound of Her Voice* doesn't focus on a single case (or two) or occur over a short time period – instead it deals with events spanning more than 20 years in Buchanan's career, and the cumulative effect of the horrors he's dealt with on his own psyche. Blackwell has zing to his prose, and takes readers into harrowing places, while delivering candid insights into the stresses criminal investigations create for all involved, rippling outwards from violent acts.

Melbourne

Given the ubiquitous nature of sports, with billions of people watching events like the Olympics and the FIFA World Cup, I'm often puzzled why so few crime novels are set in the sports world. It's a realm overflowing with passion, conflict, and big money. **JOCK SERONG** offers a sublime example of how authors can brilliantly meld sports, crime, and character study in his novel *The Rules of Backyard Cricket*. Darren and Wally Keefe are Cain and Abel cricket-loving youngsters raised by a single mother in Melbourne's suburbs. Their backyard battles graduate to representative honours, offering the sibling rivals success on the pitch and varying degrees of success off it. All leading to Darren being cable-tied and wounded in the boot of a car being driven into the remote Australian bush. Will this be his final innings? Serong delivers a beautifully written novel, a literary thriller that's also a nuanced look at suburban life, growing up, toxic masculinity, the cost of fame, and mythmaking in sporting culture. His pitch-perfect characters are fascinating individuals while being symbolic of deeper themes. Understandably shortlisted for the Edgar Award; an exquisite novel.

* * *

Melbourne author **TANIA CHANDLER** leapt with both feet into the psychological thriller pool in her debut *Please Don't Leave Me Here*, which was shortlisted for multiple writing prizes. Brigitte is a cop's wife and mother of twins who 14 years ago barely survived a hit-and-run on the same day a man was found murdered in her apartment. She says she has no recollection of that day, but do we believe her? When the investigation is reopened, and one of her husband's colleagues moves into their guesthouse, Brigitte's fragile reality begins to crumble. It's an uncomfortable read at times, as we view the world through the eyes of a rather self-absorbed as well as self-loathing character. Chandler plays with our sympathies, writes beautifully, and crafts a sense of dread as the story is told in three parts, from present to past and back again, building to an abrupt conclusion.

* * *

A standard trope of classic hardboiled crime is the moment the wisecracking, cynical private eye meets a femme fatale. In **LEIGH REDHEAD**'s 'tart noir' tetralogy those archetypes meet within a single character: Simone Kirsch. In the first novel, *Peepshow*, Kirsch's work history as an exotic dancer puts the kibosh on her dreams of joining the police, so she tops the class at a private eye course instead. Her newfound skills are called into action when her friend Chloe is kidnapped by the gangster brother of a St Kilda strip club owner who was brutally murdered. The price of Chloe's freedom? Simone must find the killer. The best way to do that is to harness skillsets old and new, going undercover at the strip club. Redhead, who shared a resume with Simone, takes readers on a vivid excursion into the intoxicating and seamy world of Melbourne's sex industry. A potent cocktail of lotharios, mobsters, and dirty cops. *Peepshow* is unabashedly sex, drugs, and rock'n'roll; a fast-paced romp laced with humour. Simone's adventures continued in *Rubdown*, *Cherry Pie*, and *Thrill City*.

* * *

Plenty of people, in real life and fiction, dream of 'escaping to the country', of trading hectic and overcrowded city lives for more space and perhaps a greater sense of community. In **SARAH BAILEY**'s assured second novel, *Into the Night*, Detective Sergeant Gemma Woodstock has gone the other way. She's jettisoned her rural hometown, her son, and her ex-husband for a lonely life in the big city, chasing killers and battling emptiness with a succession of bottles and beds. When a young actor on the cusp of a Hollywood breakthrough is stabbed to death in front of hundreds of people on a film set, other cases get sidelined and Woodstock and her new colleagues are thrown into a media maelstrom. In this outing, Bailey deepens our understanding of Woodstock, a character whose behaviour and choices may divide readers but is messily, authentically human. Some readers may miss the vivid small-town setting of Bailey's debut, *The Dark Lake*, but there's plenty here to suggest Woodstock is a character worth following. *Where the Dead Go* continues the series.

* * *

Long considered the cultural capital of Australia (despite Sydney and Brisbane trying to wrest the title away at times), Melbourne is a city overflowing with galleries, exhibitions, theatre, and world-renowned street art. Art historian and author **KATHERINE KOVACIC** taps into that scene, historical and modern, in her wisecracking mysteries featuring art dealer Alex Clayton and conservator John Porter. The accidental sleuths made their first bow in *The Portrait of Molly Dean*, which immersed readers in two eras: Melbourne on the eve of the millennium, and the city and its art scene back in the 1930s, as Clayton and Porter dug into the real-life unsolved murder of an artist's muse. Kovacic set the bar high with her fine debut, and met it well with the sequel, *Painting in the Shadows*, written recently but set in the early 2000s. At a major new exhibition, a worker collapses, a reportedly cursed painting is damaged, and then a conservator dies while repairing the work. Kovacic adroitly textures the tale with her clear love for the art world and art history without stalling the momentum of the mystery.

* * *

Within the Australian crime writing community, **LINDY CAMERON** is rather something of a Renaissance woman. A founding member when Sisters in Crime Australia was established almost 30 years ago, she has supported writers as a national convenor and magazine editor, edited anthologies, established a publishing company to provide opportunities for overlooked local authors, and written true crime. Cameron has also won awards for her own crime fiction. Her trilogy starring Melbourne cop turned private eye Kit O'Malley delivers compulsive tales of serious crimes, spiked with wit and humour, where the city shines as part of the marvellous cast. In *Bleeding Hearts*, a simple case of protecting a TV presenter who has received threatening letters soon warps into a quagmire of obligations and investigations spanning money laundering to murder. A further complication: O'Malley's inamorata Alex is back on the scene. An exciting romp full of quirky characters and fluid storytelling; smart and sexy.

* * *

While crime writing has long been considered plot-centric, many writers and readers will tell you that character is what really rules, and in terms of popular series it's the protagonist more than the author that readers really follow. **JM GREEN** laid down a great marker on that front in her debut *Good Money*, which introduced wisecracking Melbourne social worker Stella Hardy. Gruff yet engaging, Stella is full of good intentions yet often ends 'up shit creek without a paddle', as we say Downunder. She's engaging, rounded, and complex. Looking into both a murder suffered by one of her immigrant client families and the disappearance of her neighbour who turned out to be heir to a mining fortune, Stella is drawn into a dark underworld of drugs and killers. In her debut Green also captured a great sense of modern, multicultural Australia, from stratified urban life to the changing face of the countryside. She further harnessed the potential of her heroine in *Too Easy* and *Shoot Through*.

* * *

'Deaf Man Investigates Friend's Death' would be the Hollywood tagline, but **EMMA VISKIC**'s unique and award-hoarding *Resurrection Bay* is about much more than its main character Caleb Zelic's deafness. It never feels like Viskic uses Caleb's disability as a character quirk to stand out in a crowded crime field; instead it infuses his personality, his story, and how he interacts with the world. Caleb has always felt like an outsider, but when a childhood friend is murdered, he's compelled to investigate – out of guilt and to clear his own name – enlisting the help of Frankie, a troubled ex-cop. Viskic does a fine job bringing her entire cast to vivid and authentic life. Her setting, Melbourne and the rural and small-town areas surrounding it, is populated with a diverse cast that epitomises the cultural melting pot of modern-day Australia. *Resurrection Bay* is a book that will generate a reaction; Viskic adroitly draws readers into Caleb's tale and makes us care. Powered by lean and fresh prose, it's an assured debut which also brings a deaf perspective on the world to life on the page. Caleb's adventures continue in the equally excellent *And Fire Came Down* and *Darkness for Light*.

* * *

Reviewers around the world (including this one) are guilty of describing some crime writers as 'poetic', but few authors actually write crime fiction as poetry. **DOROTHY PORTER** did. Along with several collections and two operas, the iconic Australian poet wrote five verse novels including two crime tales. Her last, *El Dorado*, centres on a serial child killer in Melbourne, the detective who is trying to catch him, and the detective's childhood friend who has returned from Hollywood. Porter delivers a compulsive read that delights even as it exposes dark acts. Each poem can be enjoyed on its own, with Porter often twisting the knife to finish, and together they build into a masterful portrayal of the lives entwined in a chilling murder investigation. Pared to the bone in words, yet fully fleshed in emotion and description, *El Dorado* is a highly original, captivating crime tale. As renowned antipodean crime authority Professor Stephen Knight noted in his seminal work *Australian Crime Fiction: A 200-Year History*, Porter's untimely death in 2008 wasn't just a major blow to Australian poetry, it silenced 'probably the most original voice in world crime fiction'.

* * *

Following in the footsteps of the likes of Kathy Reichs, Melbourne forensic psychiatrist **ANNE BUIST** has created a series heroine who's a more dramatic version of her own professional career. Hopefully much more dramatic, in the case of Natalie King, a Ducati-riding bipolar badass who tries to help her patients with their damage while ameliorating her own with a variety of thrills. Like married men and going off her meds. Introduced in *Medea's Curse*, Natalie is dealing

Craig Sisterson

with several patients accused of murder as well as trying to get an ex-patient who confessed to killing her own baby out of prison. She is also receiving anonymous messages and may have a dangerous stalker among her array of professional and personal complications. Buist offers readers a plethora of characters and issues, although too many are pale satellites orbiting the powerful sun of Natalie. The erratic but fascinating psychiatrist returns in *Dangerous to Know* and *This I Would Kill For.*

* * *

Melbourne author **CHRIS WOMERSLEY** cajoled readers with the quality of his prose into a bleak, noir landscape in *The Low Road.* Two lives collide at a dingy motel on the outskirts of an Australian city. Lee is a young criminal fresh out of jail who wakes up with a suitcase of stolen money, a bullet wound, and lots of questions. He's patched up by Wild, a morphine-addicted doctor who's fleeing criminal charges and the life he torched through his habit. The unlikely duo pair up to head bush, looking for some sort of sanctuary, including from veteran crook Josef who is hunting Lee and the suitcase of money. Womersley's debut isn't an easy read; it's a violent, despairing tale of broken characters and broken places. Atmospheric without any strong sense of a particular location, *The Low Road* is a literary-tinged crime tale that could be set anywhere. Womersley followed that Ned Kelly Award-winning debut with an historical tale, *Bereft*, about a returning Gallipoli soldier and accused murderer who shelters in the bush with an orphaned girl during the flu epidemic. That book earned several crime and literary award shortlistings, winning the ABIA Award for Literary Fiction.

* * *

As the new millennium loomed there were plenty of takes on what that might entail, including conspiracy theories and those who believed the milestone date would mark the Rapture or the Second Coming of Christ. Journalist **ANDREW MASTERSON** leaned into that with his first two novels, which shared an audacious premise (each went on to win one of the early Ned Kelly Awards). In *The Last Days: The Apocryphon of Joe Panther*, Father Brendan Corrigan needs help. A local street kid has been crucified above the altar of Corrigan's church, and the police are eyeing the priest. He turns to Joe Panther, a down-on-his-luck private eye with a side gig as a heroin dealer and killer. Oh, and Joe Panther tells readers that he knows all about crucifixion, since that happened to him too, 2,000 years ago on Golgotha. Now the Son of God is wandering the streets of inner-city Melbourne. Masterson blends crime and theology and great descriptions of the city into a trippy story that may divide readers. Joe Panther returned, so to speak, in *The Second Coming*.

* * *

The first crime offering, in book form, from documentary filmmaker **ZANE LOVITT** wasn't so much a detective tale as a tale of a detective. In *The Midnight Promise* readers get a deep character study of Melbourne private inquiry agent John Dorn over the course of ten cases. Dorn is a good but flawed man eking out a drab existence as he becomes 'an expert on the shitty things people do to each other'. It's a heck of a novel, told in the form of a series of interconnected short stories. Dorn's caseload may be realistically humdrum rather than full of femme fatales and high-octane assignments, but there's still ingenuity on show and the book is more about the attritional nature of Dorn's calling on the detective himself. Snappy dialogue, dry humour, and descriptions of the city counterbalance the dreariness. Lovitt created something original that still tipped its fedora to noir traditions, then followed up with *Black Teeth*, an unusual neo-noir about a digital researcher who teams with another loner to search for an ex-cop. One man's looking for a father, the other to avenge his.

* * *

Several years before the unpublished manuscript prize at the Victorian Premier's Literary Awards paved the path to publication for fresh crime voices like Jane Harper, Christian White, JM Green, Mark Brandi and RWR McDonald, it did the same for Melbourne journalist

NICK GADD. In *Ghostlines*, Philip Trudeau is scraping a living tweaking press releases at a suburban rag, a few years in prison past his glory days as a high-flying journalist. A seemingly routine tragedy when a young boy is killed at a level crossing stirs something in the self-destructive Trudeau, especially when it appears somehow linked to an art collector found dead in his cluttered home. Gadd delivers a brooding noir centred on a haunted man whose anxious and pickled mind may struggle to decipher truth from fantasy. A strong sense of Melbourne's western suburbs and a 'hero' who tightropes readers between frustration and empathy elevates a stylish tale. After an 11-year lacuna, Gadd returned in 2019 with *Death of a Typographer*, perhaps the world's first font-focused mystery.

* * *

Long before she turned to crime fiction, Australian actress and singer **JANE CLIFTON** portrayed a criminal onscreen. In the early 1980s she appeared in more than 100 episodes of iconic Australian soap *Prisoner* (*Cell Block H* in some overseas territories) as jailhouse bookie Margo Gaffney. In the early years of the new millennium, 30 years into her five-decade acting career, Clifton added crime novelist to her resume. The cartoonish covers of *Half Past Dead* and *A Hand in the Bush* announced that, despite the dark deeds within, the fascinating heroines were anything but dour. More recently, motorcycle-riding divorcee and Melbourne psychologist Decca Brand returned in *Flush*, where a former patient tries to commit suicide and becomes the prime suspect in the murder of his wife. Engaging storytelling with a good sense of its city while deftly balancing darkness and light.

* * *

JARAD HENRY leaned into his own experiences as a criminologist and working alongside police in the criminal justice system to infuse his trilogy starring Melbourne detective Rubens McCauley with the grim realities of modern law enforcement. In the second instalment, *Blood Sunset*, something about the death of a teen runaway in an alleyway nags at McCauley, prompting him to investigate against his bosses' wishes. A needle in the arm means accidental overdose, or does it? As McCauley scratches beneath the veneer of St Kilda, he's appalled by the hidden webs of child abusers, paedophiles, and underage sex workers he finds. Recently returned to active duty after barely surviving a shooting, where will McCauley's anger lead as bushfires rage around his city during a blistering summer? Henry expertly guides readers through a gritty, troubling landscape while showcasing the inner world of investigators, the toll they endure, and the subculture in which they operate.

* * *

One night in Melbourne, lawyer David Forrester speaks his name and profession into a Dictaphone as he sits alone in his car, then says 'Tonight, at 6.10, I killed my wife. This is my statement.' So begins **ANNA GEORGE**'s superb debut *What Came Before*, a twisting literary thriller tangled with the realities of domestic violence. As a panicked David reflects on what he's done, the spirit of his wife Elle hovers over her body in their house. Readers witness the passionate beginnings, then the couple's intense and fraught relationship from the perspectives of both. With beautiful prose and consummate skill, George successfully performs a high-wire act; keeping readers invested despite knowing whodunnit from the first line, and thoroughly entranced despite the distressing themes and dislikeable protagonists. An uncomfortable read that could be triggering, and have readers reflecting on what may be going on behind closed doors in their own neighbourhood, if not their own homes. A dark, complex tale that heralded a strong new voice in antipodean suspense.

* * *

Having discovered the day-to-day reality of life working in law firms didn't match the gripping courtroom dramas he'd enjoyed growing up, South African-born **ALEX HAMMOND** said his exciting books starring Melbourne lawyer Will Harris were a little bit of wish fulfilment. In *The Unbroken Line*, Harris is still recovering from the events in *Blood Witness* when he and his girlfriend are run off the road, threatened, and attacked by masked men. But how can Harris back off something when he has no idea what their assailants were talking about? Harris has plenty of other trouble on the go, including defending a colleague's son accused of bullying a kid into suicide, then dealing with his legal partner being accused of supplying the drugs that killed a footballer. Plus his girlfriend has fled the country after the attack. Hammond deftly juggles all the threads into a gripping thriller about corruption and the misuse of power that delivers plenty of out-of-court action to keep the pages whirring.

* * *

The real-life unsolved murder of a teenager on the Mornington Peninsula in 1953 provided inspiration for **JANICE SIMPSON**'s first novel, *Murder on Mt Martha*. In the novel Nick Szabo is a PhD candidate researching defectors from the Hungarian water polo team who came to Australia for the 1956 Melbourne Olympics. It's a topic with a personal connection. While interviewing retiree Arthur Boyle for a first-hand account of what Melbourne was like at the time, conversation turns to crimes from the era, with Boyle still troubled by the killing of former work colleague Beverley Middleton (not the real victim's name). Switching between Boyle's recollections of the past, first-person perspectives from the killer, and Szabo's contemporary sleuthing, *Murder on Mt Martha* avoids rose-tinted glasses on the past. Several Melbourne suburbs are explored, along with the twin time periods. Simpson stokes the intrigue and raises interesting scenarios about what might have happened to a young woman whose life was snatched and for whom justice has not yet been found.

* * *

Want to pick a single Australian series that encapsulates the distinctive attitudes, sense of humour, colourful politics, and urban life of the nation? **SHANE MALONEY**'s sextet starring bumbling Labor Party staffer turned Member of Parliament Murray Whelan is surely a top contender. The Brunswick author artfully satirises Australian life in superlative tales that use murder like a MacGuffin while exploring the opaque world of local politics and provoking deep thought as well as deep laughter. *The Brush-Off*, which won a Ned Kelly Award and was set as a high school text in Maloney's home state, sees political fixer Whelan entangled in murder, forgery, and corruption among the arts scene. When the body of a disgruntled artist is pulled from the art gallery's ornamental moat, Whelan must scramble to protect his boss, the new state Minister for Water Supply and the Arts, from any fallout. In doing so he stumbles upon scams and rackets aplenty. Just how bad could things get? Candidly, Maloney's storytelling is quite brilliant. His prose crackles with life, full of turns of phrase both fresh and funny. His descriptions of Melbourne are exquisite. The solitary flaw of the Murray Whelan escapades? Maloney hasn't written more of them.

* * *

The idea of 'cat mysteries' may divide crime fans; delighting some while inducing eye rolls and cringes in others. But while **CAROLINE SHAW** has a 'cat detective' at the heart of her novel *Cat Catcher*, it's a far cry from the lightweight but hugely popular US-style cosies full of feline sleuths or supporters. Helena 'Lenny' Aaron was a Melbourne cop until a horrifying confrontation with a drug dealer left her scarred physically and mentally. Nerves shot, she resigns herself to a life of pill-popping, obsessive compulsions, and finding people's lost cats. When a client also asks her to investigate a series of threatening letters, Lenny is drawn into a case that turns violent and forces her to confront her lingering fears from her police past. Shaw balances Lenny's bleak view of the world with dashes of wry humour and an eclectic cast of supporting characters, including Lenny's therapist who prescribes Zen Buddhism and Bonsai trees. The cat-catching sleuth returns in *Eye to Eye*, where she goes undercover as a goth film student in order to investigate theft and vandalism at a local film school.

* * *

While **ALISON GOODMAN** is renowned for supernatural Regency and young adult fantasy novels that earned her a global audience and *New York Times* bestseller status, she has also produced a peculiar thriller. *A New Kind of Death* (originally published as *Killing the Rabbit* in the US) centres on aspiring Melbourne filmmaker Hannie Reynard whose documentary about medical oddities is collapsing. Hannie has blown her funding on a Paris trip, is being blackmailed by a former classmate, and the female subjects for her film are disappearing. Meanwhile the long-term plans of a massive Japanese pharmaceutical company may be in peril, and a Zimbabwe-based executive calls on an aging Vietnam veteran to clean things up. Goodman offers readers a variety of viewpoints from her atypical cast as events unfold. Mixing film making, corporate espionage, reproductive rights, Melbourne settings, Asian gangs, and painful illnesses sounds like a hodgepodge, but Goodman adeptly brings it all together into an action-packed thriller with a delightful dash of weirdness.

* * *

Could you get more Australian than an amateur sleuth who is also a professional cricketer? That's what special needs teacher and author **CAROLYN MORWOOD** provided with her duology starring Marlo Shaw. A first-class cricketer based in Melbourne, Marlo becomes an unintended investigator of her own family in *Uncertain Death* after her aunt Jenny dies, and Marlo can't believe it was suicide. In the sequel *A Simple Death*, Marlo and a friend discover a bludgeoned body in a Melbourne park, sparking an investigation into another family which forces Marlo to confront her unresolved grief about past events. A good example of a suburban mystery with great local colour. More recently, Morwood dug into Melbourne's past with two mysteries featuring returning First World War nurse Eleanor Jones.

* * *

The idea of high school bullies getting their just desserts years later has a visceral appeal that **ANNA SNOEKSTRA** taps into in her fourth thriller *The Spite Game*. A decade ago Ava was a timid schoolgirl willing to stay silent while popular girls Mel, Saanvi, and Cass bullied others, then targeting a teacher with them in order to win acceptance – only to be bullied and betrayed herself. With wounds festering since, she's stalking the trio as adults, looking for ways to upend their lives in return. But while Ava gets revenge on Saanvi and Cass, the bullies' ringleader Mel has caught onto her game, and is happy to play too. Snoekstra has created a fascinating tale that switches between adult viewpoints and high school recollections, told through the eyes of a vulnerable woman who was treated horribly but may be quite disturbed. Just how far will Ava and Mel go? What led up to a startling confession at a Melbourne police station? A compulsive story about some rather awful people that leans into schadenfreude and asks readers to do the same.

* * *

Looking back, 1996 was rather monumental for both Australian crime writing and a magazine editor who'd become inextricably linked with the growing appreciation for the local genre at home and abroad. That year, the Ned Kelly Awards were first held. That year, **PETER TEMPLE**, a South African who'd moved to Melbourne in the early 1980s, turned 50 and published his first novel, *Bad Debts*. Jack Irish is an ex-criminal lawyer who dulls the pain of his wife's murder with booze and betting and cabinetmaking, while doing a bit of debt collecting for cash. Confusion over a series of messages from an ex-client now out of prison turns to guilt when the client is gunned down. Jack digs into the old case, kicking over a hornet nest. From the get-go, Temple showcases his talent for diamond-sharp descriptions and dialogue, needing few words to bring intensity and nuance to his characters and Melbourne settings. The first of four excellent novels starring Jack Irish, *Bad Debts* went on to win Temple his first of a record five Ned Kelly Awards. But it was the Melbourne author's later work that really shifted the earth for Australian crime writing. *The Broken Shore* features Melbourne detective Joe Cashin, who is sent to a small country station in his hometown to rehabilitate, only to get caught up in corruption and prejudice when a prominent local businessman is bashed, and fingers get pointed at three Aborigine boys. A confronting and wonderfully evocative novel told in sparse prose, *The Broken Shore* saw Temple become the first Australian ever to win the CWA Gold Dagger (it also scooped several other awards). Its loosely linked sorta-sequel, *Truth*, about a detective investigating a murder while bushfires rage outside Melbourne, became the first crime novel ever to win the Miles Franklin Award, the Australian equivalent of the Booker Prize. The judges called *Truth* 'a stunning novel about contemporary Australian life, written with all the ambiguity and moral sophistication of the most memorable literature'. More than anyone, Temple broke down the cultural cringe long associated locally with antipodean crime. Sadly, Peter Temple passed away in 2018. Posthumously, a collection of his writings was released – *The Red Hand* – which includes part of an unfinished fifth Jack Irish novel, the script for a television movie, and stories, essays, reviews, and reflections from the legendary author.

* * *

When **JR CARROLL** spoke to his local newspaper, *The Age*, on the release of *Blindside* back in 2004, he confessed his literary life of crime was accidental: before he first put fingers to keys many years before he'd thought of writing thrillers disguised as 'serious works of fiction', à la Graham Greene. But what had naturally formed throughout several novels was far more graphic and undeniably crime fiction. In *Cheaters*, Danny is a university whiz kid earning himself extra money at the Melbourne casino who gets talent-spotted to launder money for a businessman turned porn filmmaker. Robert is a leading academic turned addict who has fallen from grace and finds himself in even greater danger when a friend witnesses the vicious killing of a young gambler in Chinatown. Carroll gives readers a thrilling rollercoaster ride in a tale that careens through the Melbourne underworld.

* * *

In sporting terms, **MARK BRANDI**'s exquisite debut *Into the River* (*Wimmera* in Australia and New Zealand) was the equivalent of a rookie cricketer striding out and hitting a century in their very first test match. His second offering, *The Rip*? Imagine the same cricketer returning to give the bowlers another pasting. Impressively, the two novels are very different in many ways, while sharing an underlying exploration of people on the margins. Whereas *Into the River* was set in small-town Victoria, *The Rip* brings readers into the rough parts of inner-city Melbourne. Our unnamed narrator is scratching out mere survival on the streets, dumpster diving for food with her friend Anton and sticking a needle in her arm to escape her reality. A vulnerable woman, beaten down in all senses. She and Anton end up crashing with Steve, a dodgy bloke, in a flat with a weird smell and a locked bedroom. Brandi lures readers in with beautiful prose, a deceptively simple storyline, and a light touch even as heartbreaking lives and violent events are portrayed. *The Rip* is a nuanced and unflinching exploration of lives that often go unseen. Hard-hitting and full of humanity.

* * *

Capital Crimes: Canberra and Wellington

It's hard to fathom now just how groundbreaking it was, as recently as the early 1990s, when a vanguard of crime writers including the likes of Val McDermid, Stella Duffy, and **ROSE BEECHAM** were increasingly placing queer characters, issues, and lives front and centre. Beecham's first trilogy, set in Wellington and featuring ex-NYPD detective Amanda Valentine, was among books blocked by customs officials at the Canadian border as 'obscene material', leading to a Supreme Court case. *Fair Play*, the coda to the Valentine tales, sees the closeted cop investigating two cases – one official, one not – that both raise questions of loyalty, keeping secrets, and culpability. Months after the high-profile head of a gay and lesbian broadcaster vanishes during a scandal, he turns up murdered. Meanwhile an enthusiastic junior brings Valentine an unusual rape allegation entwined in the local lesbian community. Although lighter in tone than Beecham's later, gritty tales starring Colorado sheriff's detective Jude Devine, *Fair Play* is an engaging read that centres on a fascinating heroine, explores tough issues, and takes a nuanced look at marginalised lives.

* * *

After a childhood ensconced in the 'working class Catholic ghetto' of Miramar in suburban Wellington, **DENIS EDWARDS** spread his wings abroad as an adult, living and working on three continents in jobs ranging from advertising to paramedic and police officer. He later returned home to an award-winning writing career spanning everything from plays and television soaps to sports journalism, memoir, and children's books, Among Edwards' oeuvre: two thrillers. The second, *Miramar Morning*, is a fast-paced and darkly fun tale that taps into his roots. A letter bomb disintegrates a woman in 1972. Her sister fears she's next. How does this tie to violence and police corruption back in 1947? Switching between eras, *Miramar Morning* exposes readers to cops good and bad, to people pushed to their limits. Sectarian struggles and a dark underbelly fester beneath seemingly innocent times. Edwards addresses serious topics in a slick read that never takes itself too seriously.

* * *

Spycraft and Islamic militancy aren't typical ingredients for a savagely funny novel, but in the accomplished hands of Wellington lawyer and author **BRANNAVAN GNANALINGAM** they're baked to perfection into a delicious tale of satire and surreal farce. *A Briefcase, Two Pies and a Penthouse* is inspired in title by a 1980s incident where a local journalist recovered a Kiwi spy's lost briefcase; rather than state secrets it contained magazines, meat pies, and a gossip-filled diary. In Gnanalingam's novel, Rachel McManus is a rookie employee at a government intelligence agency tasked with investigating a suspected terrorist. What follows is more Austin Powers than James Bond, as bumbling bureaucracy, misogynist managers, and a *laissez faire* approach to geopolitics prove equally big hurdles for McManus. An amorphous novel, at times, that's drenched in humour and intelligence.

* * *

Despite being the nation's capital and playing host to plenty of political intrigue, Canberra has rarely been featured in Australian crime fiction. Perhaps due to a (mis)perception about it being a dull backwater, a neutral 'bush capital', full of bureaucrats, only built to solve an arm-wrestle between Sydney and Melbourne 120 years ago. Conversely, **DOROTHY JOHNSTON** found it a fine setting for a quartet of intelligent thrillers starring computer crime consultant Sandra Mahoney. In *The White Tower*, Sandra is contacted by the grief-stricken mother of a young radiotherapist whose body was found at the base of a communications tower that juts like a hypodermic needle from Canberra's Black Mountain. To understand whether it was murder not suicide, Sandra must investigate not only the hospital where the victim worked, but the online gaming world to which he'd become addicted. All while raising a baby alone. Johnston draws readers into a languid mystery with a striking opening then her strong characterisation. More recently, Johnston has penned a series of 'sea change mysteries' set in coastal Victoria.

* * *

In award-bedecked television writer-producer **DONNA MALANE**'s terrific first crack at a crime novel, *Surrender*, the opening 'death knock' is a little different. Missing persons expert Diane Rowe opens her door to her policeman ex-husband, and the news he delivers leaves her anything but bereaved: a body found in Wellington's Cuba Street belongs to a recidivist low-life Diane suspects killed her troubled younger sister Niki the year before. But when Diane discovers Snow's murder was eerily akin to her sister's, she wonders whether someone else was responsible for both deaths. Diane's obsessive freelancing imploded her marriage, but she dives deeper into the seedy underbelly of New Zealand's capital city while juggling a new official case involving a decapitated body found in the Rimutaka forest. Stubborn, frustrating, funny, and beguiling, Diane is a tremendous character who gets herself into strife while trying to do the right thing, in an unconventional way. She returned in *My Brother's Keeper*, and we can only hope Malane finds time for more Diane Rowe tales, in among a jam-packed screen career (which includes recent hit crime drama *The Gulf*).

* * *

Before writing a handful of pretty great thrillers, **MICHAEL WALL** was press secretary for New Zealand Prime Minister Jim Bolger in the early 1990s. He harnessed that political experience and insider knowledge in two of his novels in particular: *Museum Street* and *Friendly Fire*. In the latter, renowned journalist Erin Florian returns to Wellington from Europe after a marriage breakup to assist the new Prime Minister, only to find herself caught up in bizarre schemes as the Government's coalition partner undergoes a leadership coup. The new leader makes outrageous demands and seems strangely confident the Prime Minister will capitulate, then Erin witnesses a killing that's covered up and finds herself under scrutiny from government security agents. More deaths and conspiracies follow, and the country teeters towards the brink of political and economic meltdown. Wall crafted a terrific political thriller, weaving together fascinating characters, global economics and international relations, the controversial Waihopai spy base, and the machinations and manipulations of the media. Twenty years on, it still seems scarily relevant.

* * *

Merely capitalising the 'O' in offbeat isn't sufficient to describe **DANYL MCLAUCHLAN**'s offbeat mysteries set in the Aro Valley, a bohemian inner-city suburb of Wellington famed for its 'liberal, artsy' soul and damp student flats. McLauchlan guides readers into this shady enclave – in sunshine terms, if not others – with tales that are offbeat in all caps, italicised, and underlined. McLauchlan took his skills as a political satirist in new directions in *Unspeakable Secrets of the Aro Valley*, a quirky tale where main character Danyl and his mate Steve bumble around, encountering an eclectic array of locals as they look into the strange activities of a local cult. The author has admitted it's a bit of a spoof of both Dan Brown-style thrillers (imagine if the mystical secrets of the universe were contained not in the Vatican, but a Wellington suburb) and thrillers where main characters are braver and more attractive versions of the author's own resume. A comic farce that works wonderfully in that regard, and many others, but won't be for everyone. Danyl the protagonist and Danyl the author both returned in *Mysterious Mysteries of the Aro Valley*.

* * *

Brisbane

Readers who enjoy stark white hat-black hat delineation between heroes and villains would be advised to steer well clear of **IAIN RYAN**'s powerful tales of tainted cops, but they'll be missing out on something a bit special. Ryan announced himself with *Four Days*, an unflinching, seamy noir set in the fetid heat of 1980s Brisbane and the Sunshine Coast. Self-destructive detective Jim Harris is awaiting a life-and-death medical verdict, having earned final condemnation many times over. A man of few redeeming qualities, perhaps he can scratch some redemption by investigating the ignored case of a dead prostitute and her missing brother, a fellow cop. Four days to traverse the swamp of Queensland policing, to uncover the truth beneath the murk and expose the killers. Ryan crafts a strong narrative drive with sparse, wry prose, meshing Aussie sensibilities with classic noir to drag readers along even as they may be grimacing. Vivid and atmospheric, stylish and shot through with sex and violence, *Four Days* was followed by three further corruption-filled noirs from Ryan.

* * *

Traditionally the lines were stark between the logic and rationality of mystery fiction and the supernatural underpinnings of horror writing, but in recent times borders have blurred. What is a serial killer, after all, but the human embodiment of a heartless monster? **GARY KEMBLE** shows how to dive successfully into genre no man's land with an adroit blend of dark mystery and dashes of paranormal in *Strange Ink* (titled *Skin Deep* in Australia and New Zealand). Harry Hendrick is meandering through life, his once-promising journalism career sabotaged years ago and now circling the drain. A mate's stag night, drunken shenanigans; he wakes with a strange tattoo on his neck. Inebriated idiocy, he presumes. Until more tattoos appear, coupled with violent visions that may tie to the war in Afghanistan and a local politician. Harry's not the only sufferer and must uncover what's going on. Kemble grounds his highly original tale with a likable if flawed hero, great sense of place, and plenty of reality: political corruption, the brutality of war, and the importance of friendship.

* * *

There's a palpable sense of righteous anger bristling through the pages of **NICOLE WATSON**'s confronting novel *The Boundary*. Within days of Justice Brosnan of the Native Title Tribunal dismissing the long-running claim made by the Corrowa indigenous people to a public park in Brisbane, the judge and two lawyers are brutally murdered. The judge's ruling relied on a legal technicality, compounded past injustices, including a colonial curfew on Aborigines, and handily freed up the park to be sold to developers. A system designed to redress injustices has instead enshrined them. When the Premier and his Aboriginal aide are added to the body count, red feathers left near each victim, it's clear someone is sick of waiting for justice. *The Boundary* is a powerful tale, passionately told from multiple perspectives (centred on troubled lawyer Miranda Eversley), that explores Brisbane's fraught indigenous history, power imbalances in politics, the Aboriginal concept of Dreamtime, and the power to change. An eye-opening read, stamped with authority given Watson (Birri Gubba) is an expert on legal issues affecting indigenous communities and has witnessed the harsh realities herself while working in legal aid and at the National Native Title Tribunal.

* * *

While **ANDREW MCGAHAN** is most remembered for his Miles Franklin Award-winning gothic novel set among Queensland's wheat fields and sheep farms (*White Earth*), or his drug-filled semi-autobiographical debut that launched the 'grunge lit' movement (*Praise*), he also scooped a Ned Kelly Award for his sole crime novel, *Last Drinks*. A murder mystery inspired by the corruption exposed by the Fitzgerald Inquiry in Queensland, *Last Drinks* centres on disgraced journalist George Verney, who returns to Brisbane ten years later following the brutal death of an old friend. Trying to find some answers, he's plunged back into memories of a booze-soaked life, of rampant corruption, of wholly unqualified people being elevated to positions of power then abusing it for personal gain. Written in 2000 to reflect on times two decades before, *Last Drinks* is still strangely relevant today, two decades later (there are plenty of echoes of Joh Bjelke-Petersen's folksy persona, reliance on public ignorance, and blatant cronyism and graft in Trump's America and elsewhere).

* * *

Other antipodean cities

Playwright **CARL NIXON** opened his first novel with a teenage boy finding the body of a teenage girl in the sand dunes near New Brighton, early one morning just before Christmas in 1980. What follows in *Rocking Horse Road* isn't a typical whodunnit or murder mystery, but an artful exploration of the ongoing human impact of violent crime. The boy and his friends become obsessed with the case: undertaking their own investigation, gathering evidence, tracking suspects, and unearthing dangerous secrets. Their lives are never the same. The narrator, now in his 40s, looks back on that scorching summer and all that followed for the teens, their small community on the outskirts of Christchurch, and the broader country as violence shattered innocence. Nixon delivered an atmospheric, layered tale that lured readers with its early hook and strong narrative voice, before taking us on a beguiling journey that's about people and place as much as solving a mystery.

* * *

If Ihaka creator Paul Thomas is the original Godfather of modern Kiwi crime writing, then **PAUL CLEAVE** is surely its Michael Corleone. The Christchurch author and former pawnbroker has said he originally wanted to write horror stories, until he read a book by an FBI profiler and realised crime fiction would allow him to explore truer monsters. He did just that in his first several novels, dark thrillers which often involved serial killers in a variety of roles. Cleave's startling debut *The Cleaner* became a smash hit abroad, including topping an annual crime bestseller list in Germany ahead of one of Cleave's storytelling idols Lee Child. A powerful tale told through the skewed view of 'Slow Joe', a good-natured, dim-witted janitor who's really a clever killer spying on the police investigation into his own crimes, *The Cleaner* was an early indicator of Cleave's talent for compromised 'heroes', dark tales laced with sly humour, and truly unforgettable moments. Famously, Australian author Jack Heath fainted while reading *The Cleaner* on a plane. Over the next dozen-plus years, Cleave has collected awards and acclaim at home and abroad while never shirking from plunging his protagonists, and readers, into moral quagmires and situations that pack an emotional, even visceral, wallop. Whether it's a son forced to reconnect with his killer father in *Blood Men*, ex-cop Theo Tate confronting his drunken past in *Collecting Cooper*, or author Jerry Grey dealing with befuddling, violent memories as Alzheimer's arrives in *Trust No One*, Cleave's heroes often face harsh consequences for even the best-intentions choices they make. The city of Christchurch casts a character-like shadow throughout Cleave's first ten thrillers, creating an atmospheric, overlapping world where the main characters in some novels appear in cameos or supporting roles in others. In recent years, Cleave has stretched his literary legs, experimenting with multiple narratives from the same fractured mind (including a rare use of second-person perspective) in *Trust No One*, and a dash of magic realism in *A Killer Harvest*. His latest is a further departure, geographically: *Whatever it Takes* is Cleave's first thriller set outside Christchurch and takes readers deep into a rural American enclave of sawmills, hiking trails, and elected lawmen. Fizzing prose and fresh storytelling.

* * *

Crime fiction can take readers into some pretty harrowing places, but from a purely emotional perspective I'd posit no amount of brutal violence, even torture, could hit someone as hard as the loss of their child. In **JANE WOODHAM**'s debut *Twister* that's the burden Detective Senior Sergeant Leo Judd and his wife Kate have borne for nine years. When a storm uncovers the body of a missing schoolgirl, it heaps stress on the city as well as Judd, who's leading an investigation that hits far too close to home. A home that has been a shadow of its former self for years; in fact Kate is about to leave Judd for her lover Rea, their former neighbour. As the pressure rises, Judd struggles to uncover the truth behind the tragedies present and past. Woodham accentuates the personal above the police investigation in a tightly plotted tale with a superb sense of its Dunedin location.

* * *

Cliffhangers are a common device in storytelling, keeping readers turning to the next chapter, or buying the next episode or instalment. But they don't often happen in the first lines, and usually don't involve a real cliff. Enter Dunedin author **FINN BELL,** who burst onto the crime scene in 2016 with *The Killing Ground* (original title *Dead Lemons*) and *One Last Kill* (originally *Pancake Money*). The first opened with its wheelchair-bound protagonist clinging to the side of a cliff, desperate to avoid discovery by his murderous neighbours. Bell's potent mix of evocative settings, complicated characters, psychology, and fresh action saw him scoop several US-based indy publishing and ebook prizes and become the first ebook author to win a Ngaio Marsh Award. In *One Last Kill*, Bobby Ress and Pollo Latu are Dunedin detectives with families who just want to make a difference. Then two Catholic priests are martyred in medieval fashion: a serial killer, or vigilante justice for past wrongs? Bell balanced a brutal page-turner with an engaging buddy cop duo backdropped by Otago's cinematic landscapes. Bell's recent novels include *Good Hot Hate* and *The Lost Dead*.

* * *

Back in 1993, controversial US college basketball coach Jimmy Valvano, dying of cancer, stood up at an awards show and gave an extraordinary speech that has been watched by millions and is still regularly shared almost three decades later. Jimmy V spoke of three things everyone should do each day, to live a great life: 'If you laugh, you think, and you cry, that's a full day'. After a couple of stylish, witty thrillers set in the corrupt worlds of law and insurance, Sydney silk **RICHARD BEASLEY** hit the Jimmy V trifecta with his 2013 novel *Me and Rory Macbeath*. Set in suburban Adelaide in the 1970s, where adolescent Jake lives with his uncompromising solo mother Harry – a barrister always up for a battle – it is an affecting story of friendship, family, and how those closest to us can build us up or tear us down. Over one summer Jake befriends Scottish immigrant Rory, who then defends Jake from high school bullies only for their whole world to be rocked by a shocking incident and its courtroom aftermath. The languid tone and nostalgic setting lure readers in before Beasley drops the hammer. An emotional, thoughtful read that intersects coming-of-age tale, literary fiction, and crime.

* * *

Legal thrillers are hugely popular and a prolific sub-genre in the United States, far rarer in the antipodes. Perhaps that's due to our different systems Downunder, with no death penalty or elected prosecutors and judges, plus less of an alphabet soup of law enforcement agencies vying for credit. Ergo, less fertile soil for drama fuelled by corrupt practices, political interference, police errors, or life-or-death cases. But as **MARK MCGINN** has shown in his Sasha Stace series, the parry-and-thrust of courtroom drama can translate Downunder. In *Presumed Guilty*, middle-aged Stace is a top Christchurch lawyer ready to chuck it all away after successfully defending a sleazy politician on a sex charge. Then her ex is accused of murdering his wife, a popular journalist. McGinn balances the intrigue of the court case with emotional oomph as Stace, a fascinating heroine, deals with complicated relationships and her own doubts and issues. An engaging tale with some nice shades of grey among 'heroes' and antagonists.

* * *

Like a shooting star, Waikato author **GAELYN GORDON**'s writing career was spectacular but all-too-brief. A high school English and Drama teacher who began writing when she took sick leave in her late 40s, Gordon produced many beloved books for children, teens, and adults before her death a decade later. Her prolific output included a trio of sly crime novels centred on Detective Senior Sergeant Rangi Roberts and Detective Constable Andy Pike. The coda to the trilogy, published shortly before Gordon's death, was *Deadlines*, which saw Roberts, one of the rare Māori detectives in crime writing, suspecting his neighbour's death was no accident. Especially since Roberts knew the deceased was the sender of a flood of anonymous letters afflicting the university. Can he find out who killed 'the little creep', while keeping his superiors at bay and courting a high-strung literary agent? Like Gordon's entire oeuvre, *Deadlines* is a delightful, engaging story that never takes itself too seriously.

* * *

Would you prefer to be poisoned or skewered? Don't let the bubbly personality fool you – **VANDA SYMON** is the epitome of 'the deadlier of the species', having trained as a pharmacist and won medals in Masters-level fencing. *En garde*. Fortunately, the Dunedin author keeps her killing on the page – as far as we know. She's damned good at it. A dozen years after I first read it, I still shiver at the gut-punch opening in Symon's superb debut, *Overkill*, a novel that introduced ambitious small-town copper Sam Shephard, a likable and headstrong heroine with a tendency to plop herself in the manure. Throughout a top shelf series Symon mixes dark deeds with lighter moments, while capturing a strong sense of Kiwi places, attitudes, and vernacular. Particularly those of the south of the South Island: a unique region of farming communities, epic *Lord of the Rings* landscapes, and a student city that proudly wears its Scottish-not-English roots. In *The Ringmaster*, Shephard has moved to Dunedin to become low woman on the detective totem pole, a junior investigator having to battle entrenched misogyny. Her first homicide is a university student found murdered in the local botanic gardens, but it quickly emerges that this isn't an isolated incident and may have links to a visiting circus. Symon populates a fine tale with great characters and fresh touches. It's no surprise the series has been shortlisted for major awards in both hemispheres. Symon was a gem hidden away Downunder; now she's getting global notice.

* * *

Modern crime fiction offers readers a veritable buffet that caters to a huge variety of tastes. For those with a gentler palate who prefer puzzles that eschew realism, violence, and sex, the 'cosy mystery' continues to be popular, particularly in the United States. Tasmanian author **LIVIA DAY** provides an antipodean spin with her series of culinary crime tales starring café owner and pastry chef Tabitha Darling. In *A Trifle Dead* gossipy Tabitha wants to run a trendy Hobart café but keeps attracting old-fashioned coppers who fondly remember Tabitha's police superintendent father and her mother, who cooked for the police canteen. When a dead musician is discovered in the upstairs flat and a series of random crimes hits Hobart, Tabitha becomes an accidental sleuth. It's a clever mystery liberally sprinkled with humour, a nice sense of the Hobart setting, and a fabulous supporting cast. Day repeats the recipe in further Tabitha escapades, with *Keep Calm and Kill the Chef* the latest dish served.

* * *

Lachie Munro, the house painting anti-hero of **ANDY MUIR**'s caper-filled novels, wants a carefree life near the beach in Newcastle but has a knack for stumbling into chaos. In *Something for Nothing*, Lachie tries to ease his gambling debts with some shellfish poaching, only to discover several kilos of heroin. A good day or a bad one? He's soon in deeper waters, stumbling across a torso on the beach, losing his job, getting punched by a bikie, and starting to fall for a cute fisheries officer while trying to avoid police scrutiny. Muir delivers a cracking romp of a tale that's distinctly Australian, packed with larrikin sensibilities, wry humour, atypical characters, and dark deeds tinted with a light touch. Muir, whose own storytelling arc traversed globally renowned Aussie soaps *Neighbours* and *Home and Away* through several years of crime inculcation on gritty drama *Underbelly*, brought Lachie Munro back in *Hiding to Nothing*. With luck, there'll be plenty more misadventures ahead.

* * *

Hobart author **DAVID OWEN** grew from mistrusting the police as a university student protesting apartheid in South Africa to writing one of the most enjoyable and wickedly funny detective series in antipodean crime. Detective Inspector Franz Heineken of the Tasmanian Police, aka 'Pufferfish' (for his prickly, even poisonous personality with those he despises, like his bosses) first appeared in a quartet of novels in the mid-1990s. After a long hiatus he returned in another five tales in the past decade, much to the delight of Aussie crime aficionados. In *13-Point Plan for a Perfect Murder* a horde of rich jetsetters arrives to play polo at a resort built by a Bahraini billionaire. When the murders of an aristocratic Englishman and a local lowlife interrupt the play-hard, party-hard atmosphere, grumpy sleuth Pufferfish is put on the case. Owen doses up the dry humour and Tasmanian locations as the cops traverse society high and low while dealing with personal distractions like stolen stamp collections and reappearing paramours from decades past.

* * *

After heralding her arrival with an award-winning trilogy featuring Sydney homicide detectives Eden Archer and Frank Bennett, **CANDICE FOX** swapped the seamy streets of her hometown for the crocodile-infested landscapes of north Queensland in *Crimson Lake*. Though the setting has switched, once again Fox offers a finely wrought, dark tale centred on an unusual, indelible pairing of investigators. Ted Conkaffey was a Sydney detective whose career and family were vaporised when he was accused of sexually assaulting a young girl. Imprisoned for months before charges were dropped, he finds freedom isn't so free and flees to Cairns where he teams with Amanda Pharrell, a peculiar private eye and convicted killer. Together the two broken souls investigate the case of a missing celebrity – a crocodile's dinner or something more sinister? – as well as peering into each other's bludgeonings by the law. Ted wants to lie low, but brutal local cops, an investigative journo from the city, and a local lynch mob are determined that, convicted or not, a 'kiddie fiddler' won't settle in their town. *Crimson Lake* is a black opal of a story: hard exterior, eye-catching and colourful characters who shift with different views, and distinctly Australian.

* * *

Adelaide scribe **KIRSTY BROOKS** gave a fresh spin to local private eye tales in the mid-noughties with her vivacious series starring video store clerk and part-time sleuth Cassidy Blair. An oddball investigator who leans more Stephanie Plum than Sam Spade, Blair has a wry one-liner for every situation and brings plenty of sassiness and sex to the mix. So much so that at the time, the books were tabbed as chick lit crime. In *The Millionaire Float*, the accident-prone Blair takes a job working undercover as an exotic dancer at a notorious local nightclub. Perhaps not a gig that will please her *amour*, local cop Sam Tusker. As Blair investigates, things go from bad to worse. Will she and her friends be able to save the day? Brooks gave fans four Cassidy Blair novels that put fun at the forefront, along with a standalone 'romantic comedy meets noir', *Lady Luck*. While Brooks spoke in interviews about two further Cassidy Blair tales, more than a decade on they've yet to be published.

* * *

Brisbane author **MARIANNE DELACOURT** dialled up the fun when she revisited her hometown in a series starring unorthodox Perth private eye Tara Sharp. We first meet Tara in *Sharp Shooter* as a rich kid turned out-of-work adult living above her parents' garage. Struggling with an unusual ability to see people's auras, and therefore their moods, Tara learns to embrace her gift/curse then gets hired by a shady lawyer to investigate the owner of a sports team. Should she be worried her new employer has ties to the local mob? Delacourt (a pen name for a successful science fiction and YA fantasy author) nicely balances both humour and peril in this award-winning debut and throughout the five-books-so-far series. Tara is a plucky, likable heroine; a Holden Monaro-driving trouble-magnet. With a fascinating cast and good sense of place, Delacourt offers plenty of entertainment.

* * *

Quis custodiet ipsos custodes? In her second novel, *The Betrayal,* former Tasmanian policewoman **YA ERSKINE** gave a chilling portrayal of the question posed by Roman poet Juvenal almost two thousand years ago: Who will guard the guards themselves? A sequel to her fine debut *The Brotherhood*, itself a confrontational exploration of modern policing, *The Betrayal* deals with crimes committed by police against their own. Weeks after waking up naked in a colleague's bed with gaps in her memory, young constable Lucy Howard lays a complaint against popular peer Nick Greaves, a member of the elite Special Operations Group, claiming Nick must have drugged and raped her. The she said-he said case sends shudders through the Hobart Station, dividing loyalties beyond gender lines. Meanwhile another case exposes high-level corruption and threatens the Police Commissioner. Told from multiple viewpoints (which somewhat distance readers from Lucy), *The Betrayal* is an all-too-realistic journey into the murky world of rape investigations. It's a deep dive into a lot of ugliness. Uncomfortable, disturbing, and well-written crime fiction.

* * *

Flour bombs dropped from a plane, cancelled games, rugby fans clashing with protesters, police in riot gear bloodying heads with batons: the 1981 Springbok Tour was one of the most divisive events in modern New Zealand history. Christchurch writer **KATHERINE HAYTON** ably taps into those chaotic times in *The Only Secret Left to Keep*, her sixth crime novel and third featuring Detective Ngaire Blakes. When a skeleton uncovered after a fire is identified as Sam Andie, a young African-American who disappeared around the time of the Tour, Blakes (of Māori descent herself) is faced with a tough case that has disturbing undertones of prejudice, racial and otherwise. Having returned to the police force after a break to try to deal with her PTSD, Blakes is put under tremendous pressure and her career is in jeopardy. As part of a clever tale propelled by a flawed and engaging heroine, Hayton addressed a mile marker in New Zealand history. More recently the prolific author has lightened things significantly with several cosy series (baking mysteries, tea shop mysteries, café mysteries, etc).

* * *

Those who prefer their crime cosy might want to avoid **TONY CAVANAUGH**'s engrossing Darian Richards series. The experienced screenwriter and producer didn't hold back on the creepier side of crime when he turned to novels, nimbly tightroping his way across the abyss, trying not to fall into gratuitousness, while also offering uncomfortable peeks into the minds of predators. In *Dead Girl Sing*, Richards gets a phone call about two dead girls and a missing cop. People flock to coastal Queensland for many reasons; Richards wanted a quiet retirement after years of hunting monsters as head of Victoria's Homicide Squad. Others have gathered for 'Schoolies Week', the notorious Aussie equivalent of spring break, where high school leavers get wild for days on end. Among all the hormones and illicit substances, young women have begun disappearing. Leaning on a hacker mate in Melbourne and a local Noosa cop for help, Richards goes back on the hunt. A conflicted protagonist whose hat hasn't been white for years plus some interesting sidekicks and a dive into the grime behind the glitter of the Gold Coast mesh into a knuckle-whitening tale. After four Richards novels, Cavanaugh switched things up in 2019 with *Blood River*. Police Commissioner Lara Ocean is forced to revisit a troubling case when a woman convicted of a series of brutal killings 20 years before as a teen (but who always protested her innocence) is paroled.

* * *

The mining boom that transformed Western Australia's urban areas didn't trickle down to everyone. *Heaven Sent* by **ALAN CARTER** is a fine crime thriller starring a Chinese-Australian detective that also explores the growing issue of homelessness in one of the world's 'most liveable cities'. After plenty of tumult in the first three novels of a terrific series, Philip 'Cato' Kwong's life is at a happy new stage; new wife, new baby, and a thawing relationship with his teenage son. He's pulled from domestic bliss (in his eyes, perhaps not his wife's) by a series of murders of Fremantle's homeless. While Cato hunts the killer, so does journalist Norman Lip, in dangerous fashion. Carter shows a great knack for balancing plot, character, and setting, delivering on all levels while advancing the gritty story with plenty of verve. Cato Kwong is a fascinating character who feels very real – a likable guy and good cop who tries to do the right thing but stuffs up at times and can be oblivious in his personal life. The books can be read as standalones while having a good character arc throughout.

* * *

KEL ROBERTSON takes readers back to one of the most bizarre moments in Australian political history in his second novel *Smoke and Mirrors*: the dismissal of Prime Minister Gough Whitlam in 1975 by the Governor-General (the Queen's representative in some former colonies within the Commonwealth, who usually only wields ceremonial powers). Australian Federal Policeman Bradman 'Brad' Chen is recovering from injuries sustained in his first outing when he's lured back to work by the murder of a former minister in Whitlam's government, and the editor who was working with him on a tell-all autobiography. Did someone want to silence an insider who could have cast light on events that have sparked plenty of conspiracy theories? Or is something else going on as South African mercenaries and Russian gangsters saunter through the capital? Robertson doses an action-packed and exciting mystery with plenty of humour, while showcasing a momentous point in Australian history as well as a hero deserving of an ongoing series.

* * *

Other urban crime writers and key books
TIM AYLIFFE: *The Greater Good* (Sydney)
CA BROADRIBB: *Nice Day for a Murder* (Sydney)
ANDREW CHRISTIE: *Left Luggage* (Sydney)
BLAIR DENHOLM: *Sold* (Gold Coast)
MICHAEL DUFFY: *Drive By* (Sydney)
STEPHEN GREENALL: *Winter Traffic* (Sydney)
SUSI FOX: *Mine* (Melbourne)
PETER GOLDSWORTHY: *Minotaur* (Adelaide)
SUSAN HURLEY: *Eight Lives* (Melbourne)
KARINA KILMORE: *Where the Truth Lies* (Melbourne)
HUGH MCGINLAY: *Jinx* (Melbourne)
NICOLA MORIARTY: *The Ex* (Sydney)
LEE MURRAY & DAN RABARTS: *Teeth of the Wolf* (Auckland)
ANDREW PORTEOUS: *A Political Affair* (Dunedin)
JENNIFER SPENCE: *The Lost Girls* (Sydney)
LEIGH STRAW: *Limestone* (Fremantle)
SUE YOUNGER: *Days Are Like Grass* (Auckland)

In the Wop-Wops – Small-town and Rural Crime

If you could collate the work histories of the world's crime writers, it's a fair bet jobs like journalist, lawyer, teacher, and law enforcement would frequently appear. Farmer, less so. Second-generation Australian cattle rancher **RICHARD ANDERSON** taps into his rarer experience to give *Retribution* a dusty verisimilitude. His debut also offers a second dose of difference: it's a rural crime tale with no murder at its heart. Instead, a stolen horse. An ensemble cast centres on an interesting quartet: a rustler with a deep connection to the countryside, a chaos-loving protester who isn't what he seems, a middle-aged politician who has fallen from grace, and a young woman who hankers for something more from life. As tensions simmer, events unfold in a fresh and fascinating way. Anderson delivers an adroit look at conflict within communities, and the melting pot of personalities and perspectives. The recent *Boxed*, another fascinating character study where violence lurks in a rural community, shows that Anderson isn't a one-book wonder.

* * *

Few novels in recent years have made me grin as much as **RWR MCDONALD**'s debut *The Nancys*. Delightful, charming, and exuberant aren't the usual go-to descriptors when musing on crime fiction, but for this tale they're very apt. Emerging from the chrysalis of the Faber Academy and Victorian Premier's Literary Awards (the latter prize for unpublished manuscripts also gave us Jane Harper's *The Dry* and Christian White's *The Nowhere Child*), *The Nancys* is a *sui generis* concoction of small-town mystery, queer fiction, and nostalgia. At its heart – and McDonald's debut has a big one – *The Nancys* centres on the misadventures of an unlikely investigative trio. Eleven-year old Tippy Chan teams with her visiting Uncle Pike, a Sydney hairdresser who could be Santa's body double, and Pike's fashionista boyfriend Devon to try to emulate her hero Nancy Drew by solving the murder of Tippy's schoolteacher. While also Queer-Eyeing a glum neighbour for a subversive assault on a local fashion show and dealing with Pike's conflicted past. Riotous characters, chaotic events, and lashings of humour; McDonald opened his authorial account with a real belter.

* * *

Fans of amateur sleuths and wilderness mysteries may want to add **TRISH MCCORMACK** to their reading list. While she's now an archivist in New Zealand's capital city, McCormack grew up near Franz Josef Glacier and previously worked in national parks and as a small-town journalist. Her passion for wild landscapes flows through her engaging mystery series featuring glacier guide Philippa Barnes. In the third instalment, *Cold Hard Murder*, Philippa has taken a job with the Department of Conservation in a coastal village on the edge of Paparoa National Park, a spectacular area of limestone caves, rainforest, and rock formations. As people start dying and Philippa's boss pushes for an unpopular commercial venture in the national park, Philippa embarks on an unofficial investigation. McCormack's storytelling echoes classic village murder mysteries, with an eccentric cast of characters, and plenty of clues, suspects, and red herrings. Secrets swirl and threats hover as both the police and Philippa try to unmask the killer, while McCormack offers readers an insight into rural issues and differing perspectives on the best use of areas of natural beauty.

* * *

The rugged magnificence of Fiordland National Park's glacier-carved landscapes has attracted adventurers, scientists, and filmmakers from all over the world and forms the backdrop for Brisbane journalist

BELINDA POLLARD's first thriller *Poison Bay*. The setting is really the star as TV reporter Callie Brown reunites a decade later with a group of her Australian high school friends for an arduous multi-day hike in the wilds of southern New Zealand. Several unprepared urbanites tackling an unforgiving landscape as secrets and grudges swirl: what could go wrong? Pollard proffers an intriguing premise – a crack at *And Then There Were None* among *The Lord of the Rings* landscapes – and sets the hook well enough that jitters with heavy exposition and light characterisation are offset by compelling moments, a good sense of menace, and a beautiful touch for the wilderness setting.

* * *

Innocent women are abducted, taken to a remote forested wilderness, and released so they can be hunted for sport: so far, so recurring premise à la one-hour American crime dramas. Queensland author **JM PEACE** gives the trope a twofold twist in her debut *A Time to Run*. The hunted is a cop, Constable Sammi Willis, as is the author herself. Having served two decades in the Queensland police, Peace textures her taut, fast-moving thriller with a strong sense of authenticity. As Sammi scrambles to survive while she's stalked through the bush by a madman, her colleague Detective Janine Postlewaite leads the investigation into her disappearance. Two hunts, simultaneously. Two determined women. Peace writes in an engaging style that doesn't hammer readers with procedural detail, and ratchets up the tension as pages whir. Her explorations of small-town Australian policing continue in *The Twisted Knot* and *An Unwatched Minute*.

* * *

Perhaps being born in London during the Blitz (before doing all his schooling in New Zealand and then moving to Australia as an adult) played a part in **DEREK HANSEN**'s first few novels having themes related to characters greatly affected by past wartime experiences. But he took a detour into new territory in *A Man You Can Bank On,* a laugh-inducing crime caper set in the overheated world of the Outback. Think Carl Hiaasen with an Aussie accent. A decade after bank manager Lambert Hampton helped save the dying outpost of Munni-Munni, 'population bugger all and declining', thanks to snatching a robbery crew's ill-gotten gains, a host of outsiders come calling for the loot: crims, big city cops, a rogue investigator, and two hitmen named Irish and The Bowler. Shenanigans ensue. The tiny town is used to dust storms, but this is a shitstorm. Hansen repeatedly jabs the reader's funny bone while dancing along the absurdity tightrope. A quirky romp full of eccentric characters, vivid moments, and a hilarious evocation of Outback life.

* * *

While growing up on a horse farm on New Zealand's volcanic plateau, as a teenager **JP POMARE** would surf off the coastal headland of Maketu. The 'little thumb of rock' jutting out between tourist-magnet towns was a gang stronghold, and Pomare says every visit felt like a dare. That atmosphere of strangeness and danger bleeds into Pomare's debut thriller, *Call Me Evie,* which splits its setting between Melbourne, where he lives now, and Maketu. Seventeen-year-old Kate has a shaved head and fractured memory; she is recuperating in a remote cabin under the watchful eye of a man she doesn't trust, who says he's looking after her after something terrible happened. But who did the terrible thing? Is the man trying to help Kate remember, or ensure she forgets? Pomare shuffles past and present as he delivers a nerve-jangling tale infused with literary flair, troubling characters, and a strong sense of place. His adroit debut marks the arrival of a strong and distinctive new voice. His excellent second novel, *In the Clearing*, takes its inspiration from a real-life Australian cult.

* * *

Some crime writers become public figures; on rare occasions public figures become crime writers. That was – briefly – the case for controversial politician and broadcaster **MICHAEL LAWS** as the new millennium loomed. On political hiatus between stints as a Member of the New Zealand Parliament and as Mayor of Whanganui, Laws penned three bestsellers: a scathing memoir, a warts-and-all biography of an All Blacks rugby player, and a good crime thriller. In *Dancing with Beelzebub*, Regan Paul hopes to heal his broken life and his suffering town by running for office. He'd returned to Whanganui after his fiancée died, but he's not the only one reeling. The town's main employer closed, and two kids have been killed. Paul's campaign is rocked by sensational, life-threatening events. However Kiwis feel about Laws the divisive public figure, he showed he could deliver a cracking crime novel full of memorable characters and clever storytelling.

* * *

Nestled between towering peaks and crashing seas, the West Coast region of New Zealand's South Island is renowned for its wildness, rugged beauty, and isolation. The final frontier of a nation that was once itself the far frontier of the British Empire. **SIMON SNOW** vividly brings that 'Coast' setting to life – the place and its people – in his debut *Devil's Apple*. Bush recluse George Todman's march to boozy oblivion is interrupted when Rainbow, a striking teen hippy, dances into his life. Fleeting happiness is snatched away when he later discovers Rainbow's mutilated body and becomes the prime suspect. Teaming with irreverent cop Linda Loveridge, together the unlikely pair infiltrate a local community rife with tensions and opposing interests. Hippies and conservatives, loggers and conservationists, distrustful of outsiders yet not as close-knit as it would seem, witchcraft, drugs, and corruption; Snow shines a light on a distinct part of New Zealand in all its eccentric glory.

* * *

It wasn't so much a case of poacher turned gamekeeper, as gatekeeper turned someone barging through the gate when **BENJAMIN STEVENSON** published his debut novel. A comedian and literary agent who has worked with some of Australia's top crime writers, Stevenson kicked the door down with his promising *She Lies in the Vines* (titled *Greenlight* in Australia and New Zealand).

Four years after grape picker Eliza Dacey was murdered in wine country north of Sydney, her case is back in the public eye. Her killer was quickly caught, or was he? Documentary maker Jack Quick has doubts about winemaker Curtis Wade's guilt, and by the end of his true crime series the wider public believes there's been a miscarriage of justice. But has Jack skewed things to tell the story he wanted? When Wade is exonerated only for another body to surface, Jack's doubts fester and he returns to the scene of the crimes. Stevenson delivers a quaffable mystery with layers of flavour; he brings the Australian wine country setting to rich and vivid life, and leaves readers with a strong finish.

* * *

Although Australia and New Zealand both maintain strong links with Britain, their rugged landscapes and the frontier feel of many rural areas harken more to the Old West than the British countryside. **TANYA MOIR** beautifully taps into that sensibility in her harrowing third novel *The Legend of Winstone Blackhat*. Straddling contemporary fiction and crime fiction and set among the small towns and rural plains of Central Otago, it's the story of a 12-year-old runaway. Something horrible happened, but is Winstone a victim, witness, or culprit? As the youngster scrabbles to survive 'on the lam', he fantasises about thrilling cowboy adventures he and his partner are having in the Wild West. Switching between past and present, and Winstone's fantasies and reality, Moir delivers a disturbing novel that is both subtle and hard-hitting, full of angst and breathtaking beauty. Not a traditional crime novel, but a haunting tale exploring the impact of crime that lingers far beyond the final page.

* * *

Distinguished wildlife photographer **GORDON ELL** brought his passion for nature to his first swing at fiction, setting his intriguing murder mystery *The Ice Shroud* against the backdrop of New Zealand's spectacular Southern Lakes region (a shooting location for *The Lord of the Rings* films). A body spotted by jet-boating tourists, half-frozen in a river canyon, is an abrupt introduction for new CIB head DS Malcolm Buchan. Especially when he recognises the woman; a fact he hides from his new colleague, local traffic Sergeant Magda Hansen. A modern Kiwi take on a classic British village mystery with working class coppers prying into the lives of the wealthy elite, and being stymied for reasons that may have nothing to do with the crime at hand. Full of suspects, red herrings, secrets, and tense business and personal relationships among the populace and police. Overall, a heartily enjoyable debut that takes readers into a gorgeous location as well as the hearts and minds of its heroes.

* * *

With her first foray into psychological thrillers, noted Australian author **EMILY MAGUIRE** skilfully subverts the 'pretty dead girl' trope in *An Isolated Incident*. When well-liked 25-year-old Bella Michaels is brutally killed in small-town New South Wales, what follows isn't your typical police investigation to uncover the killer, but instead an absorbing, at times harrowing look at the impact of violent crime on surviving family and the community. Maguire eschews lingering looks at the victim's terror, the body *in situ*, forensic detail, or the male gaze of the investigators, and instead gives us the grief, rage, and complex emotions felt by her older sister Chris, a barmaid in the local pub, and her fellow townsfolk as the investigation drags on, suspicion swirls, and Bella's life is picked over by police and the media. Both lyrical and colloquial, *An Isolated Incident* intercuts between Chris's perspective and that of May Norman, a young feminist reporter from the city. An evocative outing that explores the violence threading through everyday life, and our responses to it.

* * *

'Liked your book. You're not a bad @#%! for a Pakeha, but Kingi was too nice to be real.' In the hall of fame of reader feedback, **RAY BERARD** has a pretty great entry thanks to a follow-up email from an imposing Māori gang member who'd met Berard at his Rotorua book launch. In Berard's cracking debut, *Inside the Black Horse*, Kingi is the volatile leader of the Assassins who has a fondness for violence and the meth his gang distributes. Too nice? The story opens when a desperate youngster tries to rob the local pub, interrupting a drug deal and lighting the fuse on a violent chain of events that entwines locals and outsiders. Inspired by his diaries from years working in the betting industry, Berard crafts an authentic array of multi-layered characters, from widowed Māori publican Toni Bourke to Kingi and his cronies, ass-covering corporate executives, and an immigrant investigator. Set in a region blending tourist-enticing scenery with a blue-collar population and strong indigenous influence, *Inside the Black Horse* casts a fresh eye on the realities of modern New Zealand.

* * *

In her debut *The Floating Basin*, journalist and history buff **CAROLYN HAWES** gives readers a rich look at her hometown of Westport on the 'wild West Coast' of New Zealand's South Island. A small town that still has a frontier feel even in modern times. When a body emerges from the town's tidal lagoon, local cop Ru Clement must navigate a cast of eccentric small-town characters and past secrets to find the killer and uncover the truth. While there were moments it felt like Hawes was dipping her toe into the crime writing lagoon, overall *The Floating Basin* is a thoroughly enjoyable read that flows effortlessly with a good sense of place, interesting characters, and a solid mystery storyline.

* * *

Vegemite is an antipodean classic and a divisive breakfast spread. Many people love it; others can't stand the stuff. *Baby*, the debut slow-burn literary thriller from Wellington storyteller **ANNALEESE JOCHEMS**, may be vegemite with a capital V. A cast of noxious characters, including a self-absorbed millennial lead, is offered to readers via exquisite writing and characterisation. Cynthia is a bored 21-year-old who has left college and become obsessed with her fitness instructor Anahera. When events conspire, the pair run away to a scenic village to live on a boat, funded by Cynthia's ill-gotten gains. But what really happened back in the city, and why do strange things happen in their new paradise? Jochems keeps readers off-kilter, never sure how skewed is the perspective we see. Is Cynthia deluded, or something more sinister? Lurking unease and danger lie just out of sight. Provocative themes and a claustrophobic sense of place rule in this atypical read.

* * *

Like California, Australia's hot, dry climate makes it prone to bushfires – the worst of which can be hugely destructive and horrifically deadly. **AOIFE CLIFFORD** reflects that reality of rural Australian life in her accomplished sophomore novel *Second Sight*. Melbourne lawyer Eliza Carmody escaped her hometown of Kinsale many years ago but has now reluctantly returned for personal and professional reasons. The former includes a pregnant friend and a hospitalised father while the latter won't win her any popularity contests – Eliza is representing an electricity company many blame for a catastrophic bushfire two years before. As Eliza gets caught up in violent events in the present, she flashes back to New Year's Eve in 1996, when she and two friends met three local boys for a beach party. One disappeared. Reflection and regrets veer through small-town secrets and life-and-death events. Clifford delivers a gripping tale of fraught relationships with considerable style.

* * *

After years globetrotting as a foreign correspondent for a *60 Minutes*-style TV show, **CHRIS HAMMER** set his superb debut novel closer to home, in a drought-stricken farming region a few hours from Sydney (a region he'd explored in depth for a non-fiction book). *Scrublands* meshes sociological insights, literary stylings, and a multi-layered crime story into an epic novel that's simply superb. Martin Scarsden is sent to Riversend by his Sydney editor, ostensibly to write a human-interest tale about the town's recovery a year after a church shooting, but also to gauge his own recovery after a near-death experience in the Middle East. Some locals tell Martin there's more to the story than the 'paedophile priest' narrative that followed the shooting. When the bodies of two backpackers are found the national media descends, messily picking at the dying town's carcass. Can Martin find the truth among all the lies and manipulations? Hammer brings rural Australia, its towns and people and issues faced, to vivid life with sweat-inducing authenticity. *Silver* is a very fine sequel.

* * *

Horse-loving journalist, poet and children's author **LINDY KELLY** adopted the old adage, 'write what you know', with her crime debut *Bold Blood*, parlaying her experience as a professional equestrian rider into an enjoyable mystery set amongst the stables, saddles and sorrels of the eventing world. Big city doctor Caitlin Summerfield has happily left her rural childhood and emotionally abusive mother behind but is reluctantly called home by a suspicious fall. Playing caretaker for her stricken mother's farm, she scratches beneath the surface of high-tech horse trailers and well-fed thoroughbreds to uncover looming financial ruin, and a shot at a million-dollar breeding contract. A contract someone is willing to do anything for. Kelly populates a suspenseful tale of assaults, horse theft and murder with a fascinating cast, while impressing most with her rich portrait of life in the eventing world, and thematic questions of memory versus reality, and the stories we tell ourselves.

* * *

Every writer uses their imagination to create and breathe life into characters who go (far) beyond their own experiences yet crossing certain boundaries can draw criticism regardless of the nuance or brilliance of the storytelling. **ADRIAN HYLAND** experienced that with his superb Emily Tempest books, having been rejected early on by big publishers and received ongoing questions about his temerity; a middle-aged 'white fella' writing crime tales starring a young Aboriginal woman. How dare he? No matter that Hyland spent years living in Outback communities alongside indigenous peoples, that his storytelling is sharply observed, or that he saw his books as honouring his former neighbours and trying to bridge a cultural divide in his country. Fortunately, the brave and funny Tempest did make it into readers' hands in *Diamond Dove*, where she's a university graduate returning to her childhood home only to get caught up in the murder of her father's best friend. The sequel *Gunshot Road*, shortlisted for literary awards, may be even better. Emily's now an Aboriginal Community Police Officer in a town dominated by mining and meat works, an unexpected career. When an old friend is killed and another is blamed, she jumps into the fray. Beautifully rendered characters, humour as dry as its atmospheric setting, awkward relationships and tough social issues explored from grassroots rather than lectern; *Gunshot Road* should be considered a stone-cold classic of modern Australian crime writing.

* * *

Medical professor **CAROLINE DE COSTA** offered readers plenty of originality in the heroine, setting, and story of her intriguing 2015 debut, *Double Madness*. That book introduced Aboriginal detective Cass Diamond, a solo mother working out of Cairns and facing plenty of challenges on personal and professional fronts. In *Double Madness*, Diamond is on the team investigating the murder of a fashionista found tied up with designer scarves in the national forest. The woman's husband vanished before a cyclone, and no one seems to know much about the strange couple. The investigation takes Diamond and her colleagues in unexpected directions, including into the disturbing behind-closed-doors world of some of Far North Queensland's medical profession. The stars of the show are Diamond, richly characterised by de Costa, and an exceptional sense of place, offsetting other characters that sometimes feel like moving pieces. De Costa showed immediate promise and has followed up with *Blood Sisters* and *Missing Pieces*.

* * *

Not many crime writers can claim a plug from Bob Dylan, but **DAVE WARNER** earned a nod as the future Nobel Prize winner's favourite

Australian artist back in the late 1970s when Warner was lead singer in attitude-filled local bands. Since then Warner's creativity has veered into musical theatre, screenwriting, non-fiction, and during the final years of the old millennium, several crime novels. In 2015, Warner returned to the crime scene after a long hiatus with the exceptional *Before It Breaks*, a sharply observed tale set in the coastal town of Broome, a 24-hour drive north of Perth. City homicide detective Dan Clement is home to be closer to his daughter, working on petty incidents until a body is found in a creek. A seemingly opportunistic murder becomes something more sinister when a second body turns up. There's action aplenty as a cyclone looms and a good crime storyline, but Warner excels most in his pitch-perfect depiction of small-town Australia and its diverse array of characters. He won a Ned Kelly Award for *Before It Breaks*, then followed it with two more richly crafted crime tales, *Clear to the Horizon* and *River of Salt*. Perhaps, as his vocal contemporary Bon Scott used to sing, for Warner it's a case of 'I've been too long, I'm glad to be back'.

* * *

Australian singer-songwriter **HOLLY THROSBY** racked up major awards nominations for her folk and indie-pop tunes packed with emotive melodies and vulnerable lyrics, before turning her creative mind and talents to novels examining the impact of crime on families and small communities. Tales which likewise racked up major awards nominations. Throsby's 2016 debut *Goodwood* is set in the era of Kurt Cobain singing about teen spirit and Whitney Houston turning an old Dolly Parton track into one of the bestselling singles of all time. Seventeen-year-old Jean Brown lives in the titular small town, which is rocked when first the coolest girl in school vanishes, then another popular resident doesn't return from a fishing trip a week later. Suspicions fester in a tight-knit community, and Jean is keeping secrets of her own. Like her music, Throsby proffers a quirky, atypical crime tale that flows wonderfully and has plenty of depth beneath a simple surface. She strikes a chord with the broader cast, speckling her slow-burn tale with dry humour, truisms, and authentic characters. *Cedar Valley* showed Throsby was no one-hit wonder.

* * *

A surprise winner of the Deutz Medal in 2002, **CRAIG MARRINER** shook up the literary establishment with his unapologetically 'bogan' persona and storytelling. He was tagged as 'New Zealand's response to Irvine Welsh and Quentin Tarantino', which should be fair warning for readers. *Stonedogs* is a vivid, raw and rollicking tale, often manic and violent in language and deed. The Brotherhood are a bunch of young lads sticking together through a life of binge-drinking, drugs, trying to pick up girls, and various scrapes. When one of their number becomes gang prey, they embark on a revenge-fuelled journey into the dark underbelly of New Zealand. Blending road trip odyssey, coming of age story, and crime tale into a potent cocktail, Marriner proffers a debut that's a fictional smack to the face: compelling attention, leaving the reader feeling bloodied and slightly bewildered, and very difficult to forget.

* * *

A young woman is hitchhiking alone in the Wairarapa countryside when she's picked up by a middle-aged man with a gun in his car. The opening to **KIRSTEN MCDOUGALL**'s elegantly crafted *Tess* echoes all-too-many true crime stories in the antipodes, but what follows is a beguiling gothic suspense that's hard to categorise. Teenager Tess is running from a violent past, and ends up staying with protective Lewis, a dentist dealing with his own family traumas. A helper who may need help. Tess is afflicted by insight that can be a blessing and curse. During a hot, claustrophobic summer relationships form and danger lurks as the millennium turns. McDougall artfully keeps readers off balance as events unfold, threading together plenty of drama with strands of crime, romance, and the supernatural. There's a subtlety to McDougall's slim novel, which is deceptive and disturbing. Sparkling prose is cut with staccato bursts of violence. *Tess* offers tangled relationships with plenty of tensions; in a way, McDougall nods towards a sense of du Maurier, with a fresh Kiwi accent.

* * *

After scooping a Ned Kelly Award for her debut *Out of the Silence* that used a real-life historical murder trial to explore the plight of Australian women in 1900, **WENDY JAMES** has cast an acute eye on modern times in her recent psychological thrillers. In *The Accusation*, former soap star Suzannah Wells moves to a country town outside Sydney to care for her elderly mother and work as a drama teacher. Like many, Suzannah is at first fascinated by a bizarre story when teenager Ellie Canning is discovered on a local road, claiming to have escaped after being held captive by a woman and her crazy old mother. Then newcomer Suzannah is the one accused, and her life begins to fall apart. Ellie's DNA being found in her house and Suzannah's past being dredged up just reinforce the public's view that Suzannah is a horrid villain deserving of swift justice. As Ellie teams with a celebrity agent to milk her newfound celebrity, just who is lying? James cleverly plays with modern society's intoxication with social media, snap judgements, and news without nuance.

* * *

Like a fair few authors around the world, **JENNIFER LANE** sees herself as an 'accidental crime writer', having just written the story in her head and heart without any regard for detectives or police investigations. Her award-winning debut, *All Our Secrets*, hatched from a short story about a woman going into labour in a small-town supermarket. It's a wonderful novel of a country town gripped by murder and the fascinating adolescent at the centre of it all. Although she now lives in the city of Wellington, Lane grew up in countryside New South Wales and she brings those heat-struck landscapes of lofty gum trees and chattering wildlife to stark life in fictional Coongahoola. Gracie is a bullied 11-year-old from a troubled family whose life spirals out of control after the town's famed 'River Children' – all born nine months after an infamous town picnic and looking unlike their fathers – start vanishing. Gracie knows what no one else does: who is responsible. Lane has an assured touch for engaging readers and conveying place, but it is Gracie's voice that shines brightest.

* * *

In the delightfully madcap crime tales of **SUE WILLIAMS**, Cass Tuplin fries the fish and chips and dim sum for the locals of Rusty Bore, population 147. With her shop being one half of the town's bustling Central Business District, Cass can't resist sticking her beak into other business; although she's absolutely, definitely, not an unlicensed private investigator. Swear to God. She's just curious, and cares. Williams introduced Cass to readers in *Murder with the Lot*, where a bloodied stranger orders a burger from her shop and then later a gunshot corpse disappears, causing Cass to investigate despite her son being the local copper. I imagine Williams has a lot of fun writing this series, typing with her tongue firmly in her cheek and dialling up the laughs and zany characters among the crime. The ingredients balance better as the series progresses, with third tale *Live and Let Fry* being the high point so far. Delightfully daft.

* * *

While the northernmost point of the Australian mainland is Cape York at the top of Queensland, there are almost 300 small islands in the Torres Strait between Queensland and Papua New Guinea. Sydney-born **CATHERINE TITASEY**, who grew up in Papua New Guinea and has lived on Thursday Island as an adult, gives readers a rare fictional insight into that remote area in *My Island Homicide*. Thea Dari-Jones is looking for a fresh start and reconnection with her maternal heritage when she flees Cairns to take a job as the Officer-in-Charge of the Thursday Island police station. Hoping for a laidback tropical life of minor crimes, she's plunged into a murder case. What follows is a luscious tale where Titasey revels in the setting and the murder mystery is only one part as readers follow Thea's journey to acclimatise to the multicultural community and her own mixed heritage.

* * *

A summertime picnic by a beautiful South Island lake evokes idyllic memories for many New Zealanders, but in the talented hands of Dunedin author **PADDY RICHARDSON** the dream turns into a horrifying nightmare when a young girl vanishes, devastating her family and community. In *Hunting Blind*, the missing girl's sister Stephanie grows up to become a psychiatrist, and 17 years later she's healing damage in others' lives while never truly addressing her own. When a new patient shares a strikingly similar story, Stephanie is spurred to revisit her past, embarking on a journey that takes her around the scenic countryside and back to her long-abandoned childhood home. Can she uncover what really happened to her sister Gemma so many years ago? Richardson delivers an accomplished tale that takes readers into the aftermath of high-profile tragedies: the ongoing impact long after the media circus disperses and the rest of the country forgets. Richardson underlined her versatility and must-read status with further fine crime novels exploring media campaigns for justice (*Traces of Red*), the controversial 1981 Springbok rugby tour (*Cross Fingers*), and complex character studies (*Swimming in the Dark*).

* * *

At the 2014 Sydney Writers' Festival **ELEANOR CATTON** may have stunned some in the sold-out audience when she spoke so lovingly and at length about crime writing. A literary darling whose ambitious, sprawling tome *The Luminaries* had recently made her the youngest ever Booker Prize winner, Catton herself saw her much-lauded second novel as an 'historical, astrological murder mystery'. Egad cry the literati? Written in the style of its Victorian times and artfully structured according to the Zodiac, *The Luminaries* opens in stage-like fashion when young Walter Moody stumbles from the storm into the Crown Hotel. He interrupts an eclectic gathering of Hokitika locals who've met to parse a series of befuddling events, and is drawn into a mystery packed with greed, lust, betrayal, and murder. Catton created something quite special that won't be for all crime readers. Richly evoking the boom and bust times of a gold rush on the wild edge of the Empire, *The Luminaries* is a fiendishly clever tale full of theatricality, opium dens, doomed love, secrets and spirits that nods to the likes of Wilkie Collins while being something all of its own.

* * *

In **TINA CLOUGH**'s third novel *The Chinese Proverb*, Hunter Grant is an Afghanistan veteran just looking to enjoy the bushland around his remote cabin in Northland when he stumbles over the body of a young woman. The good news: she's alive, barely. The bad: the shackle marks on her ankle and the story she tells of fleeing the very worst kind of abuse at a coastal farm. Like the titular proverb, Hunter feels responsible for the life he's saved; nursing Dao back to health and surviving those tracking her isn't enough. Having worked in high-pay, high-danger private security, Hunter isn't the kind to call on the police for help when bringing justice to Dao's abusers. Clough delivers a cat-and-mouse tale which shines brightest in the evolving and atypical relationship between victim and saviour. The pair return in *One Single Thing*, helping a bereaved family when a journalist vanishes.

* * *

Almost 50 years before Peter Temple was shaking up the Australian literary scene as a crime writer winning the prestigious Miles Franklin Award, and two decades before Peter Corris broke through with his first Cliff Hardy tale, Queensland farm girl **ESTELLE THOMPSON** was penning Australian-set crime novels that were published all over the world and being considered by the Miles Franklin judges. While most of Thompson's bibliography (including fifteen crime novels) predates the time period of this guide, her final two novels before she passed away in 2003 are part of our 'modern era'. In 1998's *Come Home to Danger,* a man returns to Queensland for his mother's funeral only to become convinced she was murdered because she knew a secret about someone close to them all. In Thompson's swansong, *The Road to Seven-Thirty*, a young wife living in a small town becomes the prime suspect in the murder of her clergyman husband. When she's attacked in her own home by masked men she realises she may be in even greater danger.

* * *

Born in Melbourne to Polish immigrants just prior to the Second World War, **GOLDIE ALEXANDER** could barely speak English as a child but has gone on to publish almost 100 books spanning genres and age groups. Among her output is a trio of mysteries set in a small town on the Mornington Peninsula that have delightful echoes of Christie and Marsh. *Unkind Cut*, the second of the Grevillea Murder Mysteries, sees renowned Shakespearean actor Kingston Ellis, who has retired to the town, stabbed to death for real during a fundraising local production of *Julius Caesar. Et tu, Brute*, perhaps, but who was the Brutus behind the blade? Once again, DI Richard Brumby searches for the culprit with the assistance of locals including caterer Olivia Beauman and her partner Eddie, the school principal and play director. Lighter fare that's full of charm, particularly with its cast of small-town characters, while Alexander salts in a few sly observations about attitudes and assumptions.

* * *

Native Melburnian **LEE TULLOCH** has a bibliography as peripatetic as her adult life. The fashion and travel journalist has lived and worked in Paris, New York, and Australia, and written novels ranging from social satire to Gothic suspense in the fashion world. In *The Cutting*, Tulloch returns to Australian shores with an absorbing murder mystery set in seaside New South Wales. Masseuse Heidi and her screenwriter husband Beckett have fled Sydney's fast lane for a quieter coastal life, only for things to take a much darker turn when first native wildlife is butchered and then the body of a young woman is found in the quarry. Tulloch shows plenty of promise as a crime writer, furnishing a twisting plotline, some fascinating small-town characters, and a willingness to burrow into backdrops gritty rather than glossy.

* * *

The opening pages of *Sweet One* by **PETER DOCKER** may tear the breath from readers. A horrifying incident where an Aboriginal man in custody is cooked to death in the back of a van while being transported through scorching desert is, impossibly, even worse: it's based on a true event. Docker explores rather than exploits, as characters in *Sweet One* leave aside what happened in the real-life incident (multiple, drawn-out inquiries then almost everybody moving on) for a more direct response. Another Aboriginal man and fellow veteran begins taking revenge on those responsible, and is joined by others. Izzy Langford, a journalist who has reported from war zones and had stories quashed about Aboriginal deaths in custody, is sent to the Western Australian goldfields to cover the death but then finds herself on the trail of the vigilantes. Docker, who grew up on a farm outside a tiny town in a vast region that's bigger than Texas, doesn't hold back. *Sweet One* is ferociously told, the landscapes sweat-inducing, its characters nuanced and realistic. Docker wrote a grim tale, full of harshness and violence, but did it beautifully.

* * *

The realisation that general practitioners get to observe a wide range of human behaviour and 'witness the agony and ecstasy' of patients' lives inspired Melbourne doctor **BILL BATEMAN** to write. First, columns for a medical magazine, then crime novels. While he's now a city doctor, Bateman called on his 25 years as a rural GP when writing about Vince Hanrahan, an OB/GYN exiled to coastal Victoria after a medical mishap. In the second instalment, *You're Never The Same*, Vince is still hoping to reclaim his high-powered city job and family, when his life gets further complicated by the suicide of his brother, a local murder in Warrnambool, and disturbing revelations about the Catholic school he and his brother attended. An engaging whodunnit that builds steadily through the quagmire of Vince's personal and professional travails, while traversing heavy issues with a light touch.

* * *

With an all-time 'Holy Trinity' of much-loved authors consisting of Enid Blyton, Agatha Christie, and Daphne du Maurier, it's perhaps no surprise **JOSEPHINE PENNICOTT** heavily dosed her first two crime novels with country homes, tangled families, and a delicious sense of Gothic mystery. Following *Poet's Cottage*, set in a fishing village in her home state of Tasmania, Pennicott immersed readers in the Blue Mountain of NSW, where she now lives, in *Currawong Manor*. Photographer Elizabeth Thorrington is invited by the manor owners to take pictures for a new book about the life of Rupert Partridge, a notorious artist who once owned the manor and was also Elizabeth's grandfather. He vanished decades before on the same day Elizabeth's grandmother and aunt died – a family tragedy or murder? Elizabeth meets Ginger, her grandfather's only surviving life model and former live-in muse, and Pennicott guides readers deep into the mystery with twin timelines, modern and historical. Can Elizabeth clear her grandfather's besmirched reputation, or will her worst fears be realised? Wonderfully atmospheric – the property has a character-like presence – and illuminating of the 1940 arts scene, Pennicott's story gives readers a rural Australian Gothic treat.

* * *

While it took former television journalist and PR maven **JAYE FORD** a decade of effort to get her first thriller published, she certainly hit the ground running from the time she broke through. Her debut *Beyond Fear* centred on four thirty-something friends who head to a secluded barn-turned-cabin for a fun girls' weekend to recharge their batteries. But the isolation triggers terrifying flashbacks for Jodie, who survived a brutal assault as a schoolgirl almost two decades before. When she starts to believe they are being watched and begins to unravel, her friends don't believe her. But is Jodie paranoid, or perceptive? Ford unsheathes a spine-tingling tale that crackles with menace and taps into visceral fears. Having struck gold on the awards and local and international sales front first time out, Ford continued the everyday characters in peril and psychological torment formula in four more fast-paced thrillers, most recently *Darkest Place*.

* * *

The coastal NSW town of Byron Bay was long known as a laidback hippie haven, though in recent times it's become increasingly cashed up and crowded: more hipster than hippie. **MAGGIE GROFF** plays to the lingering quirkiness of the setting in her crime debut *Mad Men, Bad Girls and the Guerrilla Knitters Institute.* Freelance journalist Scout Davis has caught the scent of a couple of stories: someone is cutting up underwear at the exclusive girls' school where Scout's sister works, and perhaps more seriously, a secretive American cult has brought its strange practices and online business to town. When an old friend contacts Scout with troubling news about the cult, she's even more determined to investigate. Along the way Scout's also fighting off any boredom in her leisure hours as a member of a guerrilla knitting group which yarn-bombs the town by night, and by flirting and further with a surfer cop while her boyfriend's abroad. A fun tale full of imperfect but thoroughly human characters. Scout returned for more misadventures in *Good News, Bad News.*

* * *

When two treasure-hunters stumble across a body in an isolated canyon deep in a national park in Victoria, only for a bushfire to threaten them and the crime scene, Sergeant Quade Marsden reluctantly turns to park ranger Taylor Bridges for assistance. *The Falls* is the second thriller from **B MICHAEL RADBURN** to star the damaged park ranger, who has been mending his life following past tragedies and helping solve a multiple murder in Tasmania in *The Crossing.* Bridges teams with Sergeant Marsden, who's keen to resurrect his own career after a demotion from the city, and Detective Sandra Norton who takes over. The case gets more complex as it becomes clear the body wasn't a one-off, a witness goes missing, and events seem bizarrely tied to the legendary old gold mine inhabited by a cult led by an American preacher in the nineteenth century. Radburn crafts a claustrophobic atmosphere full of secrets and danger as he switches perspectives among those involved in the case. A deliciously disturbing tale that stands out in a crowded field.

* * *

Living in the Dandenong Ranges outside Melbourne, **SANDI WALLACE** is surrounded by bushland and tiny towns. She brings that realistic sense of countryside Victoria to her 'Rural Crime Files' series starring Melbourne writer Georgie Harvey and cop John Franklin. The pair first meet in *Tell Me Why*, when Harvey travels to Daylesford, a town famed for its mineral springs, in search of missing farmer Susan Pentecoste. Solo father Franklin is trying to track down who is sending nasty letters to young single mothers, so isn't interested in providing police help to Harvey. Until things escalate, and her investigation stirs up old secrets. *Tell Me Why* is a well-constructed mystery that shines brightest with its characters and country setting. A very promising start to what's grown into a fine series, Harvey and Franklin continuing their loose partnership in *Dead Again* and *Into the Fog*.

* * *

While writer and photographer **BEV ROBITAI** has led a nomadic life, she spent many years involved in local theatre in Nelson in the 1980s and 1990s, and later tapped into those experiences to texture her first of several crime novels, *Murder in the Second Row*. Theatre manager Jessica Jones is trying to keep Whetford's historical theatre going, under attack from repair bills, fickle audiences, and developers and councillors keen to bulldoze the landmark to make way for a shopping mall. Hope rests on a production of Agatha Christie's 'Appointment with Death', but preparations are thrown into chaos when a young actress is found dead during rehearsals. Can Jessica keep the show going on and save the theatre while helping the police investigation and dealing with an escalating series of crazed threats? Robitai has a smooth style that keeps the pages flowing in a well-constructed cosy of the Christie-Marsh mould.

* * *

A group of sixty-something music lovers reconnecting on a party-laden road trip may seem an unlikely cast for a crime tale, but Mangawhai author **ROY VAUGHAN** makes it work in *The Mereleigh*

Record Club Tour of New Zealand. Partially inspired by his own gang of pals who were immersed in the British music scene in the 1960s, Vaughan's first thriller sees tour operator Rick Foster arrange for the MRC to join him in Aotearoa for a reunion romp. When the group gets unwittingly caught up in international drug smuggling, the police and customs decide to use them for a sting. Can Rick keep his pals out of danger, while not knowing who to trust? An easy read with atypical characters set against some stunning scenery. The misadventures continued with MRC tours of Japan and the South Pacific.

* * *

How much does violence beget more violence, in terms of particularly heinous acts rippling throughout families and communities to inspire further crimes? That's one of the questions raised by **EMILY O'GRADY**'s powerful debut *The Yellow House*, a crime-drenched piece of fiction that won the 2018 Australian/Vogel Literary Award. Ten-year-old Cub lives on an isolated rural property bordering an abandoned cattle farm and knackery with her parents and two brothers – one older, one her twin. The isolation is magnified by history; her family are local pariahs for things that happened before she was born. Just over the fence sits her late grandfather's yellow house, the home of a serial killer. Animals weren't the only things to die in the knackery. When Cub's estranged aunt and cousin move into the yellow house, secrets the family wanted forgotten are stirred up and Cub must come to terms with her family legacy. Magnificently told in understated prose from the first-person perspective of a young girl carrying plenty of baggage, *The Yellow House* is a triumph.

* * *

Western Australian crime writer **FELICITY YOUNG** has shown her versatility with ten novels switching between three distinct series over the past fifteen years. While her DSS Stevie Hooper series is like a gritty Perth spin on *Law & Order: SVU* and her fine historical series featuring autopsy surgeon Dody McCleland provides an insightful look at suffragette-era London, it is Young's Cam Fraser books that perhaps connect most to her own rural life. The most recent, *Flare Up*, sees Sergeant Fraser on the brink of resignation when he discovers a body in a wool bale in a shearing shed at a friend's farm. With an arsonist lighting bush fires and livestock being rustled the small community is already on edge, and now Cam must try to damp things down while finding a killer. Young expertly and authentically portrays life in rural communities, from the volunteer fire fighters who must drop everything at their usual jobs when the siren sounds to the kinds of crimes that don't happen on city streets.

* * *

Global high priestess of paranormal romance **NALINI SINGH** shocked many when she announced she'd written a rural mystery, but *A Madness of Sunshine* proved her *New York Times* bestselling talents ably transferred to a new arena. Concert pianist Anahera returns to Golden Cove on the rugged West Coast of New Zealand, a hometown she never intended to see again. She's recuperating from loss stacked upon loss, laced with betrayal. Will is a new cop in town, exiled from the city. When a vibrant young woman about to leave on her own adventure vanishes, memories of tragedies past come hurtling back, along with fears in the present. Is a killer lurking among a tight-knit community, or has the danger arrived from the outside? Singh switches gears better than Lewis Hamilton, crafting an immersive sense of place and richly drawn characters that power an intriguing mystery. While some of her long-time fans may miss the steamy sex or vampires, archangels, and unfeeling psychics of her 40 prior novels, many other readers will hope Singh returns to the crime scene again.

* * *

While others helped set the dynamite, it was undoubtedly **JANE HARPER** who lit the fuse for the explosion of global interest in Australian-set crime in recent years. The Melbourne-based former journalist snatched worldwide attention and a flood of accolades (including the CWA Gold Dagger) for her remarkable debut *The Dry*.

A tale of a man versus the environment, a town, and his own past, it combines exquisite slow-build storytelling with a superb sense of place and richly drawn characters that provoke a range of emotions. Federal Agent Aaron Falk returns to his parched hometown Kiewarra for the funeral of a childhood friend, who seems to have broken under the strain and killed his family and himself. Falk plans a fleeting visit; he doesn't want to linger in a place he and his father fled 20 years ago after accusations swirled following the drowning of a young woman. But as he and a local detective begin to doubt the murder-suicide scenario, he finds himself digging into this latest tragedy and unearthing secrets from the past in a community struggling to survive. Harper showed she was no one-hit wonder when switching from drought-stricken farmland to rainswept bushland for her second Aaron Falk tale, *Force of Nature*, before underlining her quality while returning to the Outback in sublime standalone *The Lost Man*. The oldest and youngest Bright brothers, Nathan and Bub, meet at a barren border of their vast cattle ranches in the heat-struck expanses of inner Queensland. Their middle sibling, the family's golden child Cam, dead at their feet. Everyone who lives in the Outback knows the parched desert can quickly kill, so why would Cam abandon his car and wander to his death at the old stockman's grave? Had financial worries tipped him over the edge, concerns from his past, or something more sinister? Nathan has lived largely in exile in recent years and is thrust into a family situation full of grief, anguish, and questions. Relationships fray and long-hidden truths come to light. Harper's prose is full of taut elegance and quiet intensity as she surveys the pressures of Outback farming and the darkness that can hide within families and isolated communities. *The Lost Man* shimmers with subtext and subtlety. In short: *The Dry* was a special debut, *The Lost Man* shows Harper is a special writer.

* * *

Back in the 1980s and 1990s **JENNIFER ROWE** wrote two engaging mystery series set in Australia that were each adapted for television: the cosy-style Verity Birdwood books about a TV researcher and amateur sleuth, and a grittier urban duology starring Senior Detective Tessa Vance. Since that time, Rowe has largely concentrated on her phenomenally popular fantasy novels written for younger readers under the pen name Emily Rodda (one series alone has sold more than 15 million copies). But she briefly returned to crime in 2012. *Love, Honour, and O'Brien* sees office worker Holly Love become an accidental sleuth when the private investigator she hires to track down the fiancée who scarpered with all her money drops dead. A light-hearted romp set in the Blue Mountains that's full of zany characters and events and seasoned with a nice dose of humour.

* * *

A woman's decision to go for a horse ride into the Victorian mountains on Christmas morning turns into a deliciously menacing and claustrophobic thriller in *Dark Horse* by **HONEY BROWN**. With her marriage and her business in tatters, Sarah Barnard applies the old adage from Winston Churchill about there being nothing better for the inside of a (hu)man than the outside of a horse, and seeks solace with a ride into the rugged Mortimer Ranges. When flash floods trap her on Devil Mountain, she shelters at Hangman's Hut, only for Heath, a young bushwalker, to emerge from the wild weather and seek shelter too. Sarah's instincts tell her that there's more to Heath than the story he tells. Honey Brown dials up the tension and growing suspicion as the pair dance around each other – each hiding things – while having to hunker down to survive. Pacy and compelling, *Dark Horse* manages to submit to and subvert reader expectations while building to a stunning conclusion.

* * *

After debuting with an acclaimed coming-of-age story set against the harsh realities of an historical whaling station, Brisbane teacher **BEN HOBSON** took an even darker turn in *Snake Island*, a violent literary thriller that continues his exploration of father-son relationships. Vernon and Penelope Moore have cut off their son Caleb, ashamed after he hit his wife and went to prison. But when Vernon learns

Caleb has been getting regularly bashed in prison by local thug Brendan Cahill, with corrupt authorities looking the other way, he decides to approach Brendan's father to broker peace. The trouble being that Ernie Cahill is the patriarch of a family that switched from sheep farming to drug cultivation, and Vernon unwittingly starts a dangerous feud with the region's crime kingpin. Intercutting chapters from different perspectives, Hobson concocts a powerful tale threaded with questions about vengeance, masculinity, and frontier justice. *Snake Island* has a whiff of the great 'grit lit' tales from the American South, as well as Shakespearean tragedy, as it builds to a blood-soaked finale.

* * *

Crimes past and present collide in **ANNA ROMER**'s atmospheric rural mystery *Under the Midnight Sky*, which sees journalist Abby Bardot reflecting on her own childhood as well as digging into post-war Australia after a young woman vanishes. Abby comes across the injured teenager while running through the Deepwater Gorge Reserve, only for the girl to vanish before an ambulance arrives. Eerily, she looks like three young girls who were murdered nearby 20 years before, a traumatic time from Abby's own childhood. But that killer was caught, right? Blocked from writing about such horrors for her newspaper – a tourism-focused edict worthy of the Mayor of Amity – Abby is tasked with interviewing reclusive true crime writer Tom Gabriel, who has moved into a ramshackle manor on the edge of the reserve. Together the pair uncovers another mystery dating back several decades when a room in Tom's house starts spilling its secrets. Romer creates a riveting read full of secrets and Gothic undertones, from the manor to the bushland.

* * *

In *See You In September* by **CHARITY NORMAN**, young British holidaymaker Cassy hitches a ride with a group of friendly strangers in a rusty van after a fight with her boyfriend and then accepts their invitation to stay at a seemingly idyllic farming commune near

Rotorua. It's a decision with huge consequences for her life, and that of her family back home. As Cassy becomes entranced by the serenity of her new locale and the charisma of community leader Justin, she decides to stay. It's her new 'family'. Meanwhile her old family becomes more frantic. Norman ratchets up the tension as the story unfolds from two viewpoints: Cassy and her mother Diana. There's a lovely subtlety to the depictions of how Cassy is recruited into the fold at the commune, and Norman adroitly conveys the emotional journeys of various characters. A suspenseful, gripping psychological thriller.

* * *

Nothing Bad Happens Here signalled **NIKKI CRUTCHLEY** was a writer to watch, as the former librarian concocted an addictive read about some very bad things happening in a bucolic seaside town. Castle Bay is used to visitors answering the siren call of its laidback atmosphere and the scenic beauty of the Coromandel Peninsula, not arriving in town because someone's been murdered. But when the body of missing tourist Bethany Haliwell is discovered, the town's accommodation overflows with news crews and big-city detectives. Late to the party, troubled magazine writer Miller Hatcher is looking for a fresh angle to score herself a promotion and follows an anonymous tip that leads to another death. Meanwhile local Sergeant Kahu Parata has been sidelined in his own town. Crutchley does a fine job creating a well-paced tale shot through with brooding atmosphere; a strong sense of a bright sunny place where menace lurks just out of sight. *No One Can Hear You* underlined her talent for small town mysteries with complicated heroines.

* * *

While several fresh antipodean voices have recently garnered global attention and accolades for their outstanding tales set in rural Australia, **GARRY DISHER** showed once again in his most recent novel, *Peace*, why he's the master who paved the way. A superb tale where the violence simmers in a small community and the heat haze shimmers from the page, right from the opening lines its clear you're in the hands of a consummate storyteller. In 2018 Disher received the Ned Kelly Lifetime Achievement Award, just recognition of a rich crime writing resume, and *Peace* shows he ain't resting on his laurels. It marks the return of likable police constable Paul 'Hirsch' Hirschhausen from 2013's terrific *Bitter Wash Road*. Exiled from Adelaide to tiny Tiverton, Hirsch's beat involves a lot of long drives, welfare calls, and dealing with drunken shenanigans. At times his biggest stress may be playing Santa or doing his share at a community work bee. But things take a far nastier turn when someone brutally attacks Nan Washburn's horses, and then a secretive family on the outskirts of town suffers violence that brings big-city detectives to town. Disher delivers dirt-caked authenticity with both the countryside setting and its eclectic inhabitants. Hirsch is an engaging hero full of humanity, juggling small-town politics and trying to handle the nastiest of crimes while being marginalised by colleagues who still blame him for the fall of other cops, corrupt or not. Disher has produced another classic. Crime fans would be well advised to sample his backlist, a fine canon of crime that includes the investigations of Detective Inspector Hal Challis on the Mornington Peninsula (seven books and counting) and the exploits of Melbourne bank robber and jewel thief Wyatt (resurrected in 2010 with *Wyatt*, after six novels between 1991-1997, and continued since with *The Heat* and *Kill Shot*). Whoever the hero or whatever the story, Disher consistently delivers distinctly Australian tales with strong characters, an exquisite sense of place, and keen insights into the human condition.

* * *

First-time crime novelist **SARAH THORNTON** plays an absolute blinder with *Lapse*, a thrilling small-town tale about shame, secrets, and Aussie Rules football. When Clementine Jones flees her life as a Sydney corporate lawyer, she eschews the 'sea change' – instead heading to a dusty small town in inland Victoria, and becoming the coach for the local football team. On the cusp of the first playoffs appearance in years, and perhaps their first championship in half a century, Clem's star player quits. He's also been fired from his job for stealing. Both events are out of character for the Aboriginal man, and Clem starts asking questions. But people are also asking questions about her, ones she's desperate to avoid. Thornton's line-up includes a damaged heroine, a wonderful evocation of a footy-focused small town, an exploration of a bubbling undercurrent of racism, and plenty of intrigue. All in all, a winner.

* * *

Other small town and rural crime authors and novels
SARAH BARRIE: *Devil's Lair*
FIONA BELL: *Waterhole*
ILSA EVANS: *Nefarious Doings*
DOROTHY FOWLER: *What Remains Behind*
POPPY GEE: *Bay of Fires*
BRIGID GEORGE: *Disguising Demons*
GED GILLMORE: *Headland*
PENELOPE HAINES: *Death on D'Urville*
KYLIE KADEN: *The Day the Lies Began*
LEONIE MATEER: *Murder in the Family*
PETRONELLA MCGOVERN: *Six Minutes*
FELICITY MCLEAN: *The Van Apfel Girls Are Gone*
LAURA MELVILLE: *Bitter Business*
FAVEL PARRETT: *Past the Shallows*
BRONWYN PARRY: *As Darkness Falls*
RENÉE: *The Wild Card*
GEOFFREY ROBERT: *The Alo Release*
SD ROWELL: *The Echo of Others*
ROBERT SCHOFIELD: *Marble Bar*
JUSTIN WARREN: *The Forgotten Lands*
HELENE YOUNG: *Half Moon Bay*

Home and Away – International Settings

While the adventures of the Hardy Boys and Sherlock Holmes were my earliest introductions to mysteries, it was the novels of Alistair MacLean which first filled my thriller cup (thanks for the recommendation, Dad). Canterbury author **ANDREW GRANT**, not to be confused with Lee Child's brother, brings his own spin to the classic mix of exotic locations, intrigue, and masculine derring-do that characterised the MacLean-Fleming-Bagley-Forsyth golden age of British thrillers. From parched Texas-Mexico borders to raging Southern Ocean or sticky Southeast Asia, Grant aims to entertain. In *Death in the Kingdom*, British agent Daniel Swann is sent back to Thailand – a place he's avoided since killing the sire of an underworld boss – to recover a box from the bottom of the sea. The mission goes awry, friends and contacts are getting beheaded, and Swann doesn't know who to trust. Suspend your disbelief for a fun read that's a gritty tale with an engaging hero, good action, and locations so vivid you can feel the heat, grime, and sweat trickling down your back.

* * *

New Zealand psychologist **NIGEL LATTA** rose to prominence thanks to a dozen TV presenting gigs and a range of non-fiction books that arced from forensic psychology and true crime through parenting, money matters, and Antarctic exploration. Before all of that writing and presenting, Latta had worked with violent offenders and first dipped his toe into the publishing waters with a single assured crime novel. *Execution Lullaby* begins with Simon Chance on death row; his life the payment for seven dead girls. Like a priest at final confession, readers hear Chance's story, from happy marriage to uncovering a terrible secret and his journey to death row. But how much can we believe; who is being manipulated, and to what end? Latta delivers a slick, propulsive thriller that deals with disturbing crimes and (unsurprisingly) delves into psychological whys as much as factual who-did-whats as it powers to a strong finish. Clever and compelling, with insights into human nature and criminal minds; it's a shame we haven't had more from Latta.

* * *

As fiction editor of *Takahe* literary magazine for 16 years, **ISA MOYNIHAN** shepherded many bright writing talents to publication. A keen-eyed critic and talented short story writer herself, Moynihan was still producing her own new work, full of wry humour and sharp observation, right up until her death, aged 88, in 2013. She'd even established a writing group in her Ngaio Marsh retirement village. Earlier, Moynihan had gifted readers a single novel, *The Rashomon Factor*, during her diamond jubilee. A beguiling whodunnit, Christie meets Kurosawa, set on a Greek Islands cruise ship. Newly widowed Bridget joins a cruise after her husband dies, experiences some unusual behaviour from guests and crew, then vanishes during a shore trip to Crete. The police are faced with varying perceptions of events, and Bridget. An adroit, shimmering tale of drug-running and deception.

* * *

Long before Renaissance woman **STELLA DUFFY** was resurrecting Golden Age detectives or earning an OBE for helming Fun Palaces, a global, community-led celebration of arts and sciences, she was a queen of Tart Noir. Her Saz Martin series epitomised a vibrant part of the mystery genre that promoted sharp writing of smart, tough heroines, amply seasoned with violence, sex, and humour. In *Beneath the Blonde*, the third of the Saz quintet, the effervescent 'dyke detective' is hired to find a murderous stalker and protect Siobhan Forrester, the lead singer of a rock band. It's a globetrotting gig, as Saz joins the band on its world tour from London to New

Zealand. Duffy laces quick-fire wit, clever plotlines, and emotional oomph into a fun tale that captures the feeling of 1990s rock while exploring the divide between star personas and the human behind the celebrity. More recently, Duffy returned to the crime scene after a lengthy hiatus with *The Hidden Room*, a superb domestic thriller entwined with cults, and the pressure, secrets, and pain that can lie beneath the surface of even seemingly stable relationships.

* * *

Overseas adventures are seen as a rite of passage for many young antipodeans; for **CHRISTINA HOAG** they seem almost imprinted in her DNA. Hoag was born in New Zealand, but her parents had met travelling in Zambia, and she grew up in several countries. As an adult she worked as a foreign correspondent in Latin America; evading guerrillas and soldiers, being accused of drug trafficking, and posing as a nun to get into a Colombian jail. More recently Hoag harnessed her experiences with Latin gangs and teaching creative writing to at-risk Los Angeles teens and in a maximum-security prison into her fine thriller *Skin of Tattoos*. The underlying 'young gangbanger gets out of prison, wants to go straight, and struggles to do so' storyline could be hackneyed, but Hoag imbues her tale with thoughtfulness, insight, and a striking sense of her richly drawn characters and the world they inhabit.

* * *

Distilling a nation to a single icon is always fraught, but in some ways perhaps nothing is more unmistakably Kiwi than rugby. From the world-renowned All Blacks to thousands of schoolkids muddying their knees on fields all over the country each weekend, it's engrained in New Zealand culture. **JOHN DANIELL**, himself a former professional player, delved into the darker side of the sport in his thriller *The Fixer*, centred on Mark Stevens, a fading All Black plying his trade in France's lucrative professional league. When an exotic journalist tempts Stevens in multiple ways, and a passing comment about his team's chances in the next game leads to an expensive gift, Stevens realises he's sidestepped onto an ethical tightrope. *The*

Fixer is a taut thriller full of eclectic characters, humour, action on and off field, and undercurrents of pride, corruption, and masculinity. It takes readers deep inside the locker rooms for an unvarnished look at the pressures and politicking of top-level sport.

* * *

A beautiful woman steps into a Los Angeles private eye's office lugging a problem she desperately needs solved; a classic noir set-up played out in books, TV, and film for decades. But in **ADAM CHRISTOPHER**'s hands the result is anything but typical. With a background in comics and superhero novels, as well as writing novelisations of modern-day Sherlock Holmes TV drama *Elementary*, Christopher has no qualms with blurring genre boundaries. While there are nods to Chandler and Hammett in Christopher's daftly brilliant LA Trilogy, which begins with *Made To Kill*, there's one striking difference: the taciturn private eye is Ray Electromatic, the last robot on earth. Ray specialises in deadly jobs, managed by his office gal Ada, a controlling supercomputer who helps wipe his memory tapes each day. But when the beautiful woman triggers something in Ray, then vanishes, he can't let it go. *Made to Kill* is a fresh, smile-inducing take on hardboiled novels, full of wisecracks and action, humour among the shadows, and a strong undercurrent of enjoyable absurdity.

* * *

Crime and romance are the two biggest oceans in the world of books, but the waters where they mix (eg romantic thrillers) can be tricky for authors to navigate given their avid readerships may be looking for very different things. Case in point: *Deception Island*, the promising debut from journalist turned romantic thriller scribe **BRYNN KELLY**, had two distinct covers. One heightened the thriller vibe, the other the romance. Beneath those covers, former Legionnaire Rafe Angelito is forced to kidnap an American heiress, only to find himself double-crossed and trapped on an island with Holly Ryan, a woman who's not what she seemed. The twin leads are surrounded by danger in a tale that blends jungle-based action-thriller with slow-burn romance. There's a whiff of 'Romancing the Stone', in terms of swashbuckling action seasoned with humour and romance and two strong characters forced together by circumstance. Suspend your disbelief for a fun ride. Kelly continued her popular Legionnaire series with *Edge of Truth*, *Forbidden River*, and *A Risk Worth Taking*.

* * *

While much of the publicity at the time focused on his age, **BEN ATKINS** demonstrated a distinctive narrative voice and fine touch for atmosphere in *Drowning City*, his debut set in Prohibition-era America. Atkins was a first-year university student when the book was published, having started writing it at 15 years old. In *Drowning City*, readers follow bootlegger Fontana on a hazardous one-night search for the culprits who hijacked part of a valuable booze shipment, a small crime that could upend Fontana's operation. Atkins weaves plenty of political and sociological threads into his tale while delivering nods to many classic tropes of mid-century noir – femme fatales, hulking goons, zany characters. He leans tell-not-show at times; the story unfolding via the eyes of his wisecracking and philosophical tough guy narrator, building a stylised atmosphere that readers may love or hate. Some brave choices from a fresh and talented voice. Hopefully we'll see more from Atkins.

* * *

After a childhood spent surrounded by small towns and sheep farms in the rain shadow of the Southern Alps of New Zealand, **CHRIS NILES** spread her wings as a broadcast journalist in Australia, the UK, and Eastern Europe. Later, the small-town girl brought an outsider's eye and strong awareness of place to her gritty and funny mysteries set mainly in the world's largest English-speaking cities: London and New York. Following a trilogy centred on hard-living London radio reporter Sam Ridley, Niles turned to crime with black comedy located among the high-stakes worlds of serial killers and New York apartment hunting in *Hell's Kitchen*. Cyrus is a nerdy young millionaire looking for a life purpose. A self-help book sparks a new passion, causing his life to intersect with a variety of disparate characters floating through New York City, but is Cyrus losing his mind? Told from multiple viewpoints, *Hell's Kitchen* is an edgy urban thriller that blends grimaces with guffaws.

* * *

Is **ZIRK VAN DEN BERG** the best thriller writer in New Zealand? That was the question asked in 2004 by a prestigious magazine following the release of the Namibian-born author's first novel in English. *Nobody Dies* is a searing tale that's beautifully written and an enthralling page-turner. Erica van der Linde is a well-liked South African cop on the career fast-track who keeps her personal demons hidden. She's tasked with hiding protected witnesses, but unbeknownst to her superiors she dispatches the former criminals more permanently. Daniel Enslin has a crumbling life, made exciting by hanging out with Cape Town gangster Frank Redelinghuys. When Frank kills someone, Daniel turns to the cops for help. Can he survive a vengeful Frank, as well as his so-called protector Erica? Van den Berg delivered a tense novel in a striking setting that a decade later scooped a major South African books prize when translated into Afrikaans, before being adapted into the film *Ander Mens* (2019).

* * *

When **MARK ABERNETHY** was growing up in New Zealand he reportedly loved the books of Ian Fleming, Robert Ludlum, and Elmore Leonard. After moving to Australia to pursue his journalism career he leant into those influences with his own engaging thriller series starring Australian spy Alan McQueen. Although 'Mac' usually wore SAS fatigues rather than tuxedos, and operated in the underbelly of Southeast Asia more than any swanky hotels and cocktail bars James Bond might frequent. In *Golden Serpent*, Mac discovers that a high-profile terrorist he'd been lauded for killing has survived, partnered up with a rogue CIA agent, and armed himself with deadly nerve gas. Abernethy does a fine job balancing the catastrophic threats and derring-do required by espionage thrillers without tripping off the suspension bridge of disbelief. Mac is a reluctant hero, lured by normalcy and not untouchable or unruffled as a hero. There's a realness here and nice dashes of humour among the action as the book hurtles towards its close.

* * *

One of the finest British crime dramas of recent times, *Luther* is a cinematic showcase of both its magnetic star Idris Elba and its gritty London setting. But it was born in a suburban house half a world away. **NEIL CROSS** has penned several terrific novels, compelling television dramas for UK and US networks, and Hollywood films from his Wellington home. Like many of his screen dramas, Cross's novels centre on flawed characters thrust into emotionally harrowing situations, with menace lurking beneath bleak settings, and events spiralling horrendously out of control. In *Captured*, dying artist Kenny is determined to put things right with four people he feels he let down, but ends up investigating and harshly interrogating the husband of a woman who'd shown him much-needed kindness as a child. A woman who has gone missing. A one-sitting book that hooks early and entrances to the final page, with a hero who's both endearing and terrifying in his willingness to take things to the edge. Crisp and vivid prose power a tense tale infused with themes of justice, the importance we may place on fleeting events, memory vs reality, and the legacy we leave. Cross's most recent novel is the award-winning *Luther: The Calling*, a prequel to the first season of his Golden Globe-winning (and 11-time Emmy nominated) television series.

* * *

Canadian-born engineer and scientist **PAUL E. HARDISTY** spent many years working in conflict zones before settling in Western Australia and launching a series he says let him explore the truth of what he'd experienced. Centred on South African paratrooper turned energy contractor Clay Straker, the series intersects pulse-pounding thrills with weighty literature. In *Reconciliation for the Dead*, having barely survived adventures in Yemen and Cyprus, Straker returns 'home' to post-apartheid South Africa to face inquisition from the Truth & Reconciliation Commission. For readers, Straker's testimony about the actions of his military unit during the brutal War in Angola unlocks more of who he is, and what made him question everything he thought he knew. This superb novel is a richly evoked exposé of the horrors of a forgotten war, and the way unchecked desire for power and money can spark division, othering, and the worst consequences. A hard-hitting page-turner told in atmospheric prose that's overflowing with substance.

* * *

After topping local bestseller lists and earning awards listings with an engaging police procedural trilogy penned while he was studying engineering at Auckland University, wunderkind **BEN SANDERS** took his storytelling talents to the United States in his gritty, violent thriller *American Blood*. Marshall Grade is no longer with the NYPD, after a botched undercover operation. He now lives on the other side of the country, in New Mexico, lying low and avoiding the authorities. But the abduction of a local woman pricks his conscience, and he stumbles into a viper's nest of drug dealing, gangs, and worse. Meanwhile, his past hasn't forgotten him either, with plenty of people wanting to cash in Marshall's final chit. Powered by lean prose and dry humour, *American Blood* is a modern thriller with an expansive feel; crime meets Western. Sanders vividly evokes the Southwest, delivering action and intrigue aplenty, while creating a contemporary gunslinger with plenty of layers. Marshall Grade returned in *Marshall's Law*. Sanders's latest is standalone *The Stakes*.

* * *

Australia and New Zealand are two of the most southern nations in the world, yet there's a whole continent further south: Antarctica. After taking readers to the warmth and waters of the Mediterranean in her debut *The Lost Swimmer*, screenwriter and director **ANN TURNER** heads to the frigid south of the south in *Out of the Ice*. Environmentalist Laura Alvarado is preparing an environmental impact assessment on a long-abandoned whaling station on an Antarctic island. When Laura finds signs of recent human habitation, and during a dive thinks she sees a figure crying for help in an ice cave, her concerns are written off by others. What is going on? Turner crafts a flawed and very human heroine who may divide readers looking for likability, while being backed by a wonderfully evocative sense of place that seems to offer as many threats as the human ones.

* * *

What would you do if a random stranger told you your whole life was a lie, then proffered enough proof that you couldn't simply write them off as a crazy person? That's the dilemma faced by Melbourne photography teacher Kim Leamy in **CHRISTIAN WHITE**'S stunning debut *The Nowhere Child* after a visiting American claims Kim is actually Sammy Went, an infant girl who vanished from her Kentucky home back in 1990. Could the loving parents who raised Kim really have stolen her away from her real family? Faked her birth certificate? Or is someone trying to swindle her now, and if so, why? White intercuts past and present to build delicious tension as Kim heads to Kentucky to uncover the truth, coming face-to-face with small-town secrets and snake-handling religious fanatics who might be her 'real family'. Screenwriter White avoided any second-novel slump with his similarly dark and devious *The Wife and the Widow*, perhaps even vaulting over the high bar he set with his first bow.

* * *

If crime fiction is liberally seasoned with cold cases and troubled pasts impacting the present, then the cases 'intermillennial sleuth' Elizabeth Pimms investigates are positively frozen. Canberra author **LJM OWEN** taps into her own interests, studies, and experience as a librarian, archaeologist, and paleogeneticist to heavily texture her cosy mysteries which intertwine ancient civilisations and modern life. In *Olmec Obituary*, Pimms is a reluctant librarian who gets a chance to indulge her first love of archaeology by examining 3,000-year-old bones unearthed in Mexico. All is not as it seems with the dig or its findings. *Mayan Mendacity* and *Egyptian Enigma* continue the series. Owen has created a unique blend of mystery ingredients, and a welcome focus on often-overlooked female scientists and female leaders from ancient civilisations. Her latest novel, *The Great Divide*, is a far grittier rural mystery set in Tasmania that introduces Detective Jake Hunter.

* * *

Inspired by a famous real-life Victorian courtesan nicknamed 'Skittles', Brisbane author **MJ TJIA** has crafted a marvellous mystery heroine in Heloise Chancey, a courtesan and professional detective in 1860s London. First appearing in *She Be Damned*, Heloise rose from prostitution among the grimy streets of Waterloo to become a woman of means. When a wealthy benefactor asks her to find a missing woman thrown out of her family home, pregnant and unmarried, whom he fears has become the victim of a vicious serial killer, Heloise teams with her half-Chinese maid to investigate. The case takes her back to her old Waterloo haunts, and the prejudices of her past. Tjia has brewed an intoxicating read, nicely balancing history and mystery, giving readers an atmospheric and authentic sense of the era (pleasingly multicultural rather than whitewashed), while never overwhelming the narrative drive. The grim crimes are offset by some terrific, lively characters, and Heloise is a gem of a heroine; unusual, gutsy, resourceful, unrepentant. She screamed out for an ongoing series, and thankfully Tjia has answered the call with *A Necessary Murder* and *The Death of Me*.

* * *

Writing a novel about real-life killings that happened on the opposite side of the world in the early 1800s isn't the clearest example of 'write what you know', but what Adelaide author **HANNAH KENT** knew was she was fascinated by events surrounding Iceland's last-ever execution. A case that's also fascinated Icelanders for almost two centuries. *Burial Rites* is a lyrical and thought-provoking exploration of the final days of Agnes Magnúsdóttir, a servant who was sent to an isolated farm to await her beheading for her role in the brutal killing of a farmer and his guest (Iceland had no prisons at the time). Guarded by the members of another farming family, Agnes tends chores and receives spiritual guidance from her priest. Kent delivers a haunting tale as the family adjust to their disgraced 'guest', and the days Agnes has left evaporate. The harshness of nineteenth-century farming life, compounded by the Icelandic winter, bleeds from the page as readers view a bleak existence through Agnes's eyes and the perspectives of those who surround her. Beautiful and chilling.

* * *

From preventing fashion crimes to solving violent crimes could have been the snappy bio on former Sydney journalist **ELSA KLENSCH**'s four mystery novels. After moving to New York in the late 1960s and becoming a fashion editor at esteemed magazines like *Vogue* and *Harper's Bazaar*, Klensch shot to global fame as the leading fashion journalist on television, hosting 'Style with Elsa Klensch' on CNN for more than two decades and making cameo appearances as herself in Hollywood films and TV soaps. After retiring in 2001, Klensch underwent a costume change, emerging as a crime novelist. While still retaining some of her past wardrobe: heroine Sonya Iverson is a TV journalist and amateur sleuth. In *Shooting Script* a puff piece on the Hawaiian spa of Iverson's former network boss becomes something far darker as he's found dead in the bed he shared with his pregnant third wife. Iverson uses her outsider viewpoint and TV interviews to keep ahead of the police in the hope of a career-changing scoop. Style outshines substance in a pacy, fun tale that's perhaps more discount store than designer.

* * *

While authors may balk if you ask them which are their favourites of their own books ('it's like asking me to choose a favourite child', is a regular cry), there are always some tales that are a wee bit special. For Sydney's **MICHAEL ROBOTHAM** his masterful sixteenth book, *The Suspect*, was something of a landmark. Not because it was the subject of a publisher bidding war, though it was. Not because it introduced Parkinson's-afflicted psychologist Joe O'Loughlin, who'd go on to star in several novels, though it did. And not because it was translated into 24 languages and sold more than a million copies. No, it was rather special because it was the first of Robotham's books that had his own name on the cover. Over the previous decade the experienced journalist had ghostwritten 15 autobiographies, ranging from social workers to comedians to 1990s pop stars. In *The Suspect*, O'Loughlin is faced with a dilemma when a past patient is murdered and a current patient fits the police description of the killer. Worse, O'Loughlin is arrested himself after trying to help, and is forced to sleuth out the real killer to save his own skin. Robotham's crime debut was a laminate-you-to-your-chair kind of read, and it kick-started a brilliant sequence of tales. For me, a favourite standout in an oeuvre full of them is *Life or Death*, Robotham's masterpiece centred on a stoic convict on the run in Texas that clutches the heart while examining prison life and characters crooked and kind, backdropped by exquisite settings. It went on to make Robotham the second-ever Australian to win the CWA Gold Dagger. His latest novel, *Good Girl, Bad Girl*, also steps away from O'Loughlin but swims in similar psychological waters as protégé Cyrus Haven is called in to assess Evie Cormac, a young woman with a deeply troubled past and unusual lie-detecting abilities. An absorbing tale to kick-start a new series.

* * *

Dating back to the times of slave turned Greek philosopher Epictetus, it's been said that life isn't about what happens to you, but how you respond to it. Upper Hutt author **CAT CONNOR** could have reacted in a variety of ways when she received death threats in a poetry chat room more than a decade ago. She chose to use the experience to fuel her debut thriller, *Killerbyte*, where FBI agent Ellie Conway is confronted by a threatening former member of her own poetry chat room, only for the man to turn up dead in the boot of Conway's car. He's not the first body; all are found with poems and a killer seems to be targeting Conway and her friend Mac Connelly. A pacy tale threaded with sinister threats, *Killerbyte* instigated a long-running series centred on Conway (a tough and skilful investigator who mixes hard living with a creative soul) and her Delta A team – a series that now numbers 11 novels and several shorter works. In *Databyte*, the sixth tale, Conway gets hunted by her own when she becomes the prime suspect in the murder of her ex. Connor's tales may be catnip for readers happy to suspend disbelief for high-stakes thrills and a kick-ass, tech-savvy heroine who's regularly put through the physical and emotional wringer by her creator.

* * *

In an era where the Internet and social media seem all-pervasive, the idea of our most embarrassing or shameful moments being recorded and paraded for millions to see out of context and without consent is downright frightening. Glasgow-based Australian **HELEN FITZGERALD** tapped into such fears in *Viral*, where Su Oliphant-Brotheridge is an A-grade student who's about as wild as beige wallpaper, until one night on holiday. Su's drunken antics in a Spanish nightclub are videoed and shared worldwide, putting Su into hiding and her adopted mother, a wealthy Scottish judge, on the warpath. FitzGerald, whose star has risen with the hit BBC adaptation of her parental nightmare novel *The Cry*, adroitly raises topical issues throughout a propulsive narrative. What are the rights and wrongs of our Internet Age, where does personal responsibility lie, what should be criminalised? FitzGerald further demonstrated her originality and versatility with her recent novel *Worst Case Scenario*, where a hard-living, menopausal probation officer becomes obsessed with a recently released wife-killer and kicks over a Jenga tower of consequences that fit the title. Energetic and darkly hilarious, it's fresh and diabolical in both its heroine and overall story.

* * *

Nietzsche's aphorism about those who fight monsters taking care they don't themselves become a monster is particularly apt in crime fiction. In the case of prolific Gungahlin author **JACK HEATH**'s first foray into adult crime fiction (by age 33, Heath has written two dozen children's and YA thrillers) that isn't a concern: the monster-fighting hero in *Hangman* is already a monster himself. Timothy Blake is a professional fixer with his own fetishes, a deeply damaging past, and a working relationship with the head of the FBI's Houston field office. Operating in the shadows and called in to solve the unsolvable cases, Blake deals in life and death; those he saves and the lives he devours in payment. When a schoolboy goes missing, Blake is teamed with FBI Agent Reese Thistle, but there are warning signs from the start that the case isn't what it seems. While some readers may be put off by Blake's predilections, Heath does a fine job creating empathy for an anti-hero who is more than his revolting acts. Blake returns in *Just One Bite* (entitled *Hunter* in Australia and New Zealand).

* * *

Otago author and academic **MAXINE ALTERIO** begins her third novel and first suspense tale, *The Gulf Between*, close to home in Queenstown before taking readers on a disconcerting journey back to 1960s Naples, a city rife with corruption and unhealed wounds of war. Our narrator Julia is shocked by a phone call about an accident, and even more so by the victim: her estranged son Matteo who lives on the other side of the world and she hasn't seen for three decades. What was he doing in New Zealand? As she sits by Matteo's hospital bed, Julia reminisces on how young love curdled when she encouraged her husband to return to his native Naples so the family could be there for his ailing mother. But there were reasons why he'd fled to England, and more to the family business than olive oil. Alterio brings several ingredients to a high simmer, creating delicious suspense in a tale that brings post-war Italy to vivid life while raising plenty of questions about choices and consequences.

* * *

Fifty years ago, an unknown killer terrorised Glasgow: 'Bible John' butchered three women and was never caught. University of Otago professor **LIAM MCILVANNEY** explores the effect of those killings in his superb third crime novel, *The Quaker*, a fictional tale with strong echoes of history. DI Duncan McCormack is parachuted into the long-stalled investigation into the murders of three women, a poisoned chalice for the fast-rising Highlands copper. His new colleagues dislike him on sight, his bosses are positioning themselves politically, and McCormack is harbouring dangerous secrets of his own. Then there's a fourth murder. McIlvanney shows a deft touch for character, time, and place in an atmospheric read. 1960s Glasgow is another world, but McIlvanney salts in some modern sensibilities by giving the female victims a voice in an otherwise masculine canvas. *The Quaker* is an evocative slice of the past that's populated with an array of intriguing characters, tough issues, and some nuanced interplay between them. McIlvanney calls himself a 'slow motion crime writer', but in good news for crime fans he is reportedly working on a new McCormack tale.

* * *

Aerospace weapons systems designer turned Northland author **COLIN D PEEL** largely flew under the radar locally but earned plaudits from international media including the *New York Times* for his lean, pacy thrillers that harkened back to the heyday of Alistair MacLean and Jack Higgins. Peel produced 25 novels from the 1970s to the 2000s, full of global threats, laconic heroes, bravado and action, and topics ranging from diamond smuggling, international terrorism, and classified defence secrets akin to his former career. One of Peel's later tales, *Chicane*, blends terrorists, fast cars, and dashes of romance as photojournalist Michael Fraser is recuperating in Italy after a harrowing assignment, only to witness his best friend die while driving a Ferrari. When suspicions arise about the cause of the crash, Fraser finds himself trying to protect insurance assessor Anna Todini while uncovering an international conspiracy that threatens the military defences of the West. An engaging 'beach read' or 'airport thriller' – like Peel's entire oeuvre – that targets entertainment and reader enjoyment above all else.

* * *

Crime-lovers who prefer cosy mysteries should probably avoid **KIRSTEN MCKENZIE**'s fourth novel *Doctor Perry*, which firmly plants itself in both the horror end of the crime landscape and its

Florida setting, which includes the Rose Haven Retirement Resort. The titular doctor is a suave and fastidious psychopath who has flown under the radar even as he's constantly looking for new patients (to replace those who've vanished) and fosters children with his latest wife Myra. As undignified and hopeless as life can seem for retirees in a rest home, it's even worse when Dr Perry is providing his 'medical care' behind the scenes. A creepy and crowded tale regularly dosed with wince-inducing horror, *Doctor Perry* offers some nice touches of originality among the mayhem.

* * *

Joining the recent surge of superb fresh antipodean crime voices in 2018, Perth author **DERVLA MCTIERNAN** immediately made a big splash with her first DS Cormac Reilly novel, *The Ruin.* Set in Galway in her native Ireland, McTiernan's debut hit bestseller lists in several countries and scooped Ned Kelly, Davitt, and Barry Awards alongside other shortlistings. Here's the twist: her sophomore novel, *The Scholar,* is even better. Former anti-terrorist officer Reilly is still attempting to build trust and adjust to life in the Galway station when his hard-working partner Dr Emma Sweeney discovers a hit-and-run victim initially identified as Carline Darcy, the heir to a pharmaceutical fortune. But Carline was home safe. As O'Reilly investigates the case becomes entwined with scientific discoveries, billion-dollar business, and Emma's own work. A clever and well-crafted tale where McTiernan brings the Galway setting to rain-soaked life alongside robust characters who like the case itself are much more than they seem at first glance. O'Reilly returned in *The Good Turn* in 2020.

* * *

Horse-loving Hibiscus Coast author **ANDREA JACKA** taught herself to write a novel with several years of waking up at 4am to get words on the page before work. The result, *One for Another,* was a hugely enjoyable romp that blended mystery with Western. Set in 1880s Idaho and centred on whiskey-drinking bordello madam Hennessey Reed, Jacka's debut has the kinetic energy of a cattle drive, though occasionally her prose could be reined in. Reed is a thoroughly appealing heroine, hindered by her demons and obsessions but sparked to be a Bowie knife-wielding avenger when three young women are murdered near her town, and then her own daughter is kidnapped. Jacka richly evokes frontier life while delivering an engaging whodunnit that likely leaves readers wanting more of Hennessey Reed.

* * *

Heading abroad after a stint as a high school teacher in Queensland, **JANETTE TURNER HOSPITAL** taught at universities in Europe and North America while producing 15 books, mainly literary novels and short story collections. Following September 11, she veered into conspiracy thrillers with two tales that explored the impact of terrorism and how the fear of it penetrated everyday lives. In *Due Preparations for the Plague*, Lowell is the now-grown son of a victim of a 1987 plane hijacking who is contacted by Samantha, a now-grown woman looking for answers who survived the hijacking as a child. Did Lowell's father, a government spy who recently died and left his son a key to an airport locker, know more than he shared? Turner Hospital jams literary allusions into an award-winning tale that may divide readers as it attempts to straddle styles. In *Orpheus Lost*, the author inverts the titular myth in a story entwined with a subway bombing.

* * *

When **JULIE PARSONS** returned in 2017 with *The Therapy House* following a decade-long recess, noted Irish novelist Declan Hughes declared she 'was Irish Crime Fiction before there was Irish Crime Fiction'. Emerald Noir, like its antipodean counterparts, has increasingly (and deservedly) come more to the global fore in recent times. Parsons, a TV and radio producer who spent her childhood in a country town outside Auckland before emigrating to Ireland as an adolescent, played her part from the late 1990s with several superb character-centric thrillers that preceded the 'domestic noir' boom. Parsons's debut *Mary, Mary* was a tale of the grieving mother of a murdered daughter and an obsessed detective that played with crime conventions and became a global bestseller. Twenty years later, *The Therapy House* continued Parsons' absorbing and atypical takes on the genre as retired Garda Inspector Michael McLoughlin discovers the brutalised body of his neighbour, a renowned judge, and is hired by the judge's family to investigate. The carrot: information on the murder of his own father during an IRA robbery decades before. A rich story that surveys the ongoing trauma of violence on survivors, families, and broader society.

* * *

In her popular series starring pathologist and forensic physician Anya Crichton, Sydney doctor turned storyteller **KATHRYN FOX** has addressed a broad array of issues through the prism of page-turning mysteries. In the fifth instalment, *Death Mask*, Fox travels to New York to speak on the back of some groundbreaking research only to get caught up in a troubling case involving an alleged gang rape by five professional footballers. Crichton pairs with private investigator Ethan Rye, her minder during the summit, to uncover the truth. Written several years before the #MeToo and #TimesUp movements took hold, in *Death Mask* Fox takes readers into the darker side of male professional sport, where teamwork becomes tribalism and on-field physicality can sour into off-field brutishness and misogyny. While the setting is the United States, there have been similar issues and misconduct in Europe and Australasia. Given the importance of the topic it's perhaps understandable that Fox occasionally over-explains or sermonises. Dubbed 'Australia's answer to Patricia Cornwell and Kathy Reichs', Fox has also paired with James Patterson on *Private Sydney* and recently announced she was adapting her Anya Crichton series for television.

* * *

A host of popular young adult tales, starting with *Looking for Alibrandi*, earned Sicilian-Australian **MELINA MARCHETTA** a global reputation, film adaptation, international bestseller status, and a creaking mantelpiece full of awards. Then in 2016 she swerved, with her first adult novel, and first crime tale. In *Tell the Truth, Shame the Devil*, Chief Inspector Bashir 'Bish' Ortley is on suspension from the London

Metropolitan Police when he hears a tour bus full of British kids, including his daughter, has been bombed in France. Dashing across the Channel, he finds his daughter unharmed, but a chaotic scene swarming with French police, panicked families, and traumatised kids. To make matters worse, Violette LeBrac Zidane is missing. The granddaughter of an infamous suicide bomber. While authorities believe Violette is a victim, others paint her as the villain, and Bish must delve into crimes present and past to uncover the truth. Marchetta demonstrates her storytelling chops while leaping to a new readership, crafting a tense tale full of emotionally nuanced characters that explores the bigotry and snap judgements made when fear takes over.

* * *

The horrors of the Second World War were barely over when a brutal new regime emerged in South Africa, as the white minority entrenched its power with apartheid; new laws that enforced racial segregation and made political and economic discrimination against non-whites perfectly legal. **MALLA NUNN**, who was born in neighbouring Swaziland before immigrating to Perth as an adolescent, has probed the early years of apartheid in a sublime mystery series starring Detective Emmanuel Cooper. In *A Beautiful Place to Die*, Cooper is sent to a tiny border town to investigate the death of an Afrikaner police captain. The victim's family and the powerful Security Branch try to steer Cooper towards black communists rather than any white suspects. While Cooper is white himself, being of British descent, he's still something of an outsider. Assisted by a Zulu constable and a local shopkeeper, Cooper tries to find the truth, however politically inexpedient. He's a tortured but honourable man in a tortuous and very dishonourable world. Beautifully written despite some horrifying content; a stunning debut that kick-started a wonderful series and announced an exciting new voice who fully embraced 'crime as the modern social novel'.

* * *

Catherine Berlin, the central character in a gritty series of crime novels from **ANNIE HAUXWELL**, is flawed with a capital F. A heroine addicted to heroin, among other issues. In the fourth and most recent instalment, *House of Bones*, the London-based investigator ends up jetting to Hong Kong and China as she tries to unpick a case involving a violent assault by a Chinese teenager on scholarship at an exclusive boys' school, a missing victim, British peers with troubling proclivities, and stockpiles of looted Chinese treasures. Berlin is a tenacious investigator who barrels forward while not knowing who she can trust in a tale with more twists than a Dragon Dance in a Chinatown New Year parade.

* * *

Born in New Zealand to Cypriot parents following the Second World War, Whanganui painter and poet **CHRISTODOULOS MOISA** spent a few of his school years in his ancestral home, then revisited for 18 months just prior to the Turkish invasion in 1974. Moisa explores those turbulent times for Cyprus in his 'Wolf' trilogy, an engaging, complex set of historical thrillers. In *The Hour of the Grey Wolf*, Kiwi journalist Steve Carpenter (aka Stauvro Marange) moves to his parents' village in Cyprus to recuperate from injuries earned while reporting in Vietnam, only to get caught up in a murder mystery. Meanwhile the Mediterranean island nation is anything but a peaceful haven: the newly elected president is under threat of assassination and Cyprus teeters towards civil war. While *The Hour of the Grey Wolf* and its sequels are charming mysteries mixed with politics, in essence Moisa is delivering a textured portrait of a place and its people at a dramatic time in history. *Wolves in Dogs' Clothing* and *Thrown to the Wolves* complete the set.

* * *

Having swapped decades of high-flying corporate life for a writer's life, **JOHN M GREEN** has produced four high-stakes thrillers as well as co-founding a local publisher that has shepherded dozens of Australian authors to publication, including a few in this book. *The Tao Deception* sees Australian corporate dealmaker Dr Tori Swyft, an ex-spy who first appeared in *The Trusted*, thrust into a deadly situation. While she's brokering a deal between a Chinese billionaire and a Greek company, an obscure Chinese terrorist group claims responsibility for the death of the Pope and other world leaders. Swyft has suspicions about the bona fides of the Chinese company but finds herself in the crosshairs of foes and friends alike. Fast-paced action entwined with big money and power-hungry conspiracies.

* * *

CATHERINE LEA flipped the script on the traditionally male-dominated world of politics-tinged thrillers by putting the wife of a Senate candidate and a young female kidnapper front and centre in *The Candidate's Daughter*. Kelsey Money gets in over her head when she joins her boyfriend and his drug-addled brother in kidnapping Holly, the neglected daughter of Senate candidate Richard McClaine and his socialite wife Elizabeth. After wanting a child for so long, the high-flying parents struggled with having a disabled daughter, growing apart and becoming increasingly self-absorbed. But with Holly's life in danger, both Kelsey and Elizabeth start realising what really matters and are in a race-against-time to save the little girl. As events escalate, there's a lot going on. Lea sets the hook and reels readers through the pages, while offering some fascinating character arcs both through this book, and in the case of pickled socialite turned flawed force for justice Elizabeth McClaine, also through the follow-ups *Child of the State* and *A Stolen Woman*.

* * *

GRANT NICOL's second Grímur Karlsson tale, *The Mistake*, has a simple and effective set-up. There's been a brutal murder in Reykjavik. There's a clear prime suspect – Gunnar Atli, a very troubled man prone to blackouts who claims he just stumbled across the body. A cop and a bereaved father each want justice, but of very different kinds. Several people, all with secrets, collide. Nicol, a New Zealander who lived for several years in Iceland's capital, does a superb job taking this premise and layering in complexities and intrigue. Along with the did-Gunnar-do-it question, readers are taken down several rabbit holes as Nicol guides us into the darker sides of Icelandic society. Prostitution, the treatment of the mentally ill, domestic troubles. This is Nordic Noir with a strong emphasis on the Noir. A story of things going badly wrong beneath the snowy and peaceful veneer of Iceland. Detective Grímur's bleak investigations continued in *A Place to Bury Strangers* and *Out on the Ice*.

* * *

In Melbourne author **PD MARTIN**'s third novel featuring Australian-born FBI profiler Sophie Anderson, *Fan Mail*, someone is killing crime writers. Anderson has just moved to Los Angeles when she's called in on the murder of bestselling author Loretta Black, whom she'd met at Quantico when the author was doing research. Black had received disturbing letters from a fan and was strangled with a pair of stockings, just like a character in her latest book. Then Anderson, who gets disturbing visions as well as her psychological insights, discovers a link to the murder of a crime novelist a few months before, also matching a scene from her book. Another author is missing, and Anderson's extra ability seems to be malfunctioning. Is the killer a crazed fan? Martin delivers a fast-paced, gritty tale full of plenty of action. The most recent Sophie Anderson book, *Coming Home*, sees the profiler return to Victoria when a boy is killed in strikingly similar circumstances to her brother's murder 30 years before.

* * *

Winning second prize in a beauty contest gets you $10 in classic Monopoly but winning third prize in the 1998 Sisters in Crime Scarlet Stiletto Awards proved far more valuable for **ANGELA SAVAGE**. And rather beneficial for those of us who enjoy crime tales that thrill while also pulling back the curtain and getting our minds whirring about tough issues. Savage's fascinating heroine Jayne Keeney, an expat Aussie private eye based in Bangkok who later got reviewers grabbing for the 'feisty' descriptor, first appeared in that prize-winning short story. Several years later, after winning a Victorian Premier's Literary Award along the way, Savage gave us Keeney in full technicolour in *Behind the Night Bazaar*, the first in a series that's as beguiling, nuanced, and intoxicating as its Thailand setting. In *The Half-Child*, a distraught father calls on Keeney for help when a young Australian woman falls from a hotel balcony in beach resort Pattaya. He doesn't believe his happy daughter who'd been volunteering at a local orphanage would commit suicide. Keeney's investigation leads her to go undercover at the orphanage, hiding her language skills as well as her true purpose, and uncovering a complex world of neglected kids and overseas adoptions.

* * *

Long before the Booker judges praised a novelist for having the courage to tackle the murky history of the Troubles in Northern Ireland, crime writers were leading the way. One of the most superb explorations emanated from a house in Melbourne suburb St Kilda, as Belfast native **ADRIAN MCKINTY** turned his storyteller's eye to his homeland with his outstanding Sean Duffy trilogy-turned ongoing series. Set in 1980s Belfast, the books overflowed McKinty's mantelpiece with major crime writing prizes, including the Edgar, Barry, and Ned Kelly Awards. The fifth tale *Rain Dogs* opens with Duffy on crowd control when Muhammed Ali visits Belfast – everyone is there, from Ian Paisley to Bono to the National Front – before getting involved in a locked room mystery when a female reporter covering the visit of a Finnish trade delegation is discovered dead in Carrickfergus Castle. Echoes for Duffy. McKinty blends sharp prose with expertly crafted characters, a relentless hero, and a setting so vivid you feel the rain on your face. Over the series, from small crimes to big secrets, McKinty delivers superb historical noir seasoned with black humour, biting social commentary, and willingness to play with tropes. In the pub of crime writing, 'tis top shelf. After years of being an aficionados' favourite and 'hidden gem', McKinty deservedly broke through to a much larger audience in 2019 with standalone chiller *The Chain*.

* * *

After dabbling for years with short stories, **RACHEL AMPHLETT** certainly made up for lost time after publishing her first novel, *White Gold*, in 2011. That book kick-started a series starring scarred veteran Dan Taylor, part of a group tasked by the British Secret Service with protecting the country's energy supplies, leading to adventures in exotic locations threaded with modern counterterrorism and cyber security issues. Across three series – the Dan Taylor tales, the Detective Kay Hunter police procedurals, and the 'English Assassins' spy novels – along with a handful of standalones, the prolific Amphlett published 19 novels in less than a decade. From her Brisbane home, Amphlett gained a global readership, made the *USA Today* bestseller lists, and drew comparisons with Robert Ludlum and Michael Crichton for her heart-pounding and high-octane global thrillers. She recently returned to the UK.

* * *

TIM BAKER announced his arrival with a megaphone in early 2016 thanks to his mesmerising crime debut *Fever City*. That was a twist-filled story spanning three time periods and involving father and son investigators (one ex-cop turned private eye, one reporter) caught up in the disappearance of a young boy and the tentacles of the Kennedy assassination. Baker – an Australian living in the south of France after a globetrotting work life with stops including Brazil, India, and North Africa – then showed he was no one-hit wonder with the equally exquisite *City Without Stars*. Set in Ciudad Real, Mexico at the start of the new millennium as hundreds of female sweatshop workers have been murdered and discarded like trash, Baker's second novel unfolds from five perspectives. A union activist putting herself at risk by going up against powerful bosses; a cop who suspects many of his colleagues are on the payroll of a cartel boss; the cartel boss himself; an American journalist; and a distinguished local priest who rescues orphans. A bravura tale that's a complex and lyrical expose of a culture of corruption and exploitation, cleverly told.

* * *

Former paratrooper and banker **MARSHALL BROWNE** admitted in an interview with the *Sydney Morning Herald* that he had an ongoing interest in damaged heroes, and throughout several engaging crime novels he certainly demonstrated keen insight into those who've suffered and survived. In his Ned Kelly Award-winning *The Wooden Leg of Inspector Anders*, Browne takes readers into the Machiavellian nexus of Italian crime and politics. There's a sense of Russian dolls as the titular hero looks into the killing of a magistrate who was looking into the killing of a judge who was looking into the Mafia. It is ten years since Anders traded his leg for national hero status when he took down an anarchist group; now he's a compromised cop whose bosses hope will simplify matters by finding a way to finger anarchists for this new crime. Rather than digging into powerful networks. Or looking too closely at colleagues. An intriguing start to what became a gem of a series, with the fourth and final tale published posthumously in 2016. Browne had a great touch for character and atmosphere, and also gave us a duology set in Nazi Germany on the eve of the Second World War, and a tale starring an unstable Japanese policeman, *Rendezvous at Kamakura Inn*.

* * *

Inspired by her early days as a court reporter working biker trials in Penrith, along with meeting the likes of David E. Kelley (*The Practice, Boston Legal*) and Dick Wolf (*Law & Order*) as an Australian television executive, **SYDNEY BAUER** created a Boston-set legal thriller series. *Undertow* introduced defense attorney David Cavanaugh and saw him handling a politically charged case: a black mother and fellow lawyer accused of murder when the white daughter of a powerful senator drowns at a birthday party. The senator presses the District Attorney for harsh charges. First-time out, Bauer offers a compelling storyline and a good sense of the Boston setting, building to a thrilling conclusion. The series continued with five more novels; the latest, *The 3rd Victim*, sees Cavanaugh reluctantly coerced into defending a mother accused of brutally murdering her own baby. Bauer takes the multi-layered plot beyond the courtroom as she canvasses some tough issues.

* * *

Did you know that more than a decade before 'Jack' Lewis (aka CS Lewis) would go on to create one of the most beloved fantasy worlds of all-time, the young Oxford don was solving murder mysteries? That's the conceit behind radio host **KEL RICHARDS**' intriguing 1930s Murder Mystery series, a recent quartet among the prolific storyteller's almost 60 books. In *The Sinister Student*, Jack is hosting a meeting of the famed Inklings – whose members include his pal Tollers who'd publish a book about hobbits the following year – when a visitor is found the next morning beheaded in his locked room at Magdalen College. A readable mystery with some charm that nods to both classic mysteries and boarding school novels, elucidating past life in the City of Dreaming Spires, drenched in theological debate.

* * *

After a slow-burn debut, Melbourne author **ANNA JAQUIERY** put the accelerator down in her atmospheric second Commandant Serge Morel tale, *Death in the Rainy Season*. The Parisian detective is back in his birthplace, visiting his mother's Cambodian village and exploring the historic Angkor Wat temples, when his boss calls and sends him to Phnom Penh. A French citizen, the charismatic head of a charity and nephew of an important French government minister, has been beaten to death in a hotel room. He'd checked in under a false name. Morel teams with local Police Chief Chey Sarit to investigate the murder; the latter is keen to close the crime as a disagreement between foreigners, but the victim had stirred the hornet nests of foreign paedophiles and forced evictions, and Morel knows there are many more suspects hidden away. A rich mystery, wonderfully told, full of vivid detail about a nation of beautiful landscapes, dark history, and a complex present.

* * *

After adding a fresh voice to the domestic noir swell with her quality debut *The Girl in Kellers Way*, former foreign correspondent **MEGAN**

GOLDIN turns up the thrills in her claustrophobic second novel. *The Escape Room* sees Vincent, Sylvie, Sam, and Jules – four ruthless and money-hungry Wall Street investment bankers who've struck a flat patch – lured into a lift and trapped as part of a lethal game. Can they work out who trapped them and why? More importantly, can they get out alive? Intercutting between past and present, Goldin ramps up the tension with riddles and tests as psyches fray and revelations turn the group against each other. In a high-flying world where much is sacrificed at the altar of greed, how much will our four participants sacrifice? A seat-edge, stay-up-all-night kind of thriller that shows Goldin has taken a leap to a new level from her fine first effort.

* * *

Olivia Wolfe is the kind of heroine who can more than hold her own against the classic men of action that traditionally helmed high-octane thrillers. Introduced in **LA LARKIN**'s *Devour*, Wolfe is an investigative journalist who's more than happy to get her hands dirty, or bloody. After a fatal incident and narrow escape from a terrorist in Afghanistan, Wolfe is being stalked and her work hacked. She heads off on her next assignment, to Antarctica where she looks into sabotage and a suspicious death at the British base for a team drilling beneath an ancient lake, with plenty of things unresolved and danger still hovering. High stakes, belief suspended, plenty of action, exotic locations, and a cast of interesting characters including a superb heroine; Larkin ticks all the boxes and more to be comfortably placed alongside past thriller masters like Alistair MacLean and Michael Crichton. Olivia Wolfe returned in *Prey*.

* * *

When the sovereignty of Hong Kong was handed over to China at midnight on 1 July 1997, it not only brought an end to 156 years of British rule; in a way it also brought a natural end to a long-running crime series from globetrotting Sydneysider **WILLIAM MARSHALL**. Over the course of 16 books spanning more than two decades, Marshall took us into the surreal, comical, violent world of the police officers of Yellowthread Street station in Hong Kong. The ensemble nature of the cast – led by European-born local DCI Harry Feiffer – drew comparisons to Ed McBain, though Marshall greatly ramped up the dark humour and bizarre situations and leaned into his vivid Hong Kong setting. An ITV adaptation in 1990 failed to capture the magic of the books. The final Yellowthread Street novels dealt with the looming handover from British to Chinese rule. *To The End* sees DCI Feiffer facing an uncertain future and trying to find equilibrium by deducing whether a janitor was the true target of a shotgun blast, Inspector Yee awaiting the arrival of his new Chinese boss, and Inspectors Spencer and Auden getting caught up with mystical curses. Popular and well-reviewed during their time, Marshall's novels fell into hard-to-find status and a lingering cult following in the years following his death in 2003. Thankfully they've recently been made available again by a London publisher specialising in humorous writing.

* * *

Self-described pulp scholar **ANDREW NETTE** embraces his passion in his first novel *Ghost Money*, a taut noir set in 1990s Cambodia that takes readers on a thrilling ride while also providing insight into a country trying to recover from the wounds of a horrifying regime. Max Quinlan is a Vietnamese-Australian former cop now specialising in finding people in Southeast Asia. He's hired by Maddie Avery to find her brother Charles, a former Melbourne lawyer who's now a dodgy gem dealer. After Charles' business partner is found murdered in a Bangkok apartment, Max follows the trail deep into a country which was then far from the tourist trail, full of scarred locals and some waylaid expats. Nette worked as a journalist in Cambodia in the 1990s and brings that on-the-ground experience to the page, shading his novel with Cambodia's landscapes, culture, and politics in all their beauty and harshness.

* * *

In his Superintendent Le Fanu mysteries, **BRIAN STODDART** sets the DeLorean for 1920s India, immersing readers in the sights, sounds, and flavours (not to mention machinations) of Madras at a time when Gandhi was strengthening calls for independence from the British Raj. First spotted in *A Madras Miasma*, Chris Le Fanu is a veteran of the Great War and a thoroughly decent man operating as a detective within a society stratified by class and ethnicity. He's called into action when Jane Carstairs, a British woman who'd arrived as part of the 'fishing fleet' – unmarried women looking for husbands among the colony's officials and expat businessmen – is found dead in a canal, morphine coursing through her veins. Aided by Sergeant Habibullah, Le Fanu follows the trail to the doorstep and beyond of some powerful people among the colonial establishment. Stoddart creates a wonderful sense of time and place along with a fascinating cast of characters, while raising questions about economic and racial disparity as British rule waned. Le Fanu's sleuthing continued in *The Pallampur Predicament, A Straits Settlement,* and *A Greater God.*

* * *

Other antipodean authors with crime novels set abroad
SHAUNA BICKLEY: *Lies of the Dead*
LINDA COLES: *Hey You, Pretty Face*
KATHERINE DEWAR: *Ruby and the Blue Sky*
BARBARA EWING: *The Petticoat Men*
GREG FLYNN: *The Berlin Cross*
JUDE KNIGHT: *Revealed in Mist*
BOB MARRIOTT: *In The Lion's Throat*
FIONA MCINTOSH: *Beautiful Death*
CAROLINE OVERINGTON: *The One Who Got Away*
TONY PARK: *An Empty Coast*
MIKE PONDER: *The Windsor Conspiracy*
DEBORAH ROGERS: *The Devil's Wire*
HEATHER ROSE: *The Butterfly Man*
SARAH SCHMIDT: *See What I Have Done*
TIFFANY TSAO: *The Majesties*
YVONNE WALUS: *Murder @ Work*

Back in Time – Historical Crime

The conservative attitudes and still-relevant prejudices of post-war New Zealand are explored in **JEN SHIEFF**'s historical mysteries, which bring marginalised characters to the fore. The first of these takes readers back to 1950s Auckland with a gritty tale that exposes the seedy underbelly of a country that was often considered a land of milk and honey. *The Gentleman's Club* centres on a Hungarian bridge builder, a hairdresser who is a brothel owner by night, and a troubled teenager coming to the big city for an abortion; their lives all collide as they try to survive life on the backstreets. Weaving together exceptional historical detail and social issues, Shieff has been compared to the likes of Sarah Waters. She pierces the veneer of polite post-war society, lifting the skirts on class prejudice and other social ills. The standalone sequel, *The Vanishing Act*, is set a decade later and is another glorious romp that sees the return of some characters in a tale involving the death of a disgraced gynaecologist and set against the underground subcultures of lesbians and sex workers.

* * *

While New Zealand is usually seen as a peaceful nation with a benign government at the bottom of the world, there have been riotous events and violent clashes over the decades, such as those during the Springbok Tour in 1981. **JONOTHAN CULLINANE** explored another turbulent time in his debut *Red Herring*, set in 1951. Power grabs and backroom battles between the establishment and blue collar unions led to a long-running waterfront dispute lasting several months where more than 20,000 workers were on strike.

With scars of the Second World War still raw, and the shadow of Communism spreading through Asia, the government called in the military. Soldier-turned-private-eye Johnny Molloy is dropped into this murky world. Hired to track a supposedly dead man, he crosses paths with an ambitious reporter looking to make her mark, and the pair end up waist-deep in the muck, sloshing around among political groups and real-life figures, searching for truth, or survival. Cullinane assuredly delivered a sparkling noir full of pace and cracking dialogue, well textured by real history and realpolitik. Some characters are scheduled to return in *Yellow Peril*.

* * *

First-time crime writers come in a variety of guises, but ones like **DAME FIONA KIDMAN** are rarer than even the most endangered of New Zealand's remarkable native birds. Before she turned to crime, over the past 60 years Kidman has become a literary doyenne thanks to a diverse array of tales as an award-winning author, poet, short story writer and scriptwriter. In *This Mortal Boy* she turned her sharp eye and flowing pen to a novelisation of a real-life crime from her own childhood, and the deaths of two young men that later played a role in New Zealand abolishing the death penalty. This brilliant novel eloquently brings mid 1950s New Zealand to vivid life; a nation grappling with the scars of war and a growing youth culture. Paddy Black from Belfast escaped sectarian violence only to face a different kind of discrimination. Why did this gentle young man thrust a knife into the neck of another beside a jukebox one night? Callous murder, or more complex than the headlines? Kidman weaves together the viewpoints of many associated with the case, giving readers a textured look at a life that was more than an entry in a history book. A harrowing and haunting tale full of humanity that questions where justice lies. An important read from a master storyteller.

* * *

Begun more than 50 years before the focus of this book, during the Second World War, but not completed and published until 2018,

Money in the Morgue is an extraordinary literary tag-team between theatre-loving Kiwi crime writers **NGAIO MARSH & STELLA DUFFY**. Adding to the four of thirty-two Inspector Alleyn novels set in Dame Ngaio's home country, *Money in the Morgue* sees her gentlemanly British detective trying to juggle his secret counter-espionage work while dealing with a daring theft at an isolated quarantine hospital. Trapped by a coming storm alongside restless soldiers, besotted young staff, a dying man, a mysterious patient, and maybe a killer, can Alleyn solve the crime without breaking cover? Marsh's early chapters provided the set-up, and Duffy seamlessly delivers an absorbing mystery woven with Golden Age stylings and a richly textured sense of time and place.

* * *

Prolific Paraparaumu writer and social historian **DAVID MCGILL** has explored a wide array of lives and events through more than 50 books, ranging from riots on colonial goldfields to prisoners of war to legal biographies, landmark buildings, Kiwi slang, and thrillers. His recent series featuring Dan Delaney spans several decades of twentieth-century New Zealand history, blending real-life figures with engaging crime tales. In *The Death Ray Debacle* Delaney is a young detective in 1930s New Zealand monitoring supporters of the Nazi regime and pursuing foreign spies trying to steal secret blueprints. The following books in the series each tackle events and personalities from New Zealand in the 1940s, 1950s, and 1960s. In *Death of an Agent*, Delaney has retired to be a winemaker, but is called back into action in Wellington and gets caught up in groups protesting the Vietnam War. McGill's tales deliver an abundance of historical texture and titbits to readers.

* * *

An Australian lawyer teams with an ex-US green beret to establish a merchant bank in Sydney whose dodgy practices may extend beyond financial crimes to drug running, arms sales, and links to CIA activities during the Cold War. It all crashes down when the lawyer is found dead and the soldier flees the country, sparking multiple investigations. Sounds like the basis for a Hollywood thriller, but it's a true slice of Australian history. Dockworker turned antiquarian book dealer **WAYNE GROGAN** plunges readers headlong into gritty 1970s Sydney and the bizarre real-life Nugan Hand bank scandal in his second novel *Heavy Allies*. Grogan uses a couple of fictional characters – a cop turned hitman writing his memoirs in prison, and an Australian soldier who meets green beret Michael Hand in Vietnam and becomes bodyguard to Frank Nugan – to explore the real-life events. Did the CIA have a hand in fostering the heroin trade in Australia? Grogan writes a powerful tale with poetic touches that takes readers into a corrupt world stretching from the jungles of Southeast Asia to the backstreets and skyscrapers of Sydney.

* * *

Having a Booker Prize winner ask you to become an accomplice on a crime novel they were struggling to finish would be a pretty head-spinning thing, eh? But that was what incited a superb series about a convict turned sleuth that provides a fascinating insight into life in colonial Australia. **MEG & TOM KENEALLY** are the partners in crime behind the Monsarrat tales, which began with *The Soldier's Curse*. Or more accurately, began when Tom (*Schindler's Ark*, etc) showed his beginnings to daughter Meg and asked her to collaborate. *The Soldier's Curse* introduced gentleman convict Hugh Monsarrat, a forger transported to New South Wales who works as a clerk in the Port Macquarie penal settlement. When his intelligent yet illiterate friend, housekeeper Hannah Mulrooney, is arrested for the poisoning of the commandant's wife, Monsarrat must unmask the real killer to save Hannah from the noose. The Keneallys strike the sweet spot of mystery and history, crafting an absorbing tale that's beautifully textured by its time and place without overwhelming the whodunnit. The harshness, injustice, and deprivations of the times are on show, ameliorated by moments of compassion and humour. The excellent series continued with *The Unmourned*, *The Power Game*, and *The Ink Stain*, and fans of high-quality historical mysteries will be pleased by reports the Keneallys are planning up to a dozen books.

* * *

After a globetrotting career behind the lens, photographer **GEOFFREY MCGEACHIN** picked up the pen and began to tell thousands of words. His first books were filled with humour, action, and spies but it was a swerve into the past that put the first of two Ned Kelly Awards on McGeachin's mantelpiece. *The Diggers Rest Hotel* is set in countryside Victoria in 1947 and introduced Charlie Berlin, who has returned to the police a much-changed man after spending the war as a bomber pilot and POW. Shuffled off to Wodonga to investigate a spate of robberies, Berlin battles his wartime trauma while his assignment gets even dicier when the body of a headless girl is found in an alleyway. McGeachin beautifully beckons readers into post-war Australia, texturing the mystery with insights into the tone of the times and the lingering trauma both on the Home Front and for returning soldiers. McGeachin continued to explore Australia's changing society and turned a great book into an excellent series with *Blackwattle Creek*, set in 1957, and *St Kilda Blues*, set in 1967.

* * *

TV presenter, advocate for women and children, and former fashion model **TARA MOSS** first grabbed the attention of crime readers with her fascinating heroine Makedde 'Mak' Vanderwall. Over six gritty feminist thrillers, Mak grows from young model to forensic psychologist and private eye facing down one of Australia's most powerful and ruthless families. After several years away from the crime scene (which included a searing memoir-manifesto, *The Fictional Women*, about how society portrays and labels women), Moss made a welcome return in 2019 with brilliant historical mystery *Dead Man Switch*. In classic noir, smart and sexy Billie Walker might be the femme fatale, but here she's the private eye. The book is set in 1946 Sydney, and Billie is a former wartime journalist who has returned from Europe without her husband – missing, presumed dead – and now runs her father's detective agency. With a returned serviceman as her secretary and an indigenous woman as an aide,

Billie does things her own way as she sleuths through the Sydney underworld searching for a missing boy. Moss immerses readers in post-war Sydney with an unabashedly feminist take on the times. *Dead Man Switch* is superb, hardboiled storytelling dosed with humour, centred on an intrepid heroine.

* * *

1989 was a watershed year in Queensland; the release of the Fitzgerald Inquiry report exposed systemic corruption in the state's politics and police. Government ministers and senior police were jailed, longstanding state Premier Sir Joh Bjelke-Petersen had already resigned in disgrace. Gold Coast lawyer **CHRIS NYST** represented cops and crooks during the two-year inquiry, and it's against that backdrop he set *Cop This!* Inspired by real events and figures, Nyst's first novel begins with a homemade bomb exploding in Brisbane in 1969, killing 11 people and sparking a controversy that could threaten the government. When a small-time crook is charged, a father then son take on the state's most powerful figures in a fight for justice. A three-part saga saturated in treachery and corruption, *Cop This!* was an exciting legal thriller that saw Nyst compared to John Grisham and – he revealed later – got him a visit from some 'serious' old-time underworld figures inquiring about his intentions. He later went on to win the Ned Kelly Award for his third legal thriller, *Crook as Rookwood*.

* * *

A mixed-race soprano, a young Māori activist, and an Italian tenor take on some shady real-life figures from a lesser-known slice of New Zealand's colonial past in heritage planner and historian **DINAH HOLMAN**'s engaging novel, *A History of Crime: The Southern Double-Cross*. In 1887 the young colony is going through a depression. Singer Frédérique (Riki) Bonnell is visiting the land of her grandfather when she's hurled from a steamship, having witnessed a group of men toss another over the side. The man, Kaituhi, had been looking for evidence of a leading banker's corruption, tied to the theft of his tribe's lands. After saving each other, the pair team up to expose the conspiracy between politicians, businessmen, and other public officials to feather their own nests at the expense of the indigenous population. Unbeknownst to Riki, her fellow singer Francesco Bartellin was also conducting a secret investigation into the powerful and dangerous men. Holman delivers a rollicking historical tale, laced with crime and a dash of romance, which casts light on past misdeeds and manipulations that seem all too recognisable in our modern times.

* * *

It isn't a surprise that **STEVAN ELDRED-GRIGG**'s sole stab at a crime novel, *Blue Blood*, created a storm on its release in 1997. Over four decades and a range of non-fiction and novels, the social historian has been unafraid to take an unconventional tack whether dipping his pen into the inkwell of New Zealand's colonial past, the horrors of child abuse, or taking aim at sacred cows including the mythologising of wartime sacrifice. Set in Christchurch in 1929, *Blue Blood* was not only a parody of the detective fiction of that era, it included a future Queen of Crime as a prime suspect. Two women are brutally murdered, bodies splashed with paint. The trail leads the detective in charge to the door of Ngaio Marsh. Eldred-Grigg's depiction of Marsh as an insecure, arrogant, cross-dressing lesbian appalled some. In a TV debate, he defended his book as fantasy, with some emotional truth. Noted more for its controversy than quality, *Blue Blood* remains an interesting read. Though perhaps Eldred-Grigg – a skilful and opinionated writer – could have used some of Marsh's talents when it came to its mystery plotline. While several critics and friends of Marsh derided the book, her theatrical protégé Elric Hooper admitted he was sure the Dame herself would have enjoyed *Blue Blood* immensely.

* * *

Long-time journalist **ROBIN ADAIR**'s passion for Australia's colonial history is front and centre in his novels starring Nicodemus Dunne, a former London policeman. In *Death and the Running Patterer* it's 1828 and Dunne is working as a word-of-mouth newspaperman in Sydney after being stitched up and transported across the world. When there's a series of murders, the Governor of the colony calls on Dunne to dust off his detective skills. But how do you find one killer in a colony begun by and still flooded with criminals? Incorporating real-life as well as fictional characters into his book, Adair constructs a vivid canvas of the life of the times. While the history rather outshines the mystery, there's plenty of page-turning quality. Adair, who had family connections to the early policing of the city and turned to crime writing in his retirement years, brought Dunne back for another adventure in *The Ghost of Waterloo*.

* * *

England and Australia share a sporting rivalry that stretches back almost 150 years. **ANDREW GRIMES** sets *The Richmond Conspiracy* against one of the most controversial clashes, the infamous 'Bodyline' series of 1932-1933 in which an England team desperate to regain the Ashes resorted to questionable tactics, nearly sparking riots at cricket grounds and an international incident at a trade level. When a ruthless businessman is found brutally murdered in a grimy Melbourne warehouse, Inspector James Maclaine is charged with finding a killer who likely has a military background. Maclaine himself is a veteran, and still carries the physical and mental scars. As the summer of cricket turns into boxing with a ball, Maclaine roams his city and into the rural outskirts to find answers. Set in the Depression yet not depressing, Grimes seasons his tale with laconic humour and local vernacular. He balances details that evoke a strong sense of the time and place with continuing to advance the story and showcase the characters along with the plight of returning servicemen.

* * *

Maritime expert **JOAN DRUETT** gives readers an engaging mix of classic mystery and colourful seafaring adventures in her Wiki Coffin series. In an ocean of crime fiction, it can be tough to stand out, but Druett creates something enjoyably unique in *A Watery Grave*, both in its evocation of nineteenth-century exploration and her fabulous hero. It's 1838 and part-Māori, part American Wiki Coffin is due to join the US Exploring Expedition as a translator when his skin colour sees him arrested for murder. When freeing him, the Virginia sheriff deputises Wiki to find the real killer on board one of the seven ships. As the expedition sails for the Pacific, Wiki is confronted with an apparent suicide and a deadly accident in addition to the original murder. Druett marvellously salts in historical details that give texture while not drowning the crime story. Inspired by the real-life expedition, Druett blends fact and fiction while showcasing the beguiling mix of personalities, motivations, and perspectives on board. An entertaining mystery drenched in maritime colour, with an engaging lead. The series continued with four further novels and several short stories.

* * *

Inspired by a real-life murder, **DAVID WHISH-WILSON** plunges into a cauldron of corruption in *Line of Sight*, his excellent first novel starring Superintendent Frank Swann. It's 1975 in Perth, a time when the ranks of cops and criminals aren't mutually exclusive. Favours and dirty money flow through organised crime, big business, politics, and policing. When brothel madam Ruby Devine is gunned down on a Perth golf course, there's minimal investigation. Frank Swann is on sick leave but fears his old friend – he knew Ruby from their days in wild gold mining town Kalgoorlie – was killed by the very people investigating her murder. Money is power, and now heroin is providing plenty of money. Meanwhile Frank's teenage daughter has vanished. Frank has been outspoken about fellow cops profiting from organised crime and is a marked man as he testifies before a Royal Commission that may be toothless. Whish-Wilson creates a bleak yet compelling portrait of a time and place where crime and graft are rife, and even the honourable are tainted. Atmospheric and stylish noir more than police procedural, *Line of Sight* doesn't provide pat solutions. Frank Swann returns in *Zero at the Bone* and *Old Scores* as the seventies spill into the eighties.

* * *

In the hands of **MOIRA MCKINNON**, a tale of double murder morphs into a stunning ode to a harshly beautiful landscape and Aboriginal culture and knowledge entwined with that land. *Cicada*, the first novel from the doctor and infectious diseases specialist who has worked in the Outback, begins in the aftermath of the First World War with English heiress Lady Emily Lidscombe giving birth to a 'brown baby' at her husband William's remote property in the Kimberley. Realising Emily has cuckolded him, William reacts swiftly and with terrifying violence: killing the baby and the man he suspects of being Emily's lover. With her life also in danger, a weakened Emily escapes into the desert with her Aboriginal maid Wirritjil. Together the pair try to survive both the landscape and William, who rounds up troopers and trackers to find his wife. McKinnon concocts a lyrical story that is both an emotional thriller and an exploration of a growing friendship between two mismatched women, while highlighting Wirritjil's understanding and deep connection to her ancestral lands.

* * *

Understandably compared to Cormac McCarthy, **PAUL HOWARTH** takes an unflinching look at a horrifying and somewhat suppressed aspect of Australia's colonial history – the routine massacre of Aborigines by soldiers, white settlers, or police – in the superb *Only Killers and Thieves*. Tommy and Billy McBride are the teenage sons of a settler ranching family struggling to survive during a drought in 1885 Queensland. When the rains finally come, the brothers celebrate at a local swimming hole, only to return home to find their parents slaughtered and their sister left for dead. Calling on their most powerful neighbour for help, a wealthy landowner who runs the region like his personal fiefdom, the brothers blame their Aboriginal stockman, and are persuaded to join a posse headed by the sadistic Inspector Noone of the Native Mounted Police. A white man gleefully leading Aboriginal recruits to protect white settlements by 'dispersing' their own, by any atrocity necessary. As the true nature of the manhunt becomes sickeningly clear, the brothers choose different roads. Howarth lyrically conjures the stark realities of frontier life in colonial Queensland, with its echoes of the Old West, and doesn't let readers off the hook. The horrors of history are shown, not just told; poisonous 'us and them' seeds from which a nation has grown.

* * *

Melbourne author **ROBERT GOTT** blends mystery and history with a large dollop of hilarity in his charming crime quartet starring inept Shakespearean actor and would-be sleuth William Power. Think Inspector Clouseau meets the biggest ego at your local am-dram theatre, set in wartime Australia. In *Amongst the Dead*, military intelligence sends Power to infiltrate the top-secret Nackaroos unit that patrols Australia's Top End as Japanese forces cut a swathe down the Pacific. An insider is killing members of the elite squad, and Power is the grenade thrown into the mix to ferret out the culprit. Gott nicely flips the usual script: while our erstwhile hero and egotistical actor thinks he's chosen for his detective skills, he's really the catalyst for others to do the solving. A delightful comic caper. For those who prefer more serious historical mysteries, Gott has penned another very fine wartime series starring Constable Helen Lord and Detective Joe Sable of the newly formed Homicide Unit of the Victoria Police: *The Holiday Murders, The Port Fairy Murders,* and *The Autumn Murders*.

* * *

SULARI GENTILL offers a fresh antipodean spin on the classic gentlemen detectives of the 1930s Golden Age with her riveting series starring artist and accidental sleuth Rowland Sinclair. First sighted a decade ago in *A Few Right Thinking Men*, Rowly is the black sheep of his wealthy farming family, a scandal-magnet returning to Sydney from Europe. To the ongoing disapproval of his family, Rowly associates with bohemian, leftist pals Milton, Clyde, and Edna, and regularly stumbles into trouble and plays amateur detective. Meanwhile the Great Depression spreads suffering, and political clouds gather for the coming thunderstorm of another world war. In *Give the Devil His Due*,

Rowly prepares an art exhibit to reveal the growing horrors he saw on a visit to Germany. He also decides to race his yellow Mercedes for charity on the deadly Maroubra Speedway, only for Milt to become the prime suspect in the murder of a journalist, another man to die on the track, and dangerous figures to try to intimidate Rowly. This is storytelling with vitality and gusto in a very fine series set during turbulent times. In something completely different, Gentill also recently won a Ned Kelly Award for *Crossing the Lines*, an exceptional meta-fictional whodunnit where two writers craft each other's stories: who is the author and who the character?

* * *

A former policeman who became a familiar face on Australian television, **BRUCE VENABLES** tapped into the darker side of his first career with *A Necessary Evil,* a sweeping saga of three generations of Sydney cops. In 1956, rock'n'roll was sweeping the world and the rise of youth culture was worrying many in power. As a reward for stamping out teenage gangs in Sydney, the newly formed 33 Division was given purview over gaming and vice. Easy money. Lead by the fearsome George Everard, known as the Prince of Darlinghurst, the elite group of plainclothes cops earned the nickname 'the Dirty Tree' and became Sydney's biggest gang. George's personal tree sprouted son Harold and grandson Shayne, cops of very different types. Venables guides readers through decades of corruption and crime in New South Wales in an absorbing tale that feels all too realistic.

* * *

Political historian and biographer **EDMUND BOHAN** showed an admirable touch for blending compelling mystery plotlines into rich depictions of New Zealand's colonial history with his quintet of Inspector O'Rorke tales in the late 1990s and early 2000s. In the fourth novel, *The Irish Yankee*, readers get further insight into the charming policeman's past. It opens during the American Civil War, in which a young O'Rorke operates as a Union secret agent under the name Sean Brennan. Two decades later O'Rorke is a well-liked and respected policeman in Christchurch, when he's recognised by members of a visiting group of American lecturers. As old battle lines are redrawn, O'Rorke plans a trap and the visitors plan their vengeance. Bohan crafts an intelligent, well-written tale with a blemished but likable hero that illustrates not only the historical details but the politics and public attitudes of the times. After a 14-year hiatus, Bohan and O'Rorke made a welcome return in 2017 with *The Lost Taonga* and *A Suitable Time for Vengeance*.

* * *

In the late 1990s, **PETER DOYLE** coaxed readers into the underground culture of post-war Sydney in a fascinating trinity of books (that won two Ned Kelly Awards) centred on likable hustler and chancer Billy Glasheen. Overseas reviewers made comparisons to Elmore Leonard or 'a hopped up James M Cain'. *Get Rich Quick* saw the boozing, pill-popping Glasheen trying to avoid a murder rap by finding the real killer, dealing with a dodgy government dude, trying to hide a small fortune in jewels, and keeping the party going for Little Richard and his rock'n'roll entourage during their Sydney tour. A musician and artist himself, Doyle brings that world to energetic life with a hefty dose of Aussie vernacular. Tough and hapless people collide. Cameo appearances are made by real-life figures, from singers to future NSW Premiers and Prime Ministers. After focusing on non-fiction works inspired by Sydney police photographs and then winning the Ned Kelly Award for Lifetime Achievement in 2010, Doyle brought Billy Glasheen back for another round in 2014's *The Big Whatever*. Now a cabbie with a few side hustles in the 1970s, Glasheen is thrust into his former life when he recognises himself in a paperback novel and realises an old associate isn't dead after all.

* * *

Could there have been any more appropriate storyteller than **KERRY GREENWOOD** to become the first honoured with a lifetime achievement award by Sisters in Crime Australia? (Thus adding to her Ned Kelly Lifetime Achievement Award.) For 30 years now readers around the world have been intrigued, delighted, and thoroughly entertained by the investigations and adventures of Greenwood's utterly unique sleuth Phryne Fisher. A lady of British high society who grew up impoverished in Melbourne and returns to the city as the series begins, Phryne is a courageous and independent woman of the 1920s who is more than capable of out (derring) doing the gents. She's equally at home being an artist's model, flying a plane, taking a lover, or driving a wartime ambulance. Greenwood gives readers further insights into Phryne's past in *Murder in Montparnasse*, where her pals Bert & Cec ask for her help when two of their brothers-in-arms from the Great War are bumped off in 'accidents'. Could it have something to do with a night they were all partying together in Paris near the end of the conflict? Bert & Cec fear they may be next, and as Phryne investigates, readers get her own reflections on Parisian life in 1918, a time she was also in the city of lights. In the (late 1920s) present, Phryne also has another case – the kidnapping of a young woman about to marry an older chef at a local French restaurant – as well as dealing with the nuptials of her lover. A charming tale elevated by its heroine, setting, and the broader cast of characters. The most recent Phryne Fisher novel, *Murder and Mendelssohn*, saw the fashionable sleuth infiltrating the world of classical music to solve the murder of an orchestral conductor, and getting caught up in the world of spies and MI6. While Phryne Fisher is Greenwood's most popular creation – both through the books and the television series based upon them – this talented storyteller has also scooped five Davitt Awards for her YA crime, her contemporary Melbourne series starring baker and reluctant sleuth Corinna Chapman, and for her book about an unsolved Adelaide case from 1948.

* * *

Other historical crime authors and novels
DEBORAH BURROWS: *A Time of Secrets*
ROBERT JEFFREYS: *Man at the Window*
TONY JONES: *The Twentieth Man*
JOHN ROSANOWSKI: *Murder on Broadway*
NICK SPILL: *The Jaded Kiwi*

Start 'Em Young – YA and Juvenile Crime

High school physics teacher **KEN BENN** slept under a bridge with a group of street kids to better understand what their life was like when researching his trilogy of gritty young adult thrillers. Benn also visited youth justice centres and spoke with social workers and victims and perpetrators of youth crime during five years of research. The result: a vivid and compelling look at a world many don't see. *Lethal Deliveries* centres on siblings Rochelle and Jack, who have different fathers. Rochelle's is overseas, Jack's is training him to be a drug dealer. Their Mum is a shift worker desperate to make ends meet, and a rare male role model is their inline hockey coach, an alcoholic. Told from multiple perspectives, *Lethal Deliveries* is a tough read that tugs at reader emotions, as characters face heavy issues and harsh consequences. Homelessness, teenage drug use, murder. Benn does a fine job avoiding an unremittingly dark vibe. There's a sense of life and fun with the characters, and underlying themes relating to family, loyalty, and friendship grip on for the ride too.

* * *

My own love affair with mysteries began more than 30 years ago with the Hardy Boys, before flowing through Sherlock Holmes, Agaton Sax, and Poirot as a keen adolescent reader. While Conan Doyle and Christie were writing for adults, Franklin W Dixon (collectively) and Nils Olof Franzen were focused on younger readers, which is not the easier gig many presume. Mystery writers for that market need to deliver compelling age-appropriate plotlines and engaging characters that'll lock reader attention and resonate with kids and their worlds, while also offering humour and not patronising youngsters. Award-winner **SUZANNE MAIN** deftly managed all that in *How Not To Stop a Kidnap Plot,* as suburban pals Michael and Elvis try to foil overheard plans to kidnap their snooty schoolmate Angus, their 'mortal enemy'. Who could be behind it all? Main salted in spybots, drones and modern tech that will fascinate youngsters, alongside timeless themes of having good friends, adventures, and being worried about how you're seen by others.

* * *

One of New Zealand's most infamous wrongful conviction cases involved farmer Arthur Allan Thomas, who served nine years for the murders of a farming couple before being pardoned and compensated (a Royal Commission found numerous police improprieties including two policemen planting evidence). Having interviewed Thomas's wife as a young journalist, the case lingered with Geoff Vause for four decades before as **JACK EDEN** he wrote *Furt Bent from Aldaheit*. In this thriller, a young Kiwi shaped by delinquency and imprisonment in Australia (surviving thanks to his wits and a fair bit of chutzpah) later tries to unpick the cause célèbre conviction made by his childhood tormenter, an overly determined cop. Pacy and full of action and dry humour, with an engaging hero who's hard not to like despite his criminal proclivities, *Furt Bent from Aldaheit* fair hums along.

* * *

In **ELLA WEST**'s first young adult thriller, *Night Vision*, adolescent Viola is akin to the rare Kiwi or even rarer Kakapo (native birds) – a unique creature living a nocturnal life in the New Zealand bush. Suffering from a rare genetic condition that makes sunlight dangerous, Viola explores the family sheep farm and surrounding forest by moonlight. One night she witnesses a vicious crime and sees the culprit bury a sack. With her parents struggling, she steals the money to save their farm. While the police look elsewhere, a newspaper article about her condition sees the local drug dealer zero in on Viola. West draws readers in with first-person narration from a remarkable young woman, plus her fine touch for rural New Zealand settings shaded by serenity and danger. There's an eerie elegance to *Night Vision*, a tale that tickles readers' minds just as Viola tickles the heart. West further cemented her reputation as an adroit YA mystery writer with her recent tale *Rain Fall*.

* * *

Having written stories in other genres under another name, **HARRY ST JOHN** showed an apt hand for crime with his young adult novel *Leave Her Hanging*. 'Spade' Miller is a wayward teen looking for answers when his ex-girlfriend Ella is found dead. While some blame Spade, he can't believe Ella would kill herself. He sets out on a thrilling journey that scratches at the suburban veneer and takes him deep into Auckland's underworld, where danger lurks behind closed doors. St John isn't scared to take readers into some pretty nasty places in this very good debut; although it's tabbed as a young adult read, with a teen 'hero', there are some very adult themes. Spade is an engaging centrepiece in a fearlessly told tale.

* * *

Years spent as a mental health phone counsellor talking to people in the worst situations inspired poet and children's author **HELEN VIVIENNE FLETCHER** to explore some tough issues in her first young adult tale *Broken Silence*. Seventeen-year-old Kelsey is hurting in body and soul. Her mother's in care, her father has abandoned her, and she's moved into a shabby flat with her brother and his mates. She hides bruises. When a stranger puts her boyfriend in a coma, did she play a part? Is she being protected, or stalked? *Broken Silence* is a hard-hitting story about trauma and its effects. Fletcher doesn't shy from taking readers into dark places with a high level of authenticity, exploring bullying, domestic violence, and gaslighting. The 'messages' are adroitly textured through a tense storyline rather than being soapbox-y. A triumph of a YA tale that's an important book as well as a thrilling one.

* * *

The ethical challenges of surveillance society and the stresses of teenage life are canvassed in Wellington author **LJ RITCHIE**'s engaging young adult debut *Like Nobody's Watching*. Oscar and his friends want to be the good guys, hacking into their school's surveillance system in order to find footage to blackmail and stop the bullies. But once they've opened Pandora's Box, what will they do with their newfound power? Like Harvey Dent, will the would-be heroes see themselves last long enough to become the villains? Ritchie does a good job crafting an intriguing plot, a believable and empathetic cast of teenagers, and exploring the escalating and unforeseen consequences when they try to help fellow students. A smoothly written story about high school bullying and vigilantism gone wrong, with a cyber twist. A cracking read for teenagers while still being interesting and enjoyable for adults as well.

* * *

Sita 'Squishy' Taylor tells her friends she got her nickname from one of Australia's most notorious gangsters, Squizzy Taylor, but actually it's because she loved hugs as a baby. The 11-year-old heroine of **AILSA WILD**'s delightful 'Squishy Taylor' series for younger readers is a brilliant creation: a curious, adventurous, and mischievous girl who loves solving mysteries. Living in a crowded apartment with her father, new stepmother, twin stepsisters, and baby brother, Squishy and her 'bonus sisters' overcome their initial friction by teaming up to solve a variety of cases featuring runaways, diamond smugglers, hackers, and hauntings. Books like *Squishy Taylor and the Vase That Wasn't* and *Squishy Taylor and the Silver Suitcase* are ideal for stoking a love of mysteries in young readers, while refreshingly putting a mixed-race girl dealing with a blended family situation front and centre. Squishy is 'cheeky and sneaky' but much more than that too; a fabulous young heroine.

* * *

Two teenage outsiders who've moved to Melbourne team up as a crime-solving duo in the elegant and enjoyable 'Every' trilogy from **ELLIE MARNEY**. Rachel Watts is a country girl forced to the big city by drought. Her neighbour James Mycroft has emigrated from England following a family tragedy. The Sherlockian monikers prove apt when, in *Every Breath*, academic whiz kid and self-described 'social moron' James asks narrator Rachel to help him find a killer after their homeless friend is murdered in the local park. While being different to each other in many ways, Rachel and James are two smart and displaced kids with an interest in science, and together they discover a trail leading to the local zoo. Engaging from the get-go and accelerating throughout, *Every Breath* is a loving, light homage to Holmes that's also fresh and distinctly Australian in vernacular and attitude. The young adult series continued with *Every Word* and *Every Move*.

* * *

Given street performer turned author **MANDY SAYER** has shown a fine touch for writing a wide array of stories, scooping major awards for memoir, literary fiction, non-fiction, and crime, it's no surprise she hit a home run with her first crack at a young adult thriller. In *The Night Has a Thousand Eyes*, Mark Stamp knows he's in trouble when he's playing around and breaks the window of his father's shed. But when he peeks inside, it gets much worse and his life is upturned forever. Grabbing his older sister Ruby and their baby sibling, the trio flee in the family van, heading for the safety of relatives on the coast. Mistrustful of authority after tough stints in foster care and a few run-ins with the local law, the youngsters try to stay a step ahead of their brutal, one-legged father in his Ford Fairlane. Sayer delivers a hard-hitting young adult tale doused in local flavour, combining coming-of-age road trip story with tough issues including domestic violence, drugs, and murder.

* * *

Back in 2015 the New Zealand book industry got global attention when **TED DAWE**'s gritty coming of age story *Into the River* was briefly banned from sale or supply two years after winning the biggest local prizes for children's and young adult writing. A conservative Christian lobby group complained about the book's 'highly offensive and gratuitous language, adult themes, and graphic sexual content'. Fortunately, sanity prevailed and the interim ban (the first in 22 years) was lifted. Interestingly for crime fans, *Into the River* was not only a powerful read but an origin story for Te Arepa (Devon) Santos, one of the main characters in Dawe's award-winning debut about drugs, gangs, and boy racers. In *Thunder Road*, 19-year-old Trace wants excitement after moving from a small town to the 'big smoke' of Auckland. His roommate Devon introduces him to illegal street-racing, before doubling down on danger when a money-making scheme gets the lads entangled with the local criminal underworld. From first revs, Dawe showed a great touch for thrills and suspense while never shying away from tough but all-too-realistic issues for teenagers.

* * *

Coromandel author **MEG BUCHANAN** has written a dozen books spanning historical fiction, romance, and sci-fi genres, but teenage readers who prefer contemporary tales full of action, crime, and danger can find a wee gem in *Scavenger Hunt*. Josh Reeves is a young man in love with moto trials, racing his motorbike across challenging courses. Joining a new development team with dreams of championship glory, he and his teammates blow off steam with drunken night-time dares that escalate from silly pranks to something far riskier. With the cops sniffing around and his season in jeopardy, can Josh and his mates find a way back on track? A thoroughly enjoyable read full of action and excitement and characters who are realistic while avoiding stereotypes. Buchanan guides readers into the lesser-known sport of moto trials with enough detail to embellish the story without putting the brakes on.

* * *

After winning multiple awards for *Risk*, her debut about a young woman whose best friend vanishes after going to meet a guy she met online, former police officer and paramedic **FLEUR FERRIS** scotched any 'one hit wonder' fears thanks to a string of harrowing YA books with nuanced heroines. In *Black*, readers are plunged into the life of Ebony Marshall, a withdrawn and angry teenager whose innocuous nickname 'Black' became more sinister after three of her friends died in tragic accidents. She becomes an outcast in her small town. Then a boy who asks Ebony out on a date for a dare ends up in intensive care. Is Ebony really cursed? A local religious sect certainly thinks so and is determined to purge the evil it believes she brings. Ferris delivers an emotional, suspenseful tale about small towns, religious fervour, and a resilient heroine. Strong characterisation brings plenty of believability. Teen suspense can be hit and miss, but Ferris delivers hit after hit.

* * *

With *Small Spaces*, Melbourne storyteller and graphic designer **SARAH EPSTEIN** created one of those 'one more chapter, up all night' types of tales I (and many other booklovers I imagine) have fond memories of discovering as a voracious young reader. Or as an adult. Epstein herself has loved books all her life, scribbling stories as a youngster but shelving her writing dreams until she had children of her own. A creepy young adult tale with complex characters, *Small Spaces* focuses on Tash Carmody, a traumatised 17-year-old who witnessed her nightmarish imaginary friend Sparrow kidnap a little girl almost a decade before. Now the girl, Mallory Fisher, is 15 and mute and has moved back into town. Tash now accepts Sparrow wasn't real – though Mallory certainly went missing for a week – but begins having disturbing flashbacks. Was she a witness, or something worse? Epstein keeps readers on tenterhooks throughout a compelling debut with an unreliable narrator who is easy to empathise with as she questions her own sanity as much as readers might.

* * *

When it comes to the James sisters, it may be a case of crime (writing) running in the family, or sibling rivalry. Either way, it's their readers who are the winners. After older sibling Wendy won a Ned Kelly Award for her first novel in 2006, **REBECCA JAMES** countered a few years later with *Beautiful Malice*, a nail-biting YA psychological thriller that became a global sensation as it had publishers clawing over each other at auctions before being released in 27 countries. Katherine Patterson is looking for a fresh start in Sydney: new city, new school, new name. She's delighted to make friends with Alice and Robbie, the most popular girl in school and a boy who's smitten. The inseparable trio have lots of fun until things turn for the worse. Past secrets are revealed, Katherine's new life is threatened, and Alice shows a disturbing side. It's easy to see why *Beautiful Malice* caught eyes worldwide; James smoothly delivers an intense tale of creepy atmosphere, strong themes, and potent characters.

* * *

CATHERINE JINKS has woven a varied tapestry across 30 books for readers of all ages, from picture books to young adult sci-fi, and humour-tinged historical fiction to adult murder mysteries set against the Catholic inquisitions of medieval Europe. But the two Davitts nestled among several other awards on her shelf sit there due to Cadel Piggott. First sighted in *Evil Genius*, Cadel is a lonely child prodigy recruited to the Axis Institute for World Domination in order to learn how to become a criminal mastermind, only to begin questioning all he's been taught. In *Genius Squad*, Cadel is under police protection ahead of testifying against a powerful figure from the first novel, and still looking for somewhere to belong. Jinks writes captivating tales with plenty of suspend-disbelief-and-enjoy action, twists, and technology use on the surface, which also have a strong undercurrent of emotion, friendship, and humanity. The trilogy concluded with *The Genius Wars*.

* * *

Mystery met magic in **KAREN FOXLEE**'s unusual young adult murder mystery *The Midnight Dress*. Rose Lovell is a guarded and angry teenager who has lived a transient life with her alcoholic father since her mother died a decade before. After the pair shift to Leonora, a tiny beach town in tropical Queensland, Rose unexpectedly becomes friends with exuberant fellow teen Pearl Kelly. Among many projects, Pearl is organising the high school float for the town's Harvest Parade, so introduces Rose to Edie Baker, an eccentric seamstress who has gone from renowned to reclusive, and who townsfolk think is a witch. Together they start making a dress, Edie sharing stories as Rose sews. But who is the girl in the dress who vanishes during the Harvest Parade? With lush and lyrical storytelling, Foxlee expertly beckons readers through a tale that's enchanting and haunting. The rocky beaches, sugar cane farms and bushland that enclose Leonora add to the wild, Gothic atmosphere.

* * *

In *Kill the Music* by **NANSI KUNZE**, Lorna Powell is living every teenage girl's dream, riding in limos and globetrotting from Japan to Vienna to tropical islands by the Great Barrier Reef with Turmoil, the world's hottest boy band. But being the band mascot can be lonely when you're living in the background as millions fantasise about your brother and his friends, and you're never sure whether anyone wants to be your friend or just get closer to Turmoil. A new school might be a fresh, normal start, until Lorna discovers death threats made against the band. Can she find the faceless killer and stop the plot before he wipes out the band? A rollicking story that blends intrigue and humour as Lorna careens through unusual exploits. Like Kunze's other young adult mysteries, *Kill the Music* centres on a superb and thoroughly engaging heroine; a believable, everyday kind of girl in far-from-everyday situations.

* * *

Of all the main characters in standalones-so-far I've enjoyed over the past couple of years, the spirited heroine at the heart of *Cassie Clark: Outlaw* by **BRIAN FALKNER** may scream the loudest for an ongoing series. The author is a prolific Kiwi living on the Gold Coast who sets his award-winning books for children and young adults all over the world. The book itself is a superb YA conspiracy thriller that takes readers on an adrenaline-charged romp through the murky heart of American politics. But it's the heroine, Cassie Clark, who shines brightest of all. Having survived a hit-and-run, Cassie's world is further upturned when her father, third in line to the US Presidency, goes missing. Rumours circulate that he's run off with a journalist. Cassie doesn't believe that, and decides to investigate herself, only to be framed for crimes she didn't commit. Who is trying to stop her, and why? Full of heart as well as action, laced with thought-provoking issues, Falkner delivers a cracking page-turner with a heroine who's a riveting concoction of smart and fallible, vulnerable and kick-ass.

* * *

A young woman is attacked while walking home through a park. She's bruised and traumatised, but 'lucky' compared to the next victim. Taupo author **TINA SHAW** explores the aftermath of an all-too-common occurrence in *Make a Hard Fist*, an excellent young adult thriller which is both frightening and empowering. Lizzie Quinn is a level-headed teen with good mates who is saving up to buy her uncle's VW Beetle. After spurning a boy at school, she starts getting weird messages. Then she's attacked, draining the joy and colour from her life. Lizzie tries counselling, but still feels on edge – and the notes keep coming. Getting proactive, she starts taking self-defence, but will that stop her stalker? Shaw has masterfully written a testing, relevant tale that confronts some tough issues and gets readers thinking. There's a hovering sense of menace, while the story never gets too bleak thanks to some vibrant characters, doses of humour, and the evolution of its heroine.

* * *

Sydney author **FELICITY PULMAN** takes readers deep into medieval England in her Janna Chronicles mystery series set against the twelfth-century civil war sparked when Henry I's nephew Stephen seized the throne ahead of Henry's daughter, Empress Matilda. In *Blood Oath* (originally *Rosemary for Remembrance*), Janna is a peasant girl being taught herb lore and healing by her mother Eadgyth. When Eadgyth dies suddenly, Janna suspects poison, and there are plenty of suspects. A strong-willed teenager who often dives in before thinking, Janna seeks justice while learning to survive during harsh and bloodied times. Over the course of the six-book series, fast-paced tales beautifully embroidered with loads of historical detail, Janna roams from peasant villages to the royal court, solving a variety of crimes while looking to find the father she never knew and avenge her mother's death.

* * *

Absence hasn't just made the heart grow fonder in teenager Ryan Davis's family; it's made the absent perfect. **MELINDA SYZMANIK** ably fuses mystery, family drama, and coming-of-age story into her psychological thriller for younger readers *The Half Life of Ryan Davis*. Fifteen-year-old Ryan lives in the shadow of his sister Mallory, who vanished three years before. Now his mother compares everything he and his little sister Gemma do to her idealised version of the missing child. But where did Mallory go – was she kidnapped, did she run away, is she alive or dead? And why is a stranger watching Ryan at the skate park? Syzmanik realistically takes readers inside the head of a growing teenage boy in an unpredictable tale that twists as we ride along with characters who are easy to warm to.

* * *

Prolific storyteller **SHERRYL CLARK** is a huge fan of crime fiction as a reader and viewer but, with a couple of exceptions, has largely eschewed the genre in her 70 books for children and young adults. She did however make a fine fist of *Dying to Tell Me*, a mystery for middle grade readers that has a dash of the supernatural while dealing with realistic themes including solo parenthood and adolescent struggles. After her mother leaves, schoolgirl Sasha moves to a small country town with her father, a policeman, and her younger brother. A knock on her head leads to puzzling visions, including of a fire at an old woman's house. Befriending retired police dog King,

Sasha reluctantly gets caught up in the hunt for a killer. An exciting tale for younger readers with an interesting heroine and an engaging canine sidekick. More recently, Clark was shortlisted for the CWA Debut Dagger for her first adult crime novel, about a woman who must confront her traumatic past to find the killer of the brother she turned her back on years before. *Trust Me, I'm Dead* was published in 2019, with a sequel *Dead and Gone* due for release later in 2020.

* * *

'My name is Eliza Boans and I am a murderer.' **SHIRLEY MARR** wastes no words hooking the reader into her young adult novel *Fury*, where an angry, entitled rich girl sits in a police station confessing to a social worker. But who did she kill and why, and how much of Eliza's tale can we really believe? Through a blend of confession and flashbacks we learn how dissatisfied Eliza is with her affluent life in a gated community, the trouble she gets into at school, and the fierce rivalries and friendships among her gang of 'mean girls'. Marr does a tremendous job holding reader attention and creating a captivating narrative centred on such a spoiled and remorseless young woman. But as Eliza toys with the social worker, alternatively revealing and clamming up, is there much more going on than a terrible crime committed by Eliza and her friends? Clever and edgy storytelling with a dark vein of humour.

* * *

JC BURKE artfully explores perceptions and prejudices, including the reader's, in her confrontational and powerful novel *Pig Boy*. Damon Styles is an overweight teenager growing up in the small town of Strathven who prefers writing to sports and gets bullied at school. Ostracised since an incident at a school camp, things get worse when Damon, cruelly nicknamed 'Damoink' by his classmates, is expelled on his eighteenth birthday. He's angry, likes violent video games, has a list of names, and a plan to set things right that starts with getting his firearms licence. Damon takes a job with another outsider, a Serbian immigrant named Miro but known as the Pig Man.

Hunting pigs with Miro will teach Damon what he needs to put his plan into action. Two people on the fringe, who each have secrets and a traumatic past. Fuse lit. Burke does a remarkable job of bringing readers into Damon's world, creating a claustrophobic atmosphere where an unlikely friendship grows and menace flickers just out of view, waiting to strike. An impressive tale for older teens and adults.

* * *

Waimate writer **KEN CATRAN** has shown over a long, distinguished career in children's books and television screenwriting that he can craft compulsive stories no matter the subject or genre. Among his oeuvre is a superb young adult trilogy centred on a creepy serial killer. In *Talking to Blue*, teenager Mike Connors has had a rough time of it. A year ago, his parents died in an accident. Now he lives with a workaholic aunt, and people in his suburb are dying. When Mike stumbles onto a crime scene, he's being watched. Then the phone calls begin, from a creepy killer who knows far too much about Mike and his secrets. Can Mike survive, or will his life be destroyed? Catran delivers a tense and chilling yarn, then raises the stakes further by retelling events from a different perspective in *Blue Murder*. The trilogy is completed with *Blue Blood*, told through the eyes of Mike's girlfriend Sheril, as murders continue even after it seems the killer has finally been dealt with. Exciting stories from an author who has published more than 50 books for children and young adults, won numerous awards, and had an Emmy nomination for his TV work.

* * *

The strong voices of two young Aboriginal women are front and centre in the gripping, unusual *Catching Teller Crow* by **AMBELIN & EZEKIEL KWAYMULLINA** (Palyku). Beth Teller's father is a detective in a small town, struggling with grief after Beth's death even as he's the only one who can still see and hear her. Beth tries to help her father, including with his cases. An arson and suspicious death bring Isobel Catching into their lives (well, one life and one after-life), an unusual girl who shares her story with readers in verse chapters. The

Kwaymullina siblings craft an intriguing story threaded with relevant issues (racism, injustice, corruption) that punches far above its slim weight.

* * *

An 11-year-old boy processing grief and guilt creates a superhero persona for himself after witnessing a murder in **PETER TWOHIG**'s absorbing and unusual novel *The Cartographer*, set in Melbourne in 1959. The narrator takes readers into the bowels of the city as he creates a map for himself of safer places and he tries to avoid crossing paths with the killer. A year ago, his twin suffered a tragic accident, now he's got all too close to a killer when peering through the window of a strange house; he doesn't want to be the next to die. So he maps the city, finding adventures in all sorts of nooks and crannies, from laneways to the drainage system to deserted tram yards. An atypical novel that jitterbugs on the border of young adult and adult fiction, *The Cartographer* has good forward drive and is at its peak with the voice of its enigmatic narrator and its deep dive into the city in which he tries to survive.

* * *

Since the first time I heard it many years ago, I've loved the (likely apocryphal) Cherokee story about the two wolves fighting a battle within each of us. One prideful, greedy, negative, the other kind, truthful, and positive. The winner: whichever you feed. Talented Australian filmmaker and children's author **TRISTAN BANCKS** nodded to that idea with his terrific middle grade thriller *Two Wolves* (*On the Run* in the United States). Ben Silver is a curious, movie-loving kid who finds himself inside a real-life drama when the cops call at his house, then minutes after they leave his parents arrive and quickly pack Ben and his little sister Olive for a sudden 'holiday' in the bush. Why are they on the run? Ben tries to uncover the truth, but what if it tears his family apart? In sporting terms, Bancks hits this for six. It's an exciting and emotional tale, pacy and heartfelt. Seat-edge and more, it would fit snugly alongside middle grade classics like

The Hatchet. Bancks also writes hilarious tales for younger readers, while his most recent thriller is *Detention*, about a young refugee girl who escapes from one of the centres that have blighted Australia's international reputation.

* * *

Other young adult and children's authors and novels
JOANNA BAKER: *Devastation Road*
BERNARD BECKETT: *Jolt*
ADELE BROADBENT: *Between*
MANDY HAGER: *The Nature of Ash*
JUSTINE LARBALESTIER: *Liar*
JACLYN MORIARTY: *The Betrayal of Bindy Mackenzie*
JUDITH ROSSELL: *Wormwood Mire*
RA SPRATT: *Friday Barnes, Girl Detective*
VIKKI WAKEFIELD: *Ballad for a Mad Girl*

Section Two:
Antipodean crime on-screen

TV and film of the past 25 years

Introduction

Although Australian and New Zealand viewers have a steady buffet of northern hemisphere crime drama served on their screens, particularly from the United States and United Kingdom, over the years there has also been a decent range of locally produced films and television shows that have caught the eye. From edgy tales that push the envelope to comforting favourites, from shooting stars that light up the screen then vanish to shows that become mainstays for years and years (and have eternal life in syndication and re-runs).

Some of these Australian and New Zealand productions will be familiar to overseas viewers, with several being screened in primetime in dozens of countries or becoming cult favourites with international audiences on streaming services. Others may be unknown but are well worth digging out and trying. The following list is designed not as a comprehensive survey, but more of a tasting platter showcasing the range of Australian and New Zealand screen crime from the past 25 years. There are plenty of high points, and others that fizzled.

Note that the focus here is screen crime produced and set in Australia and New Zealand. While Kiwi and Aussie talent may appear onscreen or be the driving force behind several superb northern hemisphere crime dramas (eg *Luther*), they are not included here.

ANIMAL KINGDOM (film, 2010, written by David Michôd)
A film that raised the bar for Downunder screen thrillers and shot long-time actress Jacki Weaver to international renown and Oscar

nomination for her bravura twirl as Janine 'Smurf' Cody. A tense story full of menace begins with teenager Joshua turning to his estranged grandmother for help after a family tragedy, unaware that Smurf is the matriarch of a Melbourne crime family and the family home is under police surveillance. Joshua's trio of uncles are experienced predators in this criminal jungle, and Joshua must find his feet in an eat-or-be-eaten world full of drugs and violence. A crime thriller that is full of texture, depth and complexity. A powerful film full of powerful performances that even spawned a successful US television remake (set in California) that doesn't quite hit the same heights.

BLUE HEELERS (TV, 1994-2006)

Who knew, as the twanging guitars of the opening credits subsided on the first episode and a pretty young woman driving into town was stopped for a breath test and stood up to the flirting from local detective PJ Hasham (Martin Sacks), that both the woman, constable Maggie Doyle (Lisa McCune) and the entire show would capture viewers' hearts for so many years. Centred on the daily lives of the Victorian police officers working at a country police station in rural Mt Thomas, *Blue Heelers* struck a chord. One that rang out for more than 500 episodes over its 13-season run, picking up record numbers of Gold Logie Awards among many accolades and being shown in more than 70 countries. It made a huge star of newcomer McCune, whose character Maggie began as a probationary constable fresh out of the academy who broke up the boys club in Mt Thomas, and household names of the entire ensemble cast. I have fond memories of my parents tuning into this show when I was a teenager growing up in New Zealand, and then being sucked into all the stories myself. It was appointment television, and unsurprising in hindsight that some of the show's most dramatic episodes are some of the most-watched programmes of all time in Australia. It wouldn't be drawing too long a bow to call *Blue Heelers* the *MASH* of Australian television – a long-running show that reliably blended humour, drama, and plenty of banter, dealt at times with very dark issues despite its light tone, focused on a charming ensemble viewers grew to love, with emotional undercurrents that could make you laugh or cry. And had episodes that remain among the most watched in its nation's television history. Intriguingly, in late 2019 rumours began surfacing that a reboot of the show may be in the works.

BLUE MURDER (TV, 1995) & BLUE MURDER: KILLER COP (TV, 2017)

It may have been controversial at the time, but the original *Blue Murder* mini-series is now deservedly considered one of the finest examples of Australian television drama. A taut thriller that explored long-rumoured corruption within the NSW Police through the relationship of 'hero cop' DS Roger Rogerson (Richard Roxburgh) and notorious Sydney criminal Neddy Smith (Tony Martin), the series was banned from NSW broadcast for years due to ongoing legal proceedings. Viewers elsewhere witnessed a confrontational, exquisite drama: electric acting performances, a twisting storyline, eye-catching production. In its wake official inquiries confirmed rampant corruption and instituted police reform. Rogerson ended up in prison, first for perverting the course of justice and then, two decades later, for murder. *Blue Murder: Killer Cop* was a belated and much-welcome sequel continuing the story of Rogerson's downfall, with Roxburgh absolutely mesmerising.

THE BLUE ROSE (TV, 2013)

A reunion of sorts for the writers and two of the stars of the excellent, long-running *Outrageous Fortune*, this didn't flourish, despite showing flashes of real promise. Office temp Jane (Antonia Prebble) discovers that Rose, her PA predecessor at a prestigious Auckland law firm, isn't on leave but died under mysterious circumstances. She joins forces with Rose's confrontational bestie Linda (Siobhan Marshall) and other low-level staff to get justice for Rose, and others who need their help. A noir-ish opening becomes a dramedy mixing office politics and comic crime. Plenty to like if a little offbeat; yet the loose ends and late swerves proved superfluous when the second season didn't eventuate.

THE BOYS (1998, screenplay by Stephen Sewell)

Before he began playing some beloved characters on Australian television and regularly appearing in big Hollywood films, David

Wenham broke out with an extraordinary performance as volatile and dangerous Brett Sprague. After serving time for assaulting a store owner, Brett returns to the family home in the working-class suburbs of Sydney and begins a rapid descent into drugs, suspicion, and rage that leads to an unspeakable crime. A chilling story of the evil that can fester in the most mundane settings, and how killers can be far more recognisable and everyday than the master villains who clog some crime fiction.

THE BROKENWOOD MYSTERIES (TV, 2014-)
Bodies found in wine vats, fishing grounds, tied to rugby posts, caught up in *Lord of the Rings* tourist traps, at a colonial re-enactment village, in the ruins of an exploding Portaloo at a steampunk gathering; the talented creators of the quirkily wonderful *The Brokenwood Mysteries* have no issue leaning into various and at-times absurd elements of rural Kiwi life. A series that's more soak-into than seat-edge, it focuses on a trio of engaging detectives – DSS Mike Shepherd (Neill Rea), Detective Kristin Sims (Fern Sutherland), and DC Sam Breen (Nic Sampson) – who solve offbeat murders among eclectic locals and visitors in a small town surrounded by horticulture near the New Zealand coast. A series that grows on viewers the more they watch, just as it did with critics, upturning early scepticism to become a sustained success. There's a wonderful tone to the show, an unhurried appreciation of the landscapes and personalities that lets the clever storylines breathe. A healthy dose of humour adds the icing to a quintessentially Kiwi cake.

CHOPPER (2000, written by Andrew Dominik)
An astonishing, note-perfect portrayal by Eric Bana of one of Australia's most notorious criminals is the abiding memory of this excellent Australian film. Mark 'Chopper' Read is the epitome of a 'loose cannon', a garrulous and brutal man, fearless and funny. The kind of man who'll happily chat to anyone but can also swiftly stab fellow inmates, get stabbed, boast of murders he's got away with, shoot people, and rather democratically, be willing to assault anyone who poses an obstacle or pisses him off. Bana nails the unpredictable menace of Chopper, threaded with his hunger for

celebrity and recognition. The film follows his long stretch in prison and adjustments to life outside. A mesmerising character study.

THE CIRCUIT (TV, 2007-2010)
Taking a break from his flash Perth job, lawyer Drew Ellis (Aaron Pedersen) joins Aboriginal Legal Services and finds himself travelling on five-day 1,250-mile round trips to help bring justice to the remote communities in the Kimberley region. With court hearings held in community halls, churches, and school rooms, an in-over-his-head Drew works as part of an odd-couple duo alongside magistrate Peter Lockhart (Gary Sweet). With a predominantly indigenous cast and leads who upturn expectations, *The Circuit* regularly used everyday crimes rather than eye-catching killings to hold up a mirror to the ongoing plight of Australia's first peoples. The court officials aren't the only ones going round and round.

CITY HOMICIDE (TV, 2007-2011)
A thoroughly watchable ensemble drama set among a hard-working detective squad in Melbourne. No flashy hook of being a special unit, having an eccentric hero or consultant, or catching the most bizarre cases; this is a good quality portrayal of the relentless everyday work that goes into solving every case that crosses the desk. An Australian spin on the likes of *Hill Street Blues* or *NYPD Blue*; interesting storylines, straightforward detecting, and strong characters who engage more and more the longer you spend with them.

THE CRY (TV, 2018)
An emotionally devastating piece of television which transfixed Britain in late 2018, based upon a novel by Helen FitzGerald, a Glasgow-based Australian. Joanna (Jenna Coleman) is a struggling new mother whose stress levels are spiked when she follows her husband Alistair (Ewen Leslie) to Australia to deal with his ex-wife and a custody issue. Things go from sleep-deprived bad to horrifically worse when baby Noah vanishes from his car seat one night. Who has taken him, and why? A gut punch of a screen drama that taps into parental primal fears, *The Cry* offers a harrowing storyline, great writing, and superb acting.

DEAD HEART (1996, written by Nick Parsons)

Ray Lorkin (Bryan Brown) is a fair-minded cop and one of only a handful of 'whitefellas' living among an Aboriginal community in the remote town of Walla Walla in Australia's red centre. His efforts to keep the peace are upended when an Aboriginal prisoner is found hanged in the town jail, and then later the body of a rebellious youth (an early role for Aaron Pedersen, now a touchstone of quality Aussie crime drama) is discovered after he had taken the white wife of the local schoolteacher for a tryst on sacred ground. Fusing crime thriller with frontier sensibilities, *Dead Heart* is a strong character study that explores tricky, ongoing issues. As local pastor and Aboriginal elder David, Ernie Dingo matches and provides a fascinating foil to Brown's strong performance; two caring men striving to make a difference while caught in the complexities of the relationship between their two cultures.

THE DOCTOR BLAKE MYSTERIES (TV, 2013-2018)

A prodigal son returns to rural Victoria after the war and solves mysteries while serving as police surgeon in Ballarat in the late 1950s. Gruff and eccentric Dr Lucien Blake (Craig McLachlan) lost his wife and child in Singapore and endured a Japanese POW camp before returning to Ballarat to continue his father's practice after 30 years away. He's ably assisted by housekeeper Jean Beazley (Nadine Garner) as the duo stumble into various murder mysteries. A pleasing period crime drama that strikes the right note with its nuanced characters and rich evocation of historical Ballarat, it also struck a chord with viewers at home (top-rated local drama) and abroad (shown in 130 countries) over five intriguing seasons.

DOVES OF WAR (TV, 2006)

In this intriguing political thriller, the shared past of a group of elite Kiwi soldiers comes crashing into the present following media reports of a mass grave discovered in Bosnia. Former special forces Sergeant Lucas Crichton (Andrew Rodoreda) traverses New Zealand, from the cities to the rugged countryside, searching for his former brothers-in-arms, and answers. A decade before they shared and survived the horrors of the Bosnian War; now they share a secret about what happened on one dark day. Meanwhile ambitious Hague war crimes prosecutor Sophie Morgan (Kate Atkinson) is also on the trail, along with a journalist who leaked the story. Written by experienced crime scribe Greg McGee, this six-episode thriller is a fascinating, compulsive story.

DUGGAN (TV, 1997-1999)

Gruff DI John Duggan exiles himself to rustic life at his family bach in the picturesque Marlborough Sounds following the death of his wife. He wants to leave policing behind but is reluctantly drawn back in when a body is fished out of a nearby salmon farm. Over the course of two telemovies and a series, the enigmatic Duggan investigates a range of local murders. A rugged spin on British village mysteries; an absorbing rural noir before that became a trend. Great performances by lead John Bach and the wider cast and quality storytelling from award-winning writers Donna Malane and Ken Duncum, set against jaw-dropping scenery. Inspired by the likes of *Morse*, but in spirit and tone *Duggan* was more akin to the later slow-burn Tom Selleck adaptations of Robert B Parker's Jesse Stone novels.

EAST WEST 101 (TV, 2007-2011)

The ongoing explorations of culture clash at a global, local, and personal level in among the everyday crime solving – along with great writing and acting from a cast that reflected the multicultural nature of Sydney – elevates this intelligent police drama among its peers. Zane Malik (Don Hany) is a senior detective of the Major Crime Squad, operating among the various ethnic group of Sydney's western suburbs. A practising Muslim who faces prejudice wherever he goes in the wake of 9/11, including inside the squad room. 'You're either an Arab or a cop,' says Senior Detective Crowley (William McInnes) an old-school detective who's at odds with everyone (including himself). The antagonist-ally dance between Malik and Crowley is a feature of the first season and a microcosm of broader issues. With complex characterisation and standout performances across the cast, *East West 101* was a refreshing, compelling cop drama that was a critical darling and won numerous awards.

FELONY (2013, screenplay by Joel Edgerton)

Three Sydney detectives become embroiled in a moral quagmire and a Mexican standoff of sorts as they try to find the right measure of justice after a kid delivering newspapers is put in critical condition when clipped by a car. One is a heroic cop who accidentally injured the child, tried to save him but then kept quiet about being the cause; another is a wily veteran who tries to sweep things under the rug; the third is a zealous youngster determined to investigate, though perhaps not for pure reasons. A restrained police drama that's primarily about characters and their interplay. Deliberately slow-paced, wonderful writing and acting.

FRACTURE (2004, screenplay by Larry Parr)

When a burglary goes horribly wrong, the lives within both the victim's and the offender's families are rocked and head towards breaking point. Having been cruelly rejected by her own fundamentalist mother, young solo mother Leeanne Rosser (Kate Elliott) tries to put her son's needs first while staying close to her troubled brother Brent. She doesn't know he's a burglar, who ends up paralysing a homeowner who surprises him during his crime. A downbeat and complex character study inspired by Maurice Gee's novel *Crime Story*.

GETTIN' SQUARE (2003, written by Chris Nyst)

Three ex-cons get into all sorts of trouble on the Gold Coast in this memorable crime caper from lawyer and crime writer Chris Nyst. Barry (Sam Worthington), a small-time crim framed for murder by a crooked cop, and Spit (David Wenham), an endearing drug addict, are paroled and start working at a restaurant owned by Darren (Timothy Spall). The trio are all trying to go straight, but struggle to escape their criminal pasts, including run-ins with crime boss Chicka Martin (Gary Sweet), the crooked cop, and a government Criminal Investigation Commission. A good film made unforgettable by Wenham's scene-stealing turn as Spit.

THE GULF (TV, 2019-)

Detective Jess Savage (Kate Elliott) wakes in hospital to news she's been in a car crash, her husband is dead, and a young boy thought drowned years before has been found on a remote road, in bad shape. So begins *The Gulf*, a new series that's as moody and intense as its lead detective. Savage begins a perilous descent as she tries to function and solve other crimes on Waiheke Island while effectively investigating her own life in order to uncover the truth behind the car crash. All while juggling amnesia, an addiction to morphine, and paranoia. Understandably compared to the likes of *Broadchurch*, *The Gulf* is another triumph from outstanding writer-producer duo Donna Malane and Paula Boock.

HALIFAX FP (TV, 1994-2002)
Forensic psychologist Dr Jane Halifax (a role created especially for beloved actress Rebecca Gibney), uses her skills for delving into the darkest corners of the human mind to help the Victorian police investigate the most horrifying crimes. A suspenseful, top quality series full of twisting, intense cases. Gibney's accomplished performance provided a steady rudder throughout 21 telemovies that scooped awards, were screened in 60 countries, and included a stellar array of guest stars who'd go on to eye-catching lead roles (eg Hugh Jackman, Guy Pearce, Essie Davis, and Hugo Weaving). Gibney will reprise her iconic role as the professionally accomplished but personally troubled psychiatrist in *Halifax FP: Retribution*, a reboot mini-series shot in 2019 and scheduled for broadcast in 2020.

HUMAN TRACES (2017, written by Nic Gorman)
A sub-Antarctic research station is the setting for a slow-burn psychological thriller with shades of *Rashomon* as events are replayed three times over, building tension and revealing truths. Glenn (Mark Mitchinson) is a gruff middle-aged environmental scientist who treats Perseverance Island as a near fiefdom. He's trying to restore the island's damaged ecosystem alongside his student-turned-wife Sarah (Sophie Henderson) and new arrival Pete (Vinnie Bennett). As winter beckons and storms brew, paranoia sets in.

IN DARK PLACES (2018, written by Michael Bennett & Jane Holland)
A powerful dramatisation of an extraordinary case. In 1993 teenage

car thief Teina Pora (Richard Te Are) sat in a tiny room in a South Auckland police station, struggling to come up with stories about a rape and murder in order to please the cops and maybe earn a $20,000 reward. Instead, Pora ended up confessing to a crime he didn't commit. An action that kick-started a 22-year odyssey where he languished in prison until a small team including ex-cop Tim McKinnel (Craig Hall) managed to find enough evidence to overcome public and media disinterest and a justice system loath to admit mistakes. Writer-director Bennett was part of that small team, the storyteller alongside investigators and scientists who first returned Pora to greater public awareness with his stark 2013 documentary *The Confessions of Prisoner T.* Now this gripping feature-length film brings Bennett's exquisite true crime book *In Dark Places* to the screen. An incredible, infuriating story that goes far deeper than the standard miscarriage of justice storyline. Heartbreaking at times, yet hopeful too.

IN MY FATHER'S DEN (2004, screenplay by Brad McGann)
First-time auteur McGann brings a quiet intensity to his adaptation and updating of Maurice Gee's 1972 novel about a man forced to confront his own family secrets when a young woman is killed. Transporting the story from West Auckland to a remote small town in Central Otago, McGann's version sees cynical war photojournalist Paul Prior (Matthew Macfadyen) striking up a friendship with similarly restless 16-year-old Celia (Emily Barclay) upon his return home, only to become the prime suspect when the girl vanishes. A spellbinding story that dances a tightrope between mystery and family drama, rarely stumbling and considerably elevated by some superb performances and cinematography.

JACK IRISH (TV, 2012-2018)
Guy Pearce (*LA Confidential, Memento*) brings Peter Temple's melancholy crusader to addictive life onscreen in three telemovies and a six-part series based on Temple's own tales, then a further series of completely original adventures that continue in the same vein. There's a pleasing density to the screen versions – an all-killer, no-filler quality of which I like to think Temple would have approved

(if begrudgingly). While it can't go as deep into various social issues as the books, the series does a fine job of dragging readers through exciting episodes threaded with conspiracies and corruption festering below Melbourne's surface, from the church to exploitation of foreign students. Fine performances from series regulars Marta Dusseldorp, Aaron Pedersen, and Roy Billing burnish Pearce's portrayal.

JINDABYNE (2006, screenplay by Beatrix Christian)
An annual fishing trip deep into the mountains ends up catching heartbreak, accusations, and retaliation after Stewart (Gabriel Byrne) and his three friends discover the body of an Aboriginal girl. Choosing to finish their trip and even keep fishing rather than immediately hiking out to notify police, the men later face opprobrium from the police and their small-town community that threatens each family in various ways. Stewart's wife Claire (Laura Linney), the last to find out, tries to make reparations but receives hostility in return. Meanwhile the girl's killer hovers around the edges. Grown from a Raymond Carver short story, *Jindabyne* is a mature, complex film that explores questions of morality.

THE KILLING FIELD (TV, 2014) & WINTER (TV, 2015)
Detective Eve Winter (Rebecca Gibney) is convinced by former partner – professionally, and more – Lachlan McKenzie to join a taskforce of homicide detectives flown into the small country town of Mingara, a few hours' drive inland of Sydney, when a search for a missing girl unearths several bodies in shallow graves. An enjoyable whodunnit without being outstanding, *The Killing Field* telemovie spawned a six-episode series, *Winter*, which saw the return of the two lead detectives. When a young mother is pushed off a cliff, the investigation unlocks a Pandora's Box of cases spanning drugs, sex crimes, and corruption.

LANTANA (2001, written by Andrew Bovell)
A little jewel of a murder mystery; elegant and intricate and unconventional. Sydney detective Leon (Anthony LaPaglia of *Without a Trace* fame) is accelerating from midlife crisis to meltdown: he loves his wife but cheats, beats up suspects. His investigation into a

missing, feared dead, psychologist brings together a fine ensemble. Fractured relationships and domestic lives teetering on the edge. An undercurrent of sorrow. A stellar cast including Geoffrey Rush, Barbara Hershey, Rachael Blake and Vince Colosimo join LaPaglia in bringing shade and nuance. A stage play adapted by its creator, *Lantana* lingers in the mind.

LITTLE FISH (2005, written by Jacquelin Perske)
A small film with a stellar cast; viewers are plunged into the world of drug addiction and recovery in the Sydney suburb of Cabramatta, nicknamed Little Saigon. Tracy Heart (Cate Blanchett) is a former addict living with her mother and brother who's looking to become a small business owner. When banks turn her down, Tracy turns to her ex-boyfriend, a fellow addict who claims to now be a stockbroker, only to find herself instead entwined in a drug deal. With tragic consequences. A subtle exploration of drug dependency and its flow-on effects throughout families, notable for the potency of the acting turns, including Blanchett, Hugo Weaving as an addict and ex-rugby league player, and Sam Neill as a bisexual gangster.

MISS FISHER'S MURDER MYSTERIES (TV, 2012-2015)
These fun historical whodunnits dressed in haute couture and packing a feminist punch have proven catnip for viewers worldwide. Essie Davis stars as Phryne Fisher, a glamorous aristocrat and witty sleuth in 1920s Melbourne who has leapt to the screen from the pages of Kerry Greenwood's popular books. Over the course of three seasons Phryne fought injustice and pursued the truth while enjoying life to the full. A cosy crime show with a sharp edge. Interestingly, it's one of Australia's top five most popular series ever, in terms of global reach – broadcast into more than 170 territories. Essie Davis reprises her portrayal of Phryne Fisher in the standalone film *Miss Fisher and the Crypt of Tears* (out in Australian cinemas in 2020, then streaming internationally), while in 2019 the original series also spawned a spin-off, *Ms Fisher's Modern Murder Mysteries*, set in the 1960s with Phryne's 'gorgeously reckless' niece Peregrine Fisher taking the investigative baton.

MURDER CALL (TV, 1997-2000)

Based on characters from Jennifer Rowe's novels, this gritty Sydney cop drama focused on intense and insightful Detective Tessa Vance (Lucy Bell) and her partner Detective Steve Hayden (Peter Mochrie), a steady and laidback foil. Together the duo and their colleagues solved unusual murders, though character development was at the forefront as much as the crime over the course of the series. A show that valued substance over style (still having a dose of the latter), while evolving into a recognisable yet enjoyable formula. Good acting adds to the rather timeless storytelling, only dated by the technology used.

MY LIFE IS MURDER (TV, 2019-)

While there's nothing revolutionary about this new Melbourne-set crime drama, many viewers will be happy to see Lucy Lawless (*Xena: Warrior Princess*) back centre stage. Opening with Alexa Crowe (Lawless) making a call to a gigolo, the first episode involves the former top cop being called in by her old colleagues to help with the case of a wealthy woman who died in a fall from the hotel balcony of a male escort. Accident, suicide, or murder? A show that's more how-catch-em than whodunnit, delivered with a light tone where the fun is in riding along with engaging characters.

MYSTERY ROAD (2013) & GOLDSTONE (2016) – written by Ivan Sen

Over many years Aaron Pedersen has become near omnipresent across top quality Australian crime drama. But it his portrayal of Aboriginal detective Jay Swan that may be the masterpiece of his outstanding career. In *Mystery Road*, indigenous auteur Ivan Sen's fourth feature film, Jay Swan investigates the death of a young Aboriginal woman in a small town in the Outback. Jay's hometown, to which he's returned after many years away in 'the big smoke'. It's a case few want investigated. Swan is a man alone, estranged from his colleagues and his heritage. Displaced, untrusted. Facing a wall of silence in the community. As he scratches at the truth, he finds links to another fatality, local criminals, and his own family. It's an exquisite, slow-burn rural murder mystery deeply entwined with politics and family. Beyond that, Sen gives the film great scope, with its rugged desert landscapes and understated tone. There's a frontier sensibility. *Mystery Road* is a modern, quintessentially Australian rendering of classic Westerns that fittingly builds to a violent showdown. On the way, Sen lets his story, characters, and setting breathe, unafraid to use silence. While Pedersen is a standout, the storytelling and acting across the board is top-drawer. Swan and Sen returned in *Goldstone*, a loose sequel which can be watched as a standalone. Riding into town in the back of a police van after driving when drunk as a skunk, Swan has come to the tiny titular outpost, which services a nearby mining company, to search for a missing Chinese woman. Young cop Josh (Alex Russell) doesn't appreciate Swan's interference, or the implication he's let things slide on his patch. Local mayor Maureen (Jacki Weaver, in another formidable performance) plasters on a smile while working her rackets. Environment and the money entwine as the mining company and the local Aboriginal Council negotiate. A death complicates matters, or simplifies them. Sen again demonstrates patience to go along with his extraordinary visuals, trusting viewers to be absorbed without the need for quick cuts and mile-a-minute action. Big issues are addressed through small stories. And through it all Jay Swan roams like a lone cowboy, determined to find some measure of justice, whatever the toll it takes on his own soul.

MYSTERY ROAD (TV, 2018-)

A television spin-off from Ivan Sen's two mesmerising films, with the baton smoothly passed to fellow Aboriginal director Rachel Perkins as Aaron Pedersen reprises his role as Jay Swan. Bisecting events in *Mystery Road* and *Goldstone*, in the first season Detective Swan travels to the small town of Patterson in remote Western Australia to investigate the disappearance of two young farmhands: a local indigenous football hero and a white backpacker. He forms an uneasy team with formidable local sergeant Emma James (Judy Davis), whose brother owns and runs the cattle station from where the boys disappeared. Together they uncover nefarious local activities ranging from drug trafficking to dodgy land deals, and both have to confront realities about themselves and their own families. Absorbing, thought-spurring crime drama. A second season is schedule for broadcast in 2020.

ORANGE ROUGHIES (TV, 2006-2007)

A short-lived series, that unfortunately never lived up to its promise, about a small, experimental, elite yet underfunded taskforce in Auckland, mixing police and customs officers. High-risk scenarios and challenging issues (eg child trafficking) could have provided plenty of edge and interest yet the stories, characterisation, and delivery fell short. A missed opportunity.

OUT OF THE BLUE (film, 2006, written by Robert Sarkies & Graeme Tetley)

A chilling dramatisation of what was – until the mosque attacks of 2019 – New Zealand's worst ever mass murder. In November 1990 the idyllic seaside village of Aramoana fell under siege for 22 hours while gunman David Gray (Matthew Sunderland, in a striking performance) went on a rampage. Sarkies evokes a harrowing sense of the tension and emotional swings felt by residents, the lightly armed local police, and firefighters as they tried to save lives and survive the night. There's a beautiful restraint to the film that only adds to its power. Absorbing storytelling and unsurprisingly it scooped many local awards.

OUTRAGEOUS FORTUNE (TV, 2005-2010)

An addictive comedy crime drama that embraces bogan sensibilities and is full of great writing and acting. After her husband Wolf is sent to prison for four years, family matriarch Cheryl West (Robyn Malcolm) decides her career criminal family will go straight – no more drug running, no more thieving. A hard ask given the predilections of her kids: wannabe model Pascalle (Siobhan Marshall), devious Loretta (Antonia Prebble), slick Jethro and his boneheaded identical twin Van (both played by Antony Starr). Over the course of more than 100 episodes, the misadventures of the Wests delighted viewers at home and abroad, racked up awards wins, and spawned remakes in the United States and United Kingdom, as well as six seasons of a prequel show, *Westside*, focused on the lives of the grandparent characters Ted and Rita in the 1970s.

POLICE RESCUE (TV, 1989-1996)

An adrenalin-charged series that became iconic on both sides of the Tasman and was broadcast in several European countries. Mickey (Gary Sweet), Rattray (Sonia Todd), Angel (Steve Bastoni), and Frog (Marshall Napier) are all members of the NSW Police Rescue Squad, who spend their days crawling into tunnels, searching bushland, and abseiling off cliffs to save lives and combat crime. The character relationships as the team processes the daily traumas they face add to the strong banter and stunts in a lively show that pans from inner-city Sydney to the beaches and mountains of New South Wales. Keep an eye out for appearances from future Hollywood A-Listers like Russell Crowe and Cate Blanchett.

PREDICAMENT (2010, screenplay by Jason Stutter)

Before he drank himself to a premature death in 1972, Ronald Hugh Morrieson provided masterful snapshots of the lust and loathing, mateship and mayhem seething within small-town New Zealand. This comic-crime film completes the set of all four of his novels being brought to screen (following three in the 1980s). In 1930s small-town Taranaki, a gawky teenager meets a couple of misfits and gets roped into a scam to photograph and blackmail adulterous couples. A simple plan, until they get blood on their hands. An admirable attempt that looks good and is notable for Jemaine Clement (Flight of the Conchords) as one of the misfits, while falling short of the complexities and zing of the source material. It's worth digging out the books of a man who wrote one of the finest openers in New Zealand literature: 'The same week our fowls were stolen, Daphne Moran had her throat cut'.

REST FOR THE WICKED (2011, written by Bob Moore)

An utterly charming and delightful spin on the 'old cop haunted by an old case' trope, with Murray (Tony Barry) going undercover for one last case to try to finally bring down his nemesis and fellow septuagenarian Frank (John Bach), who lives in a flash rest home.

When another resident dies, Murray gets the sniff of murder, and tries to investigate while fighting off some amorous advances. Relaxed storytelling more than seat-edge suspense, nevertheless this is a enjoyable watch from an accomplished cast.

RUSH (TV, 2008-2011)

Rather than catching criminals after the act, the members of Melbourne's Tactical Response Unit are trained and equipped to prevent crime and defuse crises as they unfold, saving lives in the process. Specialists in non-lethal policing (as opposed to the SWAT-like Special Operations Group), the elite team cover everything from vehicle chases to protecting witnesses, defusing bombs to dealing with armed criminals. This ambitious, high quality Australian crime drama ran for four seasons, picking up awards and being broadcast across four continents. As you'd expect given the premise, there's plenty of action on offer, yet the creators and actors insert lots of heart into the characters and storylines too.

SCARFIES (1999, written by Robert & Duncan Sarkies)

The rundown flats and rowdy behaviour long associated with Otago University student life were put on full show in this quirky wee film that gear-shifts from comedy to something far darker as the minutes pass. Perhaps most notable now for being the first acting role for Oscar winning director Taika Waititi (*Thor: Ragnarok, JoJo Rabbit*), *Scarfies – Crime 101* in the United States – sees five poor students squatting in an abandoned house in Dunedin. Stoked for the ultra-cheap accommodation, their joy skyrockets when they discover a massive marijuana stash. Hello, cash windfall. Selling the drugs backfires when the owner returns, and the panicked students trap him in the basement. A comic crime film unafraid to upturn expectations and ride the absurdity curve into some ugly places.

SNAKESKIN (2001, written by Gillian Ashurst)

A road trip goes wrong for friends Alice (Melanie Lynskey) and Johnny (Dean O'Gorman) when they pick up Seth (Boyd Kestner), a cowboy boot-wearing American tourist who is hitchhiking in rural

Canterbury. The pals had wanted to take a few risks to enliven their suburban lives but may have overstepped: Seth's on the run from both a skinhead gang and drug dealers. Flipping the script on the picture postcard scenery, Seth takes Alice and Johnny – and the film takes viewers – into the darker subcultures of New Zealand.

SNOWTOWN (2011, screenplay by Shaun Grant)
A violent and disturbing dramatisation of events that led to the 'bodies in the barrels' case and the longest trial in South Australia's history. Jamie (Lucas Pittaway) is a teenager living a bleak life in Adelaide's northern suburbs who is drawn into a brutal web by John (Daniel Henshall), a wannabe father figure who appears after the police don't help when Jamie is molested. A charismatic bully and bigot, John sees Jamie as his protégé as he and his pals take escalating vengeance on paedophiles, homosexuals, and other 'weaklings'. *Snowtown* is an intense movie veering towards horror; director Justin Kurzel uses sound as much as sight to portray the gruesome nature of John's indoctrination of Jamie.

SPOOKED (2004, written by Geoff Murphy)
Inspired by real events, this conspiracy thriller is sparked by the mysterious death of Kevin (Chris Hobbs), a second-hand computer dealer who tries to sell information he found on some obsolete disks back to a merchant bank, only to reap violent harassment that upturns his personal and professional lives and threatens his sanity. Investigative journalist Mort Whitman (Cliff Curtis) becomes obsessed with digging into Kevin's death. Were secretive security forces involved, and if so, why? Told in unconventional fashion – Mort speaks directly to camera and interviews other characters – *Spooked* is a quirky, Kiwi take on a global conspiracy tale in which the story may not reach the heights of its quality cast.

STICKMEN (2001, written by Nick Ward)
Three laddish Wellington blokes who like a bit of a flutter get in over their heads when they enter a big money pool tournament run by a local Greek gangster in order to save their favourite pub – and maybe the life of the guy who runs it. Jack (Robbie Magasiva), Thomas

(Paolo Rotondo) and Wayne (Scott Wills) like to party on and off the felt, and their goal is threatened not only by an eclectic array of opposing teams, but the arrival of Karen (Simone Kessell) and Sarah (Anne Nordhaus), a couple of formidable women who are more than they seem. A slick and stylish comedy thriller that keeps up the pace and fun throughout.

STIFF (TV, 2004) & THE BRUSH OFF (TV, 2004)

Artfully helmed by legendary performers John Clarke and Sam Neill, these delicious adaptations of Shane Maloney's first two crime novels saw David Wenham bring dishevelled political staffer and struggling single father Murray Whelan to raucous telemovie life. In all his bumbling glory. Both telemovies (Clarke wrote the screenplays, he and Neill directed one each and acted in the other) captured the essence of Maloney's tales, and particularly his terrific 'hero'. This is intelligent drama, not playing down to its audience, full of wit and twists. Wenham nails Whelan, and the telemovies nail a rich sense of different parts of Melbourne: the grungy northern suburbs in *Stiff*, the art world in *The Brush Off*.

STREET LEGAL (TV, 2000-2005)

Maverick inner-city lawyer David Silesi (Jay Laga'aia) puts himself on the line for his clients while battling to save his troubled Ponsonby firm and deal with ex-lover and colleague Joni Collins (Katherine Kennard), who's now dating a relentless local detective (Charles Mesure). Courtroom drama matched by turbulent personal lives. An enjoyable and rather non-challenging series with slick production that stood out for putting a Polynesian lawyer front and centre. It enjoyed a popular run for four seasons while scooping several awards.

SUNSHINE (TV, 2017)

Throwing ingredients like underdog sports drama, crime drama, and thought-provoking tale of refugees and race relations altogether would make for a messy dish in lesser hands. But the cast and creators of this four-part mini-series not only make it work, they make it shine. Anthony LaPaglia stars as a grizzled basketball coach in the titular outer suburb of Melbourne. His charges include Jacob

Garang (Wally Elnour), a hard-working South Sudanese refugee who has NBA dreams, and several of Jacob's fellow refugees. The group gets entwined in a police investigation after a young woman in a wealthy suburb is assaulted and put into a coma. The group can be troublemakers, but that kind of trouble? The drama escalates on and off the court in a terrific mini-series.

TOP OF THE LAKE (TV, 2013) & TOP OF THE LAKE: CHINA GIRL (TV, 2017)

Atmospheric, quirky, puzzling, intricate, weird, excellent; there isn't really a word that sums up Oscar-winning film auteur Jane Campion's first return to television in more than 20 years. *Top of the Lake* is one of those shows that is hard to encapsulate; it's a simple story that has a lot going on around and underneath it, an unconventional spin on a crime drama that became resoundingly praised, although some viewers and critics were scratching their heads an episode or two in. Shades of *Twin Peaks*, perhaps. Elisabeth Moss stars as Detective Robin Griffin, who has returned to Laketop and gets involved in the case of a missing, pregnant, 12-year-old. A brooding sense of menace pervades as the case unfolds against the stunning scenery of the Southern Lakes region of New Zealand. Campion artfully gets viewers second-guessing their early impressions of various characters, offering plenty of complexity and nuance as disturbing issues and events are traversed. Detective Griffin returned in *Top of the Lake: China Girl*, having swapped rugged landscapes for the glitz and grime of Sydney, where she investigates the death of an Asian girl at Bondi Beach.

TWO HANDS (film, 1997, written by Gregor Jordan)

Long before his memorable turn as a maniacal criminal mastermind facing down Batman, a young Heath Ledger sparkled as Jimmy, a teenager scraping a living as a strip club promoter in Kings Cross. When he's robbed of $10,000 he's delivering for local mobster Pando (Bryan Brown), Jimmy fears for his life and comes up with a hare-brained scheme to repay Pando. Chaos ensues. While heavily dosed with crime and stark violence, *Two Hands* is more comedy than tragedy, and even a little heartwarming. Like if Guy Ritchie took a quirky Aussie detour, *Two Hands* is a wee ripper of a film, offbeat and highly entertaining.

UNDERBELLY (TV, 2008-2013)

I still remember passing through Sydney at the end of a year-long backpacking trip and crashing with a mate for a weekend; he popped on a DVD of season one of then-new crime drama *Underbelly*. Despite my tiredness, we ended up binging the entire season. It was a dramatisation of the infamous Melbourne gangland killings, and the rise of suburban yob Carl Williams to drug kingpin status while others in the city's criminal underworld feuded with each other. Initially banned from broadcast or DVD sales in Victoria (due to ongoing legal fallout from the events portrayed), *Underbelly* was compulsive, violent, high-end storytelling. Living more in the realm of *The Sopranos* than its Australian crime drama predecessors, it was an extraordinary portrayal of extraordinary events. An undeniable smash hit, despite the Victorian ban, the format was duplicated with several further seasons exploring criminal underworlds of other time periods in antipodean history, from the actions of corrupt NSW police in the Kings Cross red light scene during the 1980s-1990s (*Underbelly: The Golden Mile*) to the 1920s gangland war between vice queens Tilly Devine and Kate Leigh (*Underbelly: Razor*). High quality production with strong acting and storytelling, liberally dosed with violence, was a trademark across the seasons.

WARU (2017, written by Briar Grace-Smith, Ainsley Gardiner, Chelsea Cohen, Casey Kaa, Renae Maihi, Katie Wolfe, Paula Whetu Jones, and Josephine Stewart-Tewhiu)

Powerful may be too mild a word to describe this extraordinary piece of collaborative filmmaking. Centred on the all-too-realistic event of a young child killed through neglect or abuse, Waru consists of eight short films knitted together, each written and directed by a Māori woman film maker. Each segment is a single ten-minute take, beginning at the same time on the day of the *tangi* (funeral) for the child and showing the impact of the events on a different woman and those she encounters. A kaleidoscopic exploration of a tragedy and the way one life can affect so many, even in death. Bold, confronting, exquisite, important.

WATER RATS (TV, 1996-2001)
While tourists and commuters enjoy the scenic beauty of their city's world-renowned harbour, the Sydney Water Police know all too well that the sparkling surface can hide plenty of crime and corruption. Focused on the elite squad of detectives and officers whose beat was the waves rather than the streets, *Water Rats* was a thrilling police drama that ran for more than 170 episodes, even as members of a strong ensemble cast with a dash of diversity came and went. Solid storylines and reliable acting are buoyed by the range of locations where viewers are taken and the action-packed drama that ensues.

WENTWORTH (TV, 2013-)
A brilliantly acted and written prison drama series that bucks the common trend of modern reboots ending up as pale imitations of classic shows. The progeny of landmark 1970s-1980s Australian soap *Prisoner: Cell Block H*, this is a dark, gritty look at life in a modern women's prison. The series begins with middle-aged hairdresser Bea Smith (Danielle Cormack) entering Wentworth after being charged with the attempted murder of her abusive husband, then follows her and her fellow inmates, including top dog Jacs (Kris McQuade) as Bea rises through the food chain. With impeccable casting, nuanced performances, swirling relationships and shocking moments to rival the best American cable shows, *Wentworth* is masterful drama. Widely available through streaming and syndication in 140+ countries.

WHITE COLLAR BLUE (2002-2003)
A Sydney police drama that over two seasons offered a glossier façade compared to some of its grittier counterparts, highlighting the harbour city's beaches and some touches of glamour. Kick-started by a television movie where federal cop Harriet Walker (Freya Stafford) switches to the state beat as a detective for a major crime squad in Sydney's southern beaches district. A few hours into the new gig, her squad is called to a murder scene. The victim an undercover

cop, Harriet's husband. The 'white collar' cop now a prime suspect. That set the tone, with personal tensions bleeding into professional ones through the series, for Detective Walker, her new partner Detective Joe Hill (Peter O'Brien) and others at the station. A fondly remembered show that perhaps didn't quite fulfil its potential.

WILDSIDE (TV, 1997-1999)

An edgy series enhanced by its edgy production, this focused on the contentious relationship between a Sydney inner-city police station and its neighbour, a crisis centre helping those on the margins of society with medical, legal, and other issues. With the 'clientele' of each overlapping at times, there's plenty of drama as the cops and the crisis centre take different routes to protecting and serving their community. Flipping the crime drama script by focusing as much on the 'everyday battlers' as any heroic cops, *Wildside* was a hard-edged gem. Though short-lived (60 episodes over two seasons), it scooped more than a dozen major awards for its acting, writing, and the overall show. Well worth digging out.

Section Three:
The Unusual Suspects

Interviews with leading Southern Cross Crime figures

THE AUSSIE GODFATHER: PETER CORRIS

The growing wave of high-quality Australian crime writing in recent decades could arguably be traced back to a little bookshop in San Francisco, around 1970. For it was there that a young Peter Corris had a revelation.

'I was poor, I was broke, living in some crummy little hotel, and there was a bookshop nearby that had Ross Macdonald novels for about 50 cents. I think I sat down and read about a dozen of them,' says Corris. 'And the idea entered my head there that San Francisco is very like Sydney. It felt like Sydney, it looked like Sydney in some ways, and I thought, "You know, you could put a private eye in Sydney". I think that was the seed of it, the germ of the idea.'

Years later, after having little success with short stories, Corris, who had been a long-time fan of the hardboiled private eye novels of Macdonald, Dashiell Hammett, and Raymond Chandler, decided to write a local version of the books he knew and loved best.

The result, *The Dying Trade* (1980), was at first widely rejected.

'The rejections were phrased along the lines of "Australian crime readers only want to read about New York, or LA or London – they don't want to read about crime in Australia",' says Corris. But then Pan Books took a chance on the tale of Sydney private eye Cliff Hardy, who is hired by a wealthy heir to discover who has been threatening his sister, only to get caught up in murder, assault and more. And the rest, as they say, is history.

With the release of *Follow the Money* (in which the ageing investigator is unofficially hired by a slick, desperate lawyer to find out whether an embezzler faked his own death), the Hardy series now numbers almost 40 books. Although he was born and raised in Victoria, and still passionately supports the Essendon Bombers, Corris never thought of setting his private eye novels anywhere other than Sydney, where he has lived for many years.

'I'm still wide-eyed about Sydney. I still find it visually exciting,' he says. 'So my enthusiasm for Sydney, tempered by all the things I know are wrong about it – the corruption, the crime, and the political chicanery and so on – all makes for interesting texture. I've got a mixture of feelings that I can draw on when I'm writing.'

Such a layered setting is great for crime fiction, says Corris, who feels he has Sydney at his fingertips for inspiration, like Los Angeles was for Chandler and Edinburgh is for Ian Rankin.

'You have to have texture; you can't just have action, character, and so on. There has to be backdrop, the context to the story, and Sydney provides that for me in spades. And I never have any trouble finding something to refer to when making a comparison, or to explain a thing by reference to something in Sydney.'

His Sydney-based series earned Corris – a prolific author who has also written biographies, spy novels, historical novels, and stories about golf and boxing – the Ned Kelly Lifetime Achievement Award from the Crime Writers Association of Australia in 1999. In 2003, Stuart Coupe in *The Age* noted that, 'without Corris's groundbreaking early novels the majority of local crime writers would not have been published'. Not that he's slowed down since; in recent years Corris has won the Ned Kelly Award for Best Novel (for *Deep Water* in 2009), and has been shortlisted a further five times.

Despite his success, Corris comes across as a very grounded and humble man, someone who loves life and enjoys what he does. He speaks passionately and without pretension. Although he acknowledges that the acceptance of his books by local traders opened the door for the Australian crime writers who followed, he deflects any extra credit.

'I think something caught fire, and people have been able to carry on. People like Peter Temple are really terrific writers in any context.' The problem is, he adds with a laugh, 'I had the whole pie to myself in the first few years, and then all these other buggers came along and started taking slices of it. But it's been fun.'

Fun is a big part of what Corris is about as a writer. 'I basically see myself as an entertainer,' he says. 'I've never been terribly interested in philosophy and theory and the more cerebral aspects of writing. I've always been a narrative writer. It's story and action that interest me and give me pleasure to read.'

Not that a focus on exciting plots, interesting characters, and entertainment means that there can't also be more to a story. After all, much of what is now considered classic literature – from Dumas to Austen to Dickens to Stevenson – was plot-based fiction intended to entertain, while at the same time casting light on other aspects of life.

'I think if you are a reasonably talented writer and your method is action and story, inevitably other aspects of life and society and your own psychology and the psychology of characters will creep through,' says Corris. 'But with writers whose ambition is just to show how very clever they are, I find that tedious. I need things to happen. I need movement.'

Movement is very important for Corris both on and off the page. He's suffered from Type 1 diabetes since he was 16, although it was many years before he started looking after himself properly. 'To maintain your health you have to watch your weight and you have to get a lot of exercise to be a good functioning Type 1 diabetic at my age,' he says. 'So I play golf, I go to the gym, I put in about a half-hour walk in the morning and afternoon, so I spend a fair bit of time just staying fit.'

It was also through his diabetes that he met the 'most amazing person' he's come across – noted eye surgeon and humanitarian Dr Fred Hollows. Corris had neglected his diabetes in his 20s and 30s, leading to severe eyesight problems. An operation introduced to Australia by Hollows saved his eyesight.

When Corris – overweight, smoking and a beer in hand – met Hollows at a party soon after, Hollows unloaded on him, telling him to pull himself together or he'd be blind in five years and dead in 10. Though Hollows used more colourful language.

'I was a man in my 30s, and no one had ever spoken to me like that,' says Corris with a chuckle. 'That's when I started to look after myself – I started jogging, losing weight, stopped smoking, and moderated my drinking. And so Fred loomed large in my consciousness.'

When Hollows was diagnosed with terminal cancer several years later, Corris was contracted to co-write *Fred Hollows: An Autobiography* (1991) – a task he thoroughly enjoyed, and a book that sold more than 100,000 copies in Australia, raising a lot of money for the Fred Hollows Foundation.

'It was impossible to write a dull book about him,' says Corris, the admiration clear in his voice. 'There's never been anyone like him before or since. He could do microscopic eye surgery, and he could rake the diff out of a Land Rover and put in a new diff. He was a lover of poetry and music, he climbed Mount Cook and he culled wild horses with a .303 rifle in the backblocks of Queensland as a younger man. Just the range of activities, abilities and interests was amazing. And then he was politically active – a scourge of conservatism. Just wonderful.'

It's unsurprising that Corris was drawn to Hollows – after all, the eye surgeon was a unique man who loved life and broke new ground in his field. Sound familiar?

* * *

Author note: This feature was originally published in *Good Reading* magazine 2011. Peter Corris would publish another six Cliff Hardy novels and four other books covering history to true crime before he passed away on 30 August 2018. In the days following his death Corris was remembered for sparking a renaissance of Australian crime fiction, upturning the 'dead-in-the-water' status of the local genre, bringing an Australian voice to hardboiled traditions, and laying the foundations for the current golden age. *See You at the Toxteth*, a posthumous collection of Cliffy Hardy stories, Peter Corris columns on crime writing and his ABC of Crime Writing was published in late 2019.

SOLVING CRIMES IN SILENCE:
EMMA VISKIC

They'd driven from the city through the desert. Getting their kicks on stretches of Route 66 by taking snaps of the world-famous signs. But now they were on the edge of something even more famous, and significantly more ancient, than an historic highway. Flanked by her compatriots, Melbourne crime writer Emma Viskic stared into the abyss. Millions of years of history carved down through the earth, the Colorado River a snake shimmering far below.

The desert air was still, the vista grand, the only soundtrack the chattering of tourists.

Viskic and her fellow Australian crime writers Sulari Gentill, Robert Gott, and Jock Serong had been brought to the Grand Canyon for a spontaneous day trip by Tom and Karen, a local Arizona couple they'd met at their event at Poisoned Pen Bookstore the night before. But in a way, Viskic was also there thanks to someone else. A troubled man who wouldn't have been able to hear the chattering of the tourists on the southern rim of the Grand Canyon.

'I set out to write *Resurrection Bay* because I couldn't get Caleb out of my head,' says Viskic, when I ask about the inspiration behind her prize-hoarding debut, which scooped a quintet of Davitt, Ned Kelly, and iBooks Awards in Australia then was shortlisted for major crime writing prizes in the United States and United Kingdom, including the Gold Dagger.

'The seeds of his character have been growing since I was a child. Some of the inspiration came from a profoundly deaf girl I went to primary school with, but a lot of it came from my paternal grandparents who were Croatian immigrants. Baba and Dida didn't speak English and I didn't speak Croatian. Their isolation and our inability to communicate loomed pretty large in my life and those themes have been seeping into my writing all my life.'

Resurrection Bay is a strikingly original debut where deaf private eye Caleb Zelic investigates the murder of a childhood friend. Fresh prose powers a vivid tale populated by a diverse cast epitomising the cultural melting pot of modern-day Australia. Zelic returned in *And Fire Came Down*, and the soon-to-be-released *Darkness for Light*.

'I set out to write a short series,' says Viskic, without specifying. 'Even though I knew Caleb well by the time I'd finished writing *Resurrection Bay* I knew there was more to uncover. Caleb views the world very differently from me and I'm fascinated by the way he thinks.'

Character comes first for Viskic, and it was crime fiction's 'unique ability to illuminate and examine human behaviour' that strongly drew her to the genre as a first-time author, she says. 'Many of my favourite works have a crime element to them, even if they wouldn't sit in the crime section of the bookshop – *Macbeth, Lolita, Wolf Hall*.'

Wanting to deeply understand her main character, and how someone like Caleb would perceive and interact with the world, Viskic went to some unusual research lengths.

'I began researching by reading blogs and memoirs, then spoke to people in the Deaf and hard-of-hearing communities,' she says. 'I did an online lipreading course and walked around with earplugs in my ears, managing to misunderstand pretty much everyone I came across. The biggest undertaking was learning Australian sign language (Auslan).'

Viskic enrolled in a short course, then went on to study at TAFE, a national tertiary institution and vocational training provider in Australia. 'I learnt a lot that didn't directly make it into my novels, but it all informed them. Hemingway's iceberg theory really makes sense to me in terms of how much you need to know and how much you need to show.'

While determined to reflect Caleb's experience authentically, Viskic also felt the extra weight of depicting a 'disabled' character in a way that wasn't tokenistic. 'It's nerve-wracking to write outside your own experiences, and it should be,' she says. 'I think if you're blasé about it, you're not thinking deeply enough. It's important for writers to explore characters who come from different backgrounds to them, but there are dangers and responsibilities that go with it. For writers considering it, I'd say to ask yourself why. If it's for a cheap hook or tick-a-box diversity, don't do it. If it's a subject you're deeply drawn to and have a connection with, then start working. Make sure you know your facts, examine your own prejudices and assumptions, and are willing to take criticism for the final result.'

Viskic's final result has been roundly praised.

Distilling *Resurrection Bay*, and the ongoing series, to just being about Caleb's deafness would do it a disservice. Viskic strikes a superb balance, creating an absorbing, intriguing crime storyline that keeps the pages spinning, that has a deaf sleuth at its heart. Caleb's deafness isn't a character quirk, but something that infuses his personality and story in a very authentic way, without overwhelming all the other elements.

For Viskic, there are several things she enjoys about writing her Caleb Zelic books, including the surprising effect that her main character has had on her own everyday life.

'I love crafting the banter and delving into the deeper themes, but one of the unexpected joys has been the positive side of writing a deaf character. Caleb notices things most hearing people would miss, which is a huge boon for him as a detective, but also for me. I've become far more observant through writing his character. I'm not at all visual, and used to approach writing through dialogue, but I notice a lot more now– the space around me, the light, people's expressions and body language. It's been a great learning experience.'

The response to *Resurrection Bay*, both locally and internationally, was completely unexpected, says Viskic. 'It slips between the cracks of a few styles – it's plot-driven but character-focused, a thriller with literary elements. I thought people would just throw their hands up at it. That people have liked it is quite overwhelming and extremely heartening.'

It was that embrace from the crime writing community that saw Viskic standing on the rim of the Grand Canyon in October. The quartet of Australian crime writers had banded together to visit the United States, meeting their international publishers, attending Bouchercon, the world mystery-writing convention in Dallas, Texas, and meeting readers at a variety of library, bookshop, and literary salon events in New York, Arizona, and California.

Viskic has been part of the surge in international recognition and readership for Australian and New Zealand crime writing in recent years; she's one of the new Downunder Queens bringing fresh blood to the local genre. *Resurrection Bay* won the Davitt and Ned Kelly Awards the year before Jane Harper's *The Dry*, kick-starting four straight years where the Ned Kelly Award for Best First Novel has gone to a female author (and five of the past six, with Candice Fox's *Hades* winning in 2013. Only Serong has broken the recent matriarchy).

'I'm really excited by the current wave of Australian and New Zealand crime writing,' she says. 'Partly because I get to read it, but also because one of the best ways of improving your own skills is to be surrounded by people creating outstanding work.'

Viskic praises the work of the Australian Crime Writers Association and Sisters in Crime Australia for helping the crime scene flourish on her side of the Tasman, along with the influence and example of the crime writers who came before. 'We're all standing on the shoulders of writers like Peter Temple, Peter Corris, Marele Day, and Dorothy Porter.'

At a time when information and stories seem to be consumed in smaller and smaller chunks, from Twitter to clickbait articles, Viskic still sees an important place for novels and authors in the changing global landscape. Though authors need to find the right balance.

'Reading books creates empathy, and we need that more than ever in these days of polarised opinions and divisiveness,' she says. 'Despite their rumoured demise, books seem to be here to stay, but the role of authors is changing. We have to balance the need for publicity and social media with the need for quiet space for ideas to grow.'

* * *

Author note: This chapter has been written for this book based on a Q&A I conducted with Viskic in 2018 – part of which was originally published in my Māwake Crime Review column for *Crimespree* magazine in the United States – and further conversations in 2018 and 2019, including during her US road trip following Bouchercon. Emma has since published the third novel in her Caleb Zelic series, *Darkness for Light*, in both Australasia and the UK.

THE KIWI GODFATHER: PAUL THOMAS

Knight errant, ronin, wandering cowboy, hardboiled private eye – the maverick cop of modern-day crime fiction is the latest in a long lineage of loner archetypes: mysterious and conflicted heroes who for centuries have fascinated those who've sat themselves down to read a book, watch a performance, or listen to a storyteller; to absorb tales of daring, adventure, and justice brought to those in need.

'It's the "Shane" figure that rides into town and gets embroiled in a situation that may not be any of his business, but he can see it's a bad situation for people who maybe can't stand up for themselves,' says Paul Thomas, the godfather of contemporary New Zealand crime writing. 'It's that loner, that person who stands outside of society and who is maybe untroubled by some of the scruples that respectable society abides by, but when you get into that sort of situation, that sort of self-reliant person – physically tough and able to handle themselves – is what you want. It's like Charles Upham: he wasn't much good at school, and I doubt the teachers at Christ's College thought he was going to cover himself in glory in adult life, but in war he had attributes that made him an extraordinary hero.'

In the 1990s, Thomas exploded onto the local fiction scene with a series of fast-paced crime thrillers packed with mayhem, spiralling subplots, humour, and his very own maverick cop. Detective Sergeant Tito Ihaka, a hulking investigator who, like his literary antecedents, stood slightly apart from society and was somewhat untroubled by expected scruples, first appeared in *Old School Tie*, Thomas's groundbreaking 1994 debut that one critic described as 'Elmore Leonard on acid'.

Ihaka was again part of the cast in *Inside Dope*, which in 1996 won the inaugural Ned Kelly Award for Best Crime Novel (Thomas was living in Sydney at the time), before coming to the fore in *Guerrilla Season*, completing what has become known as 'The Ihaka Trilogy'. Then Ihaka disappeared. Not so much AWOL as absent without intention. 'If you'd said to me in 1996 after I'd written three of the Ihaka novels in a row that it would be 15 years before the next one came out, I wouldn't have believed you,' says Thomas, as we talk about the publication this month of *Death on Demand*, a long-awaited return to the crime fiction scene for both Ihaka and Thomas. 'There's never been a point where I thought, "I'm never going to write crime again", or "I'm never going to go back to Ihaka again".' The long absence was just the way it turned out, explains Thomas, and certainly not anything he 'sat down and planned out to do'.

Death on Demand finds Ihaka exiled in the Wairarapa five years after the way he handled the hit-and-run death of a prominent businesswoman, coupled with a bathroom brawl with a colleague, stalled any career advancement. Out of the blue, Ihaka is recalled to Auckland, where his long-held suspicions are vindicated by a confession from the hit-and-run victim's terminally ill husband (that he hired an unknown hitman) before the man is murdered himself. More deaths follow, and Ihaka finds himself dancing around police politics and old grudges as part of an investigation complicated by blackmail, gang activities and a faceless and prolific hitman who may now be hunting Ihaka.

Death on Demand puts the maverick Ihaka front and centre far more than Thomas's earlier trilogy, while still demonstrating the author's deft touch for the helter-skelter storylines and subplots, witty dialogue, and casts packed with intriguing characters that has garnered him acclaim from readers and critics alike. Local hero, local setting, world-class crime writing: Ihaka's return is a rollicking read. There's something about his character that grabs readers.

While Ihaka was in hiatus, Thomas wrote several books including standalone thrillers, short-story collections, and sports biographies featuring cricket and rugby stars and coaches, as well as working on teleplays and film scripts and numerous newspaper and magazine columns. But through all that time, it was Ihaka who readers asked about the most.

Even though the Māori copper was something of a supporting character (if a larger-than-life one) in Thomas's first two novels, which centred more on journalist Reggie Sparks and disgraced former cop Duane Ricketts, respectively. 'I just got a lot of feedback from readers saying, "We really like this character, are you going to continue with him?"' says Thomas. 'In that long hiatus between *Guerrilla Season* and *Death on Demand*, the questions when they did arise were always, "Are you going to do another Ihaka book?", rather than, "Are you going to do another Duane Ricketts book?" or whatever.'

So what is it that makes the maverick Māori cop so interesting, so memorable, that he's fondly thought of so many years later? 'I like to think he's funny,' says Thomas, 'and I think that irreverence, that kind of anarchic personality, is quite appealing.' Ihaka also has a relentless nature when it comes to solving crimes. 'There's that famous quote from Raymond Chandler talking about the emotional basis of the crime novel, talking about "that justice will not be done unless some very determined individual ensures it is done" – and that's the way I see Ihaka,' says Thomas. 'Once he decides there's something going on, he will not let go until it's resolved.'

In between book appearances, Ihaka (well, a very loose adaptation of him) has appeared onscreen in the 2000 telemovie *Ihaka: Blunt Instrument*, starring a chiselled Temuera Morrison in the lead role. Thomas wrote the teleplay, but in the end had little control of how his character was portrayed onscreen. 'Now, after that experience, I understood every tragic screenwriting story to come out of Hollywood, in terms of writing something and then what you've written getting mysteriously altered in the process,' he says, describing the whole project as 'eye-opening'.

One advantage of such a loose adaptation, however, was that when Thomas sat down to write about Ihaka again in *Death on Demand* so many years later, the image he had in his mind of the character wasn't muddied by the television version. 'I didn't recognise the character Tem played as Ihaka,' says Thomas. 'Tem did a good job, but that character who ended up onscreen certainly doesn't conform to how I see Ihaka. I didn't feel, in a nutshell, that it got the essence of the character.'

Looking back, Thomas says Ihaka was originally born from a mix of influences, including Chandler's Philip Marlowe – 'a hero character who gave you an insight into his own psychological make-up, and his own depressions and concerns and self-loathing' – and formidable Māori rugby players and soldiers Thomas met growing up. 'People you would love to have beside you if you were in the shit but on the other hand you would hate to have coming after you. And that's the sort of character I wanted.'

Of course, the twist with Ihaka is that although he has the formidable and relentless nature of those soldiers and rugby players Thomas knew, the author also imbued him with less creditworthy traits. 'He was the complete opposite in his personal behaviour – undisciplined in his personal habits, he was overweight, he drank too much and he was just a bit of a slob.' That contrast is just part of what makes Ihaka, a modern-day knight errant, so complex and compelling. It's great to see him riding back into town.

* * *

Author note: This feature was originally published in the *New Zealand Listener* magazine in February 2012. *Death on Demand* would go on to win the 2013 Ngaio Marsh Award for Best Novel, making Thomas the first author to win the major crime writing prizes in both Australia and New Zealand. His next Detective Ihaka tale, *Fallout*, became a finalist for the 2015 Ngaio Marsh Awards. Thomas is currently working on a sixth Ihaka novel.

BREAKING THE DROUGHT:
JANE HARPER

Mud squelches beneath Australian federal agent Aaron Falk's boots as a chill wind whips through the Giralang Ranges, a rugged wilderness east of Melbourne. It's a beautiful, unforgiving landscape where forests blanket hillsides veined with walking tracks and mountain creeks. Waterfalls rumble, kookaburras chortle, and the wise stay on the path. An ancient place, offering both faces of Mother Nature: beauty and danger.

It's the latter worrying Falk. Alice Russell's disappearance the day before she was to hand over evidence of high-level fraud triggers red flags, and has Falk stomping about in hypothermic conditions. He may still be in the same state, but it's a far cry from Kiewarra, the drought-stricken Outback town where Falk solved a brutal farmhouse killing months before. That was a case that saw Falk's name splashed across newspapers all over the globe; although it was Jane Harper getting the accolades.

'Writing *The Dry* was a personal project,' says Harper of her debut that earned global accolades and turned readers' and publishers' eyes south. 'I wanted to finish a manuscript. I had no expectations that anyone would read it, let alone publish it. So I just wrote what I wanted to write.'

Harper had been a journalist for more than a decade when she decided to scratch her novel-writing itch, and knew she'd write the kind of book she loved to read. 'My parents were really into crime novels, and a lot of my reading was influenced by them,' she says. 'We read Val McDermid, Jo Nesbo, Lee Child, people like that. I really like anything that is quite fast-paced, has a strong plot, and keeps you guessing. I loved to be surprised in books.'

When it came to the setting for her first crack at a novel, the choice was also clear.

'I definitely wanted to set my book in Australia,' she says. 'I started with the idea of a death in a community where things aren't what they seem. I wanted a setting where people are under extreme pressure. The idea of a drought-stricken community came very quickly.'

Harper's first journalism job had been with a rural newspaper in the UK, having returned to her country of birth as a teenager following a childhood spent in Australia. She'd reported on farming communities dealing with the foot-and-mouth crisis. 'Then when I moved back to Australia in 2008, the newspaper I worked for in Victoria stretched out into the rural areas. A lot of *The Dry* is inspired by snippets of conversations from people in such communities, how they reacted in different ways to different pressures.'

In *The Dry*, Kiewarra is a farming community struggling to survive in a tinder-dry landscape. Agent Falk reluctantly returns to his childhood hometown for the funeral of an old friend who seems to have broken under the strain, shooting his wife and son, then himself. It's a shocking event, even in a community that faces life and death choices each day. Falk has no desire to linger, but he and a local detective begin to doubt the murder-suicide scenario.

While Harper may have started writing *The Dry* for herself, as 'a practise novel', the end result was loved by publishers, readers, critics, and awards judges around the world.

When Harper was recently named the winner of the 2017 CWA Gold Dagger, it was the ninth major writing award scooped by *The Dry*. Reese Witherspoon has bought the film rights, and the Outback-set crime debut has been translated into 24 languages. All of this in less than three years since Harper took an online novel writing course as a cattle prod to herself.

But after the fanfare dies down, what's next? Writing her second novel *Force of Nature* was an entirely different experience, says Harper. 'With *Force of Nature* I had a publishing contract, so there were different expectations. I was also pregnant with my daughter!'

Harper relied on her journalist training to write *Force of Nature*: working to deadlines, under pressure, producing copy when you had to. 'At the time, overseas deals were coming in for *The Dry*, and people were asking, "What's next?" I'd already been working on *Force of Nature*; it was a story that had been simmering away for some time before *The Dry* took off.'

So even though Harper's life then seems something of a blur in hindsight, quickly going from online writing student to 'overnight sensation', while being pregnant, leaving her career, and adjusting to everything that changed in such a short space of time, she kept writing.

Force of Nature, like *The Dry*, has an evocative, textured setting that's almost character-like, but this time it's frigid rainforest, rather than a parched and heat-struck landscape. Where Harper's debut could make readers reach for a glass of water, her second induces shivers.

As the details emerge in the wake of Alice Russell's disappearance on a workplace team-building exercise, Falk uncovers a tale of brittle group dynamics, suspicion, and eroding trust. Among the mud and strain of an arduous hike, something went badly wrong.

Force of Nature has an eerie quality, with the simmering power of the landscapes and the ghosts of lives that have passed through them (including Falk's own father, and the spectre of a vicious killer who hunted his prey near there years before).

Harper has a real knack for vivid settings, and beautifully rich characterisation too. So it might surprise some to discover her book ideas don't begin with a person or place.

'My ideas come to me about the plot rather than any specific characters,' she says. 'Once I'm happy with the plot and how it falls, I then build in character backstory, motivations, and relationships, and add touches of scenery and more.'

While some authors, like Stephen King, write long then pare things back, distilling the power of their tales as they cut, Harper does the opposite. 'I think it's a newspaper thing, not to write too much, but then build it up. Start with the basics, a skeleton, then add more in.'

Harper says she'd wanted to take a writing course because she knew she responds better to deadlines and external pressure. 'I found the Curtis Brown Creative one and during the 12 weeks of the course, I finished a 40,000 word first draft.'

In the months following the course, Harper fleshed that out during second and third drafts, and won a prestigious unpublished novel prize with a 60,000 word draft. She got an agent, and was sending out a 75,000 word draft to publishers. The final book is 90,000 words.

While some scoff at writing courses or the idea that creativity can be taught in a classroom, Harper believes writing is a skill more than an inherent talent that you've either got or not. 'Some people will find it comes more naturally than others, but like any other creative skill such as painting and dancing, most people benefit from expert tuition and advice.'

Harper found her writing course invaluable. 'I had tried a few times and never got past the first few chapters. I found the external pressure and feedback of the online course helped make me progress, and start to believe I could actually finish my book.'

Of course, she couldn't have predicted what would happen. Less than three years after Harper was learning on the go as she pieced together the skeleton alongside tutors and fellow classmates, her name was being read out as the winner of the CWA Gold Dagger. 'I was so thankful to be shortlisted,' she says. 'Peter Temple and Michael Robotham were the only other Australians to have won it. It was such an honour. I hope it encourages more people to read Australian writing and give other Australian writers a go.'

* * *

Author note: This is a condensed version (a double Stephen King cut, for those who've read *On Writing* – and if you haven't, you should) of a feature published in *Mystery Scene*, a quarterly American magazine, during the northern winter of 2017/2018. *Force of Nature* went on to win the 2018 Davitt Award for Readers' Choice and the Polar de Cognac prize for Best International Thriller in France. Jane Harper's third novel, *The Lost Man*, a standalone mystery set among the remote, heat-struck cattle farms of inner Queensland, won the 2019 Ned Kelly Award for Best Crime Novel and the 2019 Davitt Award for Readers' Choice.

SOUTHERN SASSINESS: VANDA SYMON

Aspiring authors all over the world are often told to 'write what you know', though such sentiments aren't to be taken too literally, of course, as few of us encounter spies or serial killers, boy wizards or Victorian gentry in our everyday lives. Our fictional worlds would be far less rich and interesting without imagination blending with authenticity. But what writers can do is inject what they know about life into their tales, infusing even the most fantastical settings and stories with recognisable viewpoints, emotions, and humanity.

Dunedin crime writer Vanda Symon didn't have many cold-blooded killers on speed dial when she sat down over 15 years ago to write what became her first Sam Shephard tale, *Overkill*. But what she did know were the swirling emotions and do-anything protectiveness felt by new mothers. And a few things about rare drugs, thanks to her first career as a pharmacist. The result: a gut-punch of a prologue where a nondescript man comes to a young mother's door in a small farming town, bringing a terrible ultimatum rather than Roses chocolates.

'You know, I wrote that first chapter, and I still cry at the end every time I read it,' says Symon, who'd wanted to be a writer since childhood but didn't seriously put fingers to keys until she had children of her own. '*Overkill*'s prologue was born out of the mind of a young mum who was sleep deprived to the point of being paranoid and vaguely hallucinating, up in the middle of the night feeding a baby, and imagining all of the worst things that could happen to her and her child.'

While the prologue is bruising, it is headstrong country cop Sam Shephard who makes *Overkill* such a knockout crime debut. Feisty, passionate, and flawed, Sam finds herself deep in the manure as she tries to investigate a local tragedy in a small community that's a spider's web of personal and professional overlap.

'What I love about Sam is her optimism and her imperfections,' says Symon. 'She is occasionally over-emotional, and that's okay. She's impulsive and gets into trouble, but she does it with the very best motives at heart, and she will stand up for what she thinks is right even where others may not share the same opinion. She is also a character who is developing. She's a bit immature and inexperienced in *Overkill*, but like the rest of us she grows and matures with each experience, and hopefully learns from it.'

Symon wrote four excellent Sam Shephard novels and a superb standalone thriller *The Faceless*, about people on the margins in inner-city Auckland, before going on hiatus to complete a doctorate that combined her loves of science and crime writing.

'The PhD came about because I did a University of Otago summer school paper in forensic biology as research for my novel writing,' says Symon. 'I loved the course so much I decided to do more study, but I wanted to do something relevant to what I loved.'

Symon examined the communication of science in crime fiction, using the works of Golden Age Queen of Crime Fiction and fellow New Zealander Dame Ngaio Marsh as a case study to contextualise two surveys examining reader and author attitudes. 'I surveyed readers of crime fiction to see if, amongst other things, they believed the science they encountered in crime fiction, and if they cared if it was accurate or not,' says Symon. 'I also surveyed crime writers to assess their approach to science.'

Unsurprisingly, says Symon, her research confirmed that readers care a lot about accuracy, with many saying that, if they found a scientific error, it broke their trust in the author across all elements, 'plot, character, everything'. Most authors took care to ensure any science they included was accurate, feeling both an ethical obligation and a desire to avoid being challenged by readers!

Symon learned another thing too while successfully completing her PhD – that writing a thesis was awful for a crime writer. 'In academic writing you have to give away the point in the first sentence, then provide the evidence to justify it,' she explains. 'For a crime writer who normally doesn't reveal everything until the end, that was really hard. I even asked my supervisors whether I could please write a thesis with a great surprise for them at the end – I told them they'd love reading it. Alas, they said no.'

After completing her PhD, Symon looked forward to returning to her old pal Sam Shephard – especially as the series had been picked up for northern hemisphere publication while she was studying. The changing global landscape for Australian and New Zealand crime writers was underlined as Symon updated the early Sam tales for overseas audiences. 'My amazing publisher Karen Sullivan of Orenda Books warned me to make the books more New Zealand, which was music to my ears as like almost every other New Zealand author I knew I'd been told I'd never be able to sell the books overseas if they were too Kiwi, and to tone down the New Zealand content, make them more homogenous, because that was what sold. So I was utterly thrilled when Karen said, "Give me more Kiwi".'

Talking to Symon is in many ways like reading one of her Sam Shephard novels – there's a real sense of fun, even when the subject matter might be serious; a southern sassiness among the dark deeds. She is now working on a new Sam Shephard adventure that continues her heroine's evolution from small-town country cop to respected city detective who must battle the misogyny of the 'old boys club' as well as plenty of personal travails.

'I love writing about Sam, doing mean and nasty things to her, she's fun to hassle,' says Symon, reflecting on her early books. 'Right from the outset, I wanted to have a character who wasn't static and who was affected by the events that happened in each book.'

Sam has plenty of personality, and is a protagonist whom readers love to follow. Her flaws and foibles are particularly important to Symon, who believes the best characters in crime fiction, such as Michael Connelly's longstanding LA detective Harry Bosch, aren't impervious super-cops who are always right. 'They make mistakes, they get themselves into the pool. I wanted that, I wanted Sam to be human.'

Perhaps surprisingly, given the character of Sam (along with vivid Otago settings, snappy repartee, and lashings of humour) is a key part of what makes Symon's storytelling stand out, the stroppy heroine wasn't originally slated to be the star. Symon envisaged a male hero for *Overkill* until a real-life incident completely overturned her plans.

'I can't even remember exactly what it was, but my husband did something completely daft, and I went "Oh my God, I can't even understand my own husband, how could I get into the head of a male cop?", so I changed it,' says Symon with a chuckle. 'And the moment I changed direction to have a female protagonist, Sam Shephard stepped up, fully formed as a character, and it was like she attituded her way into my life.'

* * *

Author note: This chapter is an amalgam created from past interviews with Vanda Symon for features in Australian magazine *Good Reading* in 2009, the *New Zealand Herald* newspaper in 2011, and American magazine *Crimespree* in 2019. Vanda Symon is the author of five crime novels and is a three-time Ngaio Marsh Awards finalist, a CWA Dagger Awards finalist, and a current judge of the Ngaio Marsh Award for Best First Novel. Two of her novels have been published in Germany and three in the United Kingdom and USA. She is currently working on her sixth crime novel, the fifth instalment in her Sam Shephard series.

DARK PRINCE OF THE PEN
– PAUL CLEAVE

You have to be a touch careful around Christchurch crime writer Paul Cleave.

Not because he shares any of the violent or (self) destructive tendencies of the memorable and morally conflicted characters packing the pages of his international bestsellers. But because he tends to, well, 'take the piss'. Mainly of himself.

Like his compelling tales, which on the surface seem rather serious – dark thrillers sprinkled with a fair bit of carnage – with Cleave there's often a fair bit of sly humour and self-deprecation going on underneath; easy to miss if you're not paying full attention.

Relaxing in his home in the northern suburbs of his city, the soft-spoken author admits he was 'pretty hard on Christchurch' in *Blood Men*, his fourth novel that saw him snapped up by a giant international publisher for a US launch in July 2010 – a rare achievement for a Kiwi author. It will be a big month for Cleave, as he's also appearing at the prestigious Theakston Old Peculier Crime Writing Festival in the United Kingdom, rubbing shoulders with the biggest names in the business. Overseas, his gritty and well-written thrillers have seen him touted as 'the New Zealand Ian Rankin'.

The story in *Blood Men* centres on accountant Edward Hunter, a happily married family man with a great life but a dark past; he's the son of a notorious serial killer who has been in Christchurch Prison for 20 years and will never be coming out. The son of a man of blood.

When tragedy strikes, Edward suddenly needs the help of a man he's spent all his life trying to separate himself from, and as things spiral out of control Edward starts wondering whether deep down he might be a man of blood too.

Cleave doesn't write boring stories, that's for sure; *Blood Men* crackles with freshness and energy. As in his previous international bestsellers (he's particularly popular in Germany, where his debut *The Cleaner* was the #1 bestselling crime novel on Amazon.de in 2007), sporadic moments of violence may be too much for those who favour mysteries of the Agatha Christie style. But Cleave masterfully mixes compelling characters, sly humour, and taut plotlines with enough tension and twists to keep pages whirring. It takes a talented writer to have readers stifling chuckles moments after wanting to huddle under their covers, but the laidback local has the rare touch, weaving laughs amongst the darkness.

'I always try for some humour,' he says. 'Sometimes it will be really subtle, but I definitely aim for humour. It's taken me a long time to develop that style, because I started writing novels when I was nineteen. It took me ten years to write and develop and get published.'

Another trademark of Cleave's writing is his well-evoked, if sometimes malevolent and sinister, version of his hometown. Readers and reviewers could be mistaken for thinking Cleave doesn't think much of the Garden City, given he portrays Christchurch as an unpredictable place, full of murder, mystery and mayhem. But the 35-year-old laughs that off, saying, away from his writing desk, he enjoys living here. 'I really like Christchurch... kind of,' he says, playfully deadpanning the last words. 'I don't see it in the dark way I write about it. I take everything bad I've learned about Christchurch and I exaggerate it for the books to create an atmosphere more suitable for a crime novel. It's not what I think of it, but my characters see it that way. Plus, it's a more entertaining angle to write.'

Perhaps surprisingly, given his fictionalised Christchurch is such a strength, originally Cleave wasn't going to set his stories locally. 'When I first started writing, I just made up... some kind of generic US city,' he recalls. He was learning his trade, churning out unpublished horror manuscripts in his early 20s (that he says will remain firmly ensconced in the bottom drawer, never to see the light of day), having always been fascinated by what scares us.

Then two things changed; he made the switch from horror to dark crime, realising that 'horror fiction isn't really horror... the scariest stuff in the world is true stuff, stuff that's real, like serial killers'. And he read advice from one of his favourite authors, Dean Koontz, about writing what you know. 'I started setting things in Christchurch, and it just changed everything. You know how things look; you know the feel of the city and how long it takes a character to get somewhere. It was just the best thing I ever did.'

Away from the page, Cleave likes spending time with friends and family, and enjoys getting active with his mates at the parks, beaches, and golf courses of Canterbury. He used to enjoy 'aggressively' hitting some of the great local mountain bike trails, until a couple of serious crashes put paid to that (he still has a few scars). Now he goes for the odd low-key ride with mates, as well trying to enjoy golf. 'I just love doing stuff, being athletic,' he says, before confessing with a laugh that he hasn't always been that way, having grown up 'small and geeky and underweight and just a bit of a nerd' through his years at Papanui High.

'I like to frustrate myself on a golf course and see if I can go around without throwing my clubs into the trees or breaking them all in half,' he says. 'I figure if I can use up all my swear words on the golf course, then there won't be any left for my writing.'

Cleave is also a big fan of Frisbee. 'Frisbee is the coolest thing in the world, and we'd all be better off if we made time for it,' he says, giving his serious face. 'It bonds people. I've seen it happen. I once played Frisbee in Egypt by a beach with a guy from Slovakia and a guy from Austria and I'd never met them before and for those ten minutes we were all best friends. Imagine how well peace talks would go if Presidents were tossing Frisbees back and forth – "Hey good catch, Barack" – "Hey, cheers, great throw".'

Once again, I'm not sure if he's serious or joking. Probably both; after all, he has a valid point – something important to say, even if I imagine I can see a mischievous glint in his eye.

Just like his writing.

* * *

Author note: This is a lightly edited version of a feature published in the Winter 2011 issue of *Latitude* magazine. *Blood Men* went on to win the 2011 Ngaio Marsh Award for Best Novel, the first of a record three times Cleave has won that award. He's also won the Prix Saint-Maur Crime Novel of the Year in France and been shortlisted for the Edgar and Barry Awards in the United States. His eleventh and latest thriller is *Whatever it Takes* (2019).

STRIKING GOLD: MICHAEL ROBOTHAM

'You hope it's a dinosaur,' says Michael Robotham, with a nod to Stephen King's analogy of authors as archaeologists, of wandering along the road and spying a fragment of bone jutting out of the dirt. Novel writing is an act of faith, sparked by an idea that may or may not go anywhere. 'You begin brushing away the dirt, unsure of whether it's a dog bone or a dinosaur... A dinosaur will make a novel. A dog bone will, well, feed the dog.'

Almost 20 years ago, Robotham saw a piece of bone when he read about convicted killer turned model prisoner Tony Lanigan, who escaped days before his release. 'The idea stuck in my head,' he admits. 'The big question was why? Like all lovers of crime fiction, I can't resist a mystery.'

A decade would pass before Robotham exploded onto the fiction scene with *The Suspect*, a chilling and beautifully written thriller where Parkinson's-afflicted clinical psychologist Joe O'Loughlin tries to make sense of the brutal death of a former colleague as well as the violent dreams of a current patient. It sparked a publishers' bidding war, was translated into 22 languages, and a million copies were sold.

That debut was a milestone. Robotham already had successful careers as a London journalist and ghostwriter of several bestselling celebrity 'autobiographies', but fiction writing had been the dream. Journalism and ghostwriting were always 'stepping stones', he says, to a life he'd desired since his earliest days in Gundagai, a former Gold Rush town in the Australian Outback.

A life exciting and terrifying: sitting before the blank page, having to invent everything. 'I love the freedom of writing fiction but sometimes it feels like I'm standing naked on a high wire above Niagara Falls with everything hanging out in the breeze,' he says. For a man who writes such dark tales, there's a grounded lightness and warmth about Robotham. He's nicknamed his writing room by the North Sydney beaches 'the Cabana of Cruelty'.

Around the time he wrote *The Suspect*, Robotham had somewhat solved the mystery of 'why' someone might escape the day before they were to be released from prison – he'd found a compelling reason. But he didn't feel ready to write that story. In King's terms, he'd found a dinosaur bone, but needed more time to excavate it. 'It took nine novels before I felt I had the skills to tell the story properly,' he says. 'I needed to practise. I needed to learn. I needed to get better.'

It was worth the wait. Robotham has been writing intriguing and intelligent psychological thrillers for a decade, scooping awards, acclaim, and places on bestseller lists around the world. But *Life or Death* – a departure from his usual heroes, O'Loughlin and tough investigator Vincent Ruiz, and his usual setting, the United Kingdom – may be Robotham's masterpiece.

It's the story he feels he was meant to tell. 'Most writers will tell you that the story in their heads is never quite the one that makes it to the page,' he explains. 'They can never quite capture exactly what they envisage. With *Life or Death* I think I've come closest to matching the two stories. It's never going to be perfect, but it's very close to what I wanted to achieve.'

In the novel, Audie Palmer nearly dies during a botched armoured car robbery where $7 million went missing. Many people have wanted him dead since. He avoided life as a vegetable, avoided a death sentence, then survived years of stabbings and beatings in a Texas prison, only to escape the day before his release. He's on the run, trying to save someone else, very much wanted dead not alive.

Robotham says he considered setting his story in the UK, or even Australia, but settled on the United States due to its history of prison-based films and novels, and because he 'needed a setting where the political and justice systems are so intertwined at a local level that corruption can sometimes flourish'. It is that exquisite evocation of the Texas setting, along with the emotional oomph of Audie's tale meshed with Robotham's page-turning plotting, that really raises the storytelling bar in *Life or Death*.

For research, Robotham read prison memoirs, corresponded with a prisoner who reviewed one of his earlier novels for a prison magazine, and immersed himself in audio books by Cormac McCarthy, William Faulkner, James Lee Burke and the like. 'On top of this I spent almost a month in Texas, Arizona, and Arkansas researching elements of the story such as the justice system, people smuggling across the border, and soaking up the local atmosphere… Eventually I found myself talking in a Texan accent as I was writing.'

It was while researching in the Ozark Mountains of Arkansas that Robotham had a memorable encounter with a small-town sheriff, who knocked on his door late one night, hand hovering over his sidearm, suspicious of why Robotham had been taking photos of Jasper's bank and courthouse. When humour failed to soothe, Robotham explained he was a writer researching a story about a prisoner who escaped the day before his release.

'Well, that'd make him dumber than shit on a biscuit,' said the sheriff, who was finally appeased when Robotham seemed open to the idea of Audie being shot, and a sheriff being the hero of the novel. Did the novelist follow through on the sheriff's suggestions?

'I'm never going back to Jasper,' says Robotham.

* * *

Author note: This feature was originally published in the *New Zealand Listener* magazine in September 2014. *Life or Death* was Robotham's tenth novel and would go on to win the CWA Gold Dagger from the Crime Writers' Association in the United Kingdom and be shortlisted for the Edgar Award for Best Novel from the Mystery Writers of America. During the same time period Michael served as President of the Australian Crime Writers Association. His standalone psychological thriller *The Secrets She Keeps* won the Australian Book Industry Association (ABIA) General Fiction Award in 2018, and *Good Girl. Bad Girl* was nominated for the 2020 Edgar Awards.

SCOTLAND IN THE SOUTH:
LIAM MCILVANNEY

Looking up at the bronze likeness of iconic poet Robbie Burns, listening to bagpipes wafting on the chill air, Scotsman Liam McIlvanney feels remarkably 'at home' considering he's 11,000 miles from his Kilmarnock birthplace. Professor McIlvanney, who immigrated to Dunedin with his young family to become the Stuart Chair in Scottish Studies at the University of Otago, says he's been experiencing an interesting mix of 'the foreign and the familiar' in his new home. 'It's been fantastic,' he says. 'It's quite extraordinary to see all the streets named after Edinburgh streets. It's a great city; compact, but vibrant and a lot going on culturally.'

In a way, McIlvanney has come full circle. 'I grew up in Ayrshire, the epicentre of Burns country, where Burns is absolutely inescapable... just part of the air we breathed', he says. After a break from the Scottish poet while studying in Glasgow, he returned to his roots with a Burns-themed doctoral thesis at Oxford on the way to becoming an expert in Scottish literature. Now he's teaching a new generation, in another Burns-mad city, about the man dubbed 'Scotland's favourite son'.

He's also come full circle in another way – penning his first fictional tale after years of producing academic articles and non-fiction books on Scottish (and Irish) culture and society. For when his debut *All the Colours of the Town* was published recently, McIlvanney joined his famous father William, a former schoolteacher, in the ranks of published novelists. The older McIlvanney is a renowned Scottish writer, who won a Whitbread Award (now the Costa Book Awards) for his literary novels and CWA Daggers for his ground-breaking 'Laidlaw' detective novels.

Perhaps surprisingly, given his knowledge of eighteenth-century Scottish culture, McIlvanney's own remarkable debut is a contemporary thriller (although deeply influenced by historical events). *All the Colours of the Town* centres on Glasgow political journo Gerry Conway, who receives a tip-off about the unsavoury past of the Scottish Justice Minister, one of his best sources. Initially unimpressed, Conway is eventually drawn into a journey from Glasgow to Belfast, attempting to uncover a shocking story laced with sectarian violence and dangerous secrets.

Liam McIlvanney's debut has been well-received by critics, with *The Observer* calling it 'a perfect example of why talented writers ought not to shy away from tackling genre novels' and *The Independent* saying 'the prose crackles with the sort of neat descriptions Chandler would have been happy to copyright'.

The latter compliment particularly pleases McIlvanney, who considers the American creator of the Philip Marlowe novels 'the absolute gold standard for hardboiled crime, and quality of prose'. Despite (or perhaps because of) the fact he studies and teaches 'literature', McIlvanney firmly believes crime and thriller-writing can have an importance beyond mere page-turning entertainment. He points out that the wave of Scottish crime writing, fuelled by the success of Ian Rankin (who incidentally credits William McIlvanney's Laidlaw books as an important influence) and those who followed, has played a potent role in contemporary Scotland by providing a fertile forum for pressing political and social issues to be explored. 'Literary fiction can be sort of detached from contemporary realities,' he says. 'It's been left to the genre writers to... hold a mirror up to contemporary Britain.'

Furthermore, says McIlvanney, many books that are now considered great literature were in fact the 'popular fiction' of their time. 'In my courses on Scottish literature I teach Robert Louis Stevenson's *Strange Case of Dr Jekyll and Mr Hyde*, which is now of course a classic, but at the time was a shilling shocker.'

It took McIlvanney, who is now snatching time for the second Gerry Conway thriller in between his teaching and family commitments, two years to complete *All the Colours of the Town*. What started as an evocative vignette of the famous Orange Walk in Glasgow, a highly charged sectarian celebration of William of Orange's victory over King James II in 1690, quickly became a book deal after it was read by an agent. 'It was just something which had always stuck in my imagination, that I really wanted to write about ... it was the germ of the novel,' says McIlvanney. 'Then I created my journalist, and the politician whom he's investigating, and it just developed from there.'

While even in the antipodes many are aware of the 'Troubles' between Catholics and Protestants in Northern Ireland, McIlvanney says less is known about sectarianism in Scotland. 'Unlike Northern Ireland, there is no segregation in terms of housing, and job discrimination is a thing of the past, but the attitudes that were ingrained because of sectarianism are still ingrained to some extent,' he says, noting his book explores the aftershocks and ongoing effects of the Troubles, including from a Scottish perspective.

'It is a slightly unexplored aspect of contemporary Scotland, which is one of the reasons I found it useful to write a crime novel,' says McIlvanney. 'We have so many ties to Northern Ireland in terms of family, and cultural links... there's an interesting Scottish experience, so I wanted to explore that... some of the issues that are being discussed at a policy level in Scotland.'

If McIlvanney's debut is anything to go by, perhaps (quality) crime writing can indeed pull double duty as great entertainment and the modern social novel.

* * *

Author note: This chapter was originally published as a feature in the *Canvas* magazine of the *Weekend Herald* in October 2009. In the decade since, McIlvanney has published another Gerry Conway novel, *Where The Dead Men Go*, which went on to win the 2014 Ngaio Marsh Award for Best Novel. He became a New Zealand citizen, and saw his third crime novel *The Quaker* win the 2018 McIlvanney Prize in Scotland (named after his father William) and get shortlisted for multiple awards in the United Kingdom and New Zealand. In 2019, Liam McIlvanney helped establish the Celtic Noir festival in Dunedin.

DOIN' IT FOR THEMSELVES
– LINDY CAMERON

One Sunday almost 30 years ago, Lindy Cameron headed along to the Democritus Club in Carlton, a lively suburb just north of downtown Melbourne. She didn't know anyone there, but she was interested in a debate being held as part of the Feminist Book Fortnight.

Lindy had no idea that day would change the trajectory of her life.

'I'd gone along mostly to see Kerry Greenwood on the panel,' says Cameron. The author of the Phryne Fisher mysteries was one of only a few female Australian crime novelists at the time (along with the likes of Marele Day and Jennifer Rowe). Greenwood was joined onstage at the Democritus Club by Mary-Ann Metcalf and Alison Littler, with Carmel Shute chairing, to debate whether 'feminist crime fiction confronted the hard-boiled head on'.

And on that day, Sisters in Crime Australia was born.

'I joined at the launch so am a founding member,' says Cameron, who before then had never really been a joiner. She says she succumbed to the feeling of fun. 'Before long, however, I had volunteered to take over the newsletter – a printed affair, this being last century – which later became a physical magazine. I became a Convenor in 1994.'

Forty women joined up that first day. A movement had begun.

'The establishment of Sisters in Crime Australia is all down to Carmel Shute and a small group of Melbourne crime fans,' says Cameron. 'Unlike our American "mother" association – which was founded by Sara Paretsky as a writers' association designed to improve the exposure of women crime writers – our founders were all readers not writers of the genre.'

The early days of the group were focused simply on celebrating the genre the members all loved, while also promoting local writers and emerging voices and trying to get the media to notice, says Cameron. 'We also had a lot of fun – our other prime objective – hosting events with panels of authors, or real-life specialists and practitioners of crime solving.'

Fun and beyond, by any measure the organisation has been a huge success. In 1994, the Scarlet Stiletto Awards were introduced: national prizes for short stories by Australian women featuring a strong female protagonist. And a pipeline for new talent to emerge.

Over the past quarter century, more than 3,500 stories have been entered by women from all walks of life. Dozens of entrants have later become published novelists, including the likes of Tara Moss, Angela Savage, and Aoife Clifford.

To mark the tenth anniversary of Sisters in Crime Australia, Cameron, Shute and their comrades held the SheKilda conference in 2001, and launched the Davitt Awards. 'Ellen Davitt, who wrote one of the first crime novels published anywhere – by man or woman – was the natural fit for our own awards,' says Cameron.

Nowadays there are more than 500 members of Sisters in Crime Australia, and Cameron is the President. In 1991 Greenwood had few peers; by 2019 there were 127 books entered in that year's Davitt Awards, which celebrate the best crime books by Australian women.

What began as a group of passionate crime readers has grown into one of the driving forces behind a welcome explosion of Australian women writing crime fiction, getting it published and being appreciated by readers at home and abroad. The Sisters are doin' it for themselves.

'I've always loved a good mystery,' says Cameron, who herself graduated from keen reader to published author during her time with Sisters in Crime Australia.

'I started with the Famous Five and never looked back, travelling via Biggles, James Bond, and Agatha Christie all the way to my "grown-up" reading when I discovered modern crime writers like Sara Paretsky and Val McDermid,' she says. 'There was no question, as a writer, that I'd start with anything else but crime, although I have slid sideways into science fiction and historical. But even those stories have killer plots and more than a few dead bodies.'

Perhaps appropriately, when Cameron became a published crime novelist herself a few years after that fateful Sunday in Carlton, her debut had an unusual nod to the genre's past: like *The Moonstone* by Wilkie Collins and the Sherlock Holmes stories of Sir Arthur Conan Doyle, *Golden Relic* (originally *Stolen Property*) was first published in serialised form.

Not for a Victorian-era literary magazine, but a modern equivalent.

A mystery entwined with the world of museums, ancient artefacts, and obsessive collectors, Cameron's first book was published chapter by chapter on the internet in the lead-up to the International Council of Museums' triennial conference, hosted in Melbourne in 1998. The conference committee had the, well, 'novel' idea to showcase its international gathering and promote its host city by commissioning a mystery novel, and Cameron obliged.

In *Golden Relic*, Detective Sam Diamond investigates the murder of a professor at the Museum of Victoria, assisted by archaeologist Maggie Tremaine, who ends up whisking Sam around the world from Melbourne to Egypt to Peru and back as they search for the truth.

But even before the serialisation, Cameron had been working on another crime tale, featuring a lesbian private eye in Melbourne. Once *Blood Guilt* was published, it was that heroine which legendary Queen of Crime Val McDermid praised as 'smart-mouthed, sharp-witted, and sexy', and 'a welcome addition to the list of female crime-fighters'. And it was that heroine, Kit O'Malley, who sparked an acclaimed trilogy of locally-set novels.

'I always intended to write a series,' says Cameron. 'I love Kit. Weird to say when she's both fiction and my fictional character. But I wanted to create a memorable protagonist who was both funny and cluey and had friends and family that mattered to her and were all more than cut-out clichés. I like to think I managed that.'

Cameron says she worked hard to make Melbourne a character itself, to embed Kit O'Malley and her friends in 'a recognisable and interesting version' of her own city, which in the two decades since has grown to become arguably the heart of crime writing in Australia.

'They say write what you know, but to me that really only applies (sometimes) to writing where you know,' she adds. 'One of the best things about most crime fiction is its sense of place. So for me, making Melbourne a "character" was intentional and a given. It's my city and I love it, and when I started there was pretty much only Kerry Greenwood setting crime fiction here. Shane Maloney and I happened almost at the same time – so his books were a joy from the get-go. Maybe there's something in the water here now, when we are producing so many crime writers in Victoria. Who knows, but it's bloody marvellous.'

In recent years, Cameron's own novel writing has taken a back seat. She's edited anthologies, written true crime, organised events, and established Clan Destine Press, an inclusive publisher of new and established Australian genre writers that also republished Ellen Davitt's groundbreaking 1865 novel *Force and Fraud*, the original 'Outback Noir'.

When I ask Cameron about wearing so many hats, and how that affects her own writing, there's a smile in her answer. 'I'm a hat-wielding lunatic, she says. 'Truly, I should learn to say no; or stop having ideas. But, again, I am what I love – and I love books: reading them, writing them, publishing others who write them; encouraging and helping to promote the many more who I don't publish; hosting or going to events so they/we can talk about them.'

Not that the writing itch will go unscratched indefinitely for the woman whose life was changed, along with many others who weren't even there, by that afternoon in Carlton in 1991. Lindy Cameron, President of Sisters in Crime Australia, makes a final confession. 'I have clawed back a day a week for myself and am embarking on a new crime series.'

* * *

Author note: This chapter has been written specifically for this book, based on an interview with author and Sisters in Crime Australia President Lindy Cameron in September 2019.

THE GOLD STANDARD – PETER TEMPLE

'You've done the crime, you do the time,' said Peter Temple, drawing laughs.

It was Sydney, ten years after the Olympics. The crowd had gathered for the presentation dinner for the Miles Franklin Award, Australia's most prestigious literary prize. Seared salmon, chardonnay, and literary backslapping. But there was a twist in this tale.

For the first time in its 63-year history, the annual prize for a novel 'which is of the highest literary merit and presents Australian life in any of its phases' went to – shock horror – a detective novel. Admittedly, it was a rather special one. *Truth* wasn't so much a sequel as a companion novel to Temple's outstanding *The Broken Shore*, which three years before had made the South African-born writer the first antipodean winner of the CWA Gold Dagger.

Now, a crime writer had crossed the Rubicon of the Australian literary scene.

Truth is a novel of a man and his city, both facing destruction. Inspector Stephen Villani, a friend of the main character in *The Broken Shore*, is acting head of homicide in Victoria. For a man whose work is his life, a botched operation and a string of unsolved cases have him teetering. With a murder in a luxury Melbourne apartment and bush fires raging across his state, personal and professional crises conflate into a spiral towards meltdown.

It's a towering novel that won three major literary awards in Australia including the Miles Franklin, and later the International German Crime Prize. It didn't add to Temple's five Ned Kelly Awards because he withdrew it from contention, wanting to clear space for 'the many talented crime writers' who hadn't yet been recognised.

The Miles Franklin judges praised *Truth* as a 'stunning novel' that had 'all the ambiguity and moral sophistication of the most memorable literature'. Still, on that night in Sydney, the former magazine editor was disbelieving that his name had now joined a list alongside 'Australia's greatest writers'.

'I'll thank the judges anyway,' he said. 'They'll have to take the flak for giving the Miles Franklin to a crime writer and all I can say, my advice to them is cop it sweet.'

Being a crime writer at the podium wasn't the only way Temple stood out during that awards evening, with Stephen Romei, editor of the *Australian Literary Review*, later telling ABC News that Temple 'must be the first Miles Franklin winner to cite the Melbourne Cup in an acceptance speech … and even remembered the jockey, which was fantastic'.

A tiny insight into a *sui generis* storyteller who in many ways broke the mould.

For Michael Robotham, who a few years later became the second Australian crime writer to win the CWA Gold Dagger, Temple receiving the Miles Franklin Award 'shrugged off the literary snobbery that often regards genre writing as being a lesser form of literature'.

Speaking after Temple passed away from cancer in 2018, Robotham called Temple one of their country's literary giants, and said the death of a remarkable writer and remarkable man was a huge loss far beyond the crime writing fraternity. 'He didn't fight against the term "crime writer" but he just used crime as a vehicle to tell lots of other important stories about truth, justice, family, politics, and the corruption of power.'

At an event a few years ago, Temple spoke to Robotham about his choice to write crime fiction. 'In everything I've written, the crime has always just been an occasion to write about other things,' he said. 'I don't have a picture of myself as writing crime novels. I like fairly strong narratives, but it's a way of getting a plot moving. I'm not trying to say that I don't write crime novels, but I don't sit down and think I'm writing a crime novel.'

Temple was pleased about the growing realisation that crime fiction was a storytelling form that could deal with a wide range of issues. 'Indeed, often deals with them better; family issues, personal issues and character and conduct of human beings, power, political power, economic power. All of these things are easily encompassed in the crime novel, and other things too: flower arranging, aesthetics of carpentry and things of that kind.'

But what makes Temple's own crime writing so damned good? Is it the way he uses crime as a starting point to explore big themes, often entwined with conspiracies and corruption festering out of plain view? Temple himself said he was never interested in writing a straight police procedural, that he always found himself grasping for something larger, even if he fell short. 'The vision almost always includes political corruption, financial corruption, questions of morality, of behaviour or decency,' he said. 'Because I think those are issues you should write about, if you are a crime writer or not.'

Or is it his distilled prose suffused with insights? Robotham praises the taut sparseness and beauty of Temple's writing, how he 'pared back his sentences and polished them like diamonds'. Reflecting on his time as a journalism teacher, Temple had said that he tried to teach his students to write by teaching them to write less. He practised what he preached. 'It seemed to me that you needed to subtract stuff down to some sort of irreducible minimum, and at that point you developed a style.'

A quintessentially, unashamedly Australian author who captured local vernacular and attitudes like few others, and wouldn't water them down over any worries of being 'too Australian' for non-Australian readers, the genius of Peter Temple lay in all those things.

As Morag Fraser, a long-time judge of the Miles Franklin Award who regularly reads crime fiction, said to Alison Flood of *The Guardian* after *Truth* won, typical crime novels don't have a shot at the biggest literary prizes as they don't 'work language hard enough' and 'think originally with sufficient depth and imagination' – they gratify without surprising.

But Peter Temple, and *Truth*, were anything but typical. In that book the divide between genre and 'literary' was so comprehensively crossed, said Fraser, that the judges didn't have to think much about crime conventions, 'except to note that Temple was able to observe them rather as a poet observes the 14-line convention of the sonnet or a musician the sonata form: as a useful disciplinary structure from which to expand, bend or depart.'

Temple was a generous man when it came to doling out praise to others, but struggled to accept such plaudits for himself, remembers Robotham. Winning the Miles Franklin Award was both immensely satisfying to him, but also created a burden of self-expectation.

In the years before his death, Temple was said to be working on a third instalment in the loose series comprising of *The Broken Shore* and *Truth*, a coda entitled *The Light on the Hill*.

It remains unfinished. Sadly, for once, Peter Temple pared things back too far.

* * *

Author note: This chapter has been written specifically for this book and hasn't been published elsewhere. Unfortunately, I was unable to interview Peter Temple before his passing, so it has been created from other sources. I would like to thank Michael Robotham for sharing his personal reminiscences of his crime writing colleague and friend with me.

THE CO-CONSPIRATOR – CANDICE FOX

Her first two novels put two Ned Kelly Awards on her mantelpiece, and she's hit the top of the *New York Times* bestseller list with her criminal co-writing, but the first four manuscripts a young Candice Fox wrote while she was a student in Sydney were supernatural novels.

'I was into vampires and werewolves and things,' she confesses.

Looking back further though, Fox was likely destined for a life of crime, fictionally. 'I was always interested in crime,' she says. 'I grew up in a household where my mother fostered 155 kids and they were always being dropped off by cops and coming in with their own sort of crime story. My mother was a huge true crime fan, she used to drive us into the Belanglo Forest and tell us the story of Ivan Milat, you know try to scare us in the middle of the night. My dad worked at a prison as well, and he would come home with all these crime stories.'

Even before she was a teenager, Fox used to run home from school to tap out 'shoot 'em up gangster tales' on a computer, mimicking the Scorsese films she loved, despite her brothers mocking her efforts when they got their hands on them. But later, when Fox first sat down to try her hand at a novel, she plumped for supernatural stories because she felt intimidated by crime writing. 'I didn't feel like I had all the procedural knowledge, all the policing and proper terms and that kind of thing,' she explains. 'Then I read John Connolly's *Every Dead Thing*, which a friend recommended to me. It was a crime novel with supernatural leanings, so it was a good bridging book between the two genres, and I just thought you know what, supernatural stuff is just not working for me in terms of getting things published, so I might write something that's a bit more crime-y. So, I just gave it a whirl.'

It was a winning whirl. Fox's first crime novel, *Hades*, was a grim, fresh crime tale that burrowed into disturbing parts of society. Eden and Eric Archer are siblings who work for the Sydney police, capable of charm and cold efficiency. A result of their scarred childhood? Homicide detective Frank Bennett is excited to get Eden as his new partner, then the team is on full alert when toolboxes full of body parts are pulled from the Sydney Harbour. What could the grisly case have to do with Eden and Eric's childhood, or the shambling criminal who raised them?

While Fox switched supernatural manuscripts for police stories, there remains a strong thread of horror running through *Hades*, and its sequels *Eden* and *Fall*. 'You can see from the whole trilogy that the characters are quite vampy, it's all a bit Gothic,' she says.

With *Hades* winning the Ned Kelly Award for Best First Novel in 2014, and then *Eden* winning the Best Novel prize in 2015, it was a rapid arrival for Fox on the crime scene, going from unpublished unknown to being lauded by readers and critics and celebrated by her peers. Having been a kid who'd always felt a bit out of place, it was a little head-spinning for Fox.

'Yeah, it was good,' she says, pausing. 'I struggled to find a sense of belonging though because, ah, I've just never been very popular and my natural instinct is like "I won't fit in here" whenever I turn up anywhere. So winning the two awards made me feel like I had some street cred and people were reading my novel to see who I was, so it was good to have that kind of attention. People like Adrian McKinty and Michael Robotham were very welcoming of me into the crime writing community as well, so it was good.'

Then something even more head-spinning happened. Fox was shoulder-tapped to team up with the world's biggest-selling thriller writer, James Patterson. 'He'd already collaborated with two authors in Australia, Michael White and Kathryn Fox, and was out here promoting his book with Kathryn,' recalls Candice. Being 'a huge fan' of Patterson's storytelling, when her publisher asked if she'd be interested in going on a list of authors to be proposed to Patterson for future collaborations, there was no hesitation. 'It was like offering a treat to a dog and almost having your hand snapped off, with the enthusiasm,' she says, 'But I didn't have any hopes of it actually panning out.'

Fox's debut was among the books Patterson took with him after a trip to Australia. He read *Hades* on the plane home to Florida and picked her. 'I got the phone call maybe two weeks later. It was really good.' The work quickly started. Fox had already begun writing her own fourth novel, the start of a new series after her Sydney trilogy, and now had to fit in another book. She would write *Crimson Lake* in the morning, and *Never Never* (her first co-write with Patterson) in the afternoon and evening. The latter book required different things to Fox's solo efforts; for example, she had to refrain from flashbacks or multiple perspectives, which she'd regularly used in the past. 'It was just an adjustment period, learning how to do that, and how to keep the chapters under 1,000 words, so I would write them then cut them back, this kind of thing,' says Fox. 'So, I had the two styles side by side, and I was putting on very distinct hats, switching from one to the other each day.'

In a strange coincidence, after three urban crime novels set in her home, both new books sprang from rural Australia. *Never Never*'s setting is a remote Outback mining camp, and Fox had already decided on Cairns for *Crimson Lake*. But both still involved Sydney detectives. 'I had spent a lot of time up in Cairns and the Sunshine Coast, and I'd thought to myself "where would I run if I wanted to disappear inside Australia?", because it was probably not a good idea for Ted to leave the country with his case the way it is.'

In *Crimson Lake*, Ted Conkaffey was a Sydney detective accused of assaulting a young woman – and still looked at askew despite charges being dropped – who joins forces in Cairns with convicted killer turned private eye Amanda Pharell to find a missing celebrity.

Fox loved the atmosphere of Cairns for a crime novel. 'In Sydney the crime to me is very obvious, you can point to the dangerous parts, you can see the sinister-ness of Sydney, if that's a word,' she says. 'But with Cairns I think it's a bit more mysterious. You see these crocodile signs everywhere but don't see a single crocodile like ever, they have this menacing presence just under the surface. I wanted to capture a place that was a bit more subtle in its evil nature.'

In *Never Never*, Harriet Blue is a hotheaded Sydney detective sent against her will to Bandya Mine in the dusty interior of Western Australia after three people disappear. Meanwhile back in the city her brother has been accused of being a serial killer.

Both books spawned ongoing series, keeping Fox extremely busy in recent years. When I ask if her rapid success and full slate have changed the way she approaches writing a crime novel now, compared to when she was working on *Hades* as an aspiring author, Fox points out a few differences. 'I'm a lot less precious now, in every way,' she says. 'I have to move fast, at high quality, so there's not a lot of room for lying around waiting for the muse, or getting writer's block, or having a bunch of ideas to test out and see which is best.'

Having to deal with six editors spread across Australia, the UK, the United States, and Germany, who all consider the manuscripts and provide feedback based on what they want for their own markets, Fox has also had to develop a thick skin. 'So whereas it used to be that I'd get feedback, saying something like "Frank is the most boring character" and I'd fall into a heap and cry for five hours, I just can't do that anymore. I get so much criticism all the time, I just have to make it work for what's best for the novel, rather than my artistic ego.'

Keeping writing in the face of criticism, and coping with her brothers' childhood teasing, paid off.

* * *

Author note: This chapter has been written specifically for this book and hasn't been published elsewhere. It is based on an interview with Candice Fox in October 2019.

LIKE A DAME – STELLA DUFFY

Twenty years before writer and theatre-maker Stella Duffy was born, war raged across the globe. Her father Tom, a young man from the New Zealand countryside who'd joined his nation's air force to fight fascism, was being passed around German POW camps.

'Both my parents had a really tough war,' says Duffy as we sit looking over the Thames. 'Some people had a good war, but they didn't. Both had left school at 14. Dad was shot down and was a prisoner of war for four years. My mum got bombed out of three homes.'

During that time, back in Tom's homeland a woman named Ngaio was volunteering as an ambulance driver in Christchurch, transporting wounded soldiers from ships to hospitals. She began producing Shakespeare plays, while continuing to write the murder mysteries that saw her become one of the Queens of Crime of the Golden Age of Detective Fiction.

It was around then that Ngaio Marsh jotted down a few short chapters, setting up a locked-room mystery occurring over the course of one night at a quarantine hospital in rural Canterbury, and scribbled further notes on the back of an *Antony and Cleopatra* script. There were no hints of a solution, no motive, and the detective had yet to appear. Before putting it in a drawer, Marsh also gave the mystery a title: *Money in the Morgue.*

It would be more than 70 years before Marsh's beloved gentleman sleuth, Chief Inspector Roderick Alleyn, would finally solve that locked room mystery. And it would be Duffy who dusted him off and showed him the way, after his original creator passed away in 1982. 'I was contacted out of the blue by David Brawn from HarperCollins, who told me about these chapters they'd known about for 20 years, and that they'd recently found some notes too,' says Duffy, a 'Pakeha Londoner' who grew up in the timber town of Tokoroa and had written 15 novels ranging from edgy lesbian mysteries to award-winning historical fiction.

Dame Ngaio had likely abandoned this book because the war ended, and she turned her attention to writing *Final Curtain* (1947), which 'brought Alleyn back to London for a more light-hearted post-war adventure,' says Brawn, Publisher of Estates at HarperCollins. After failing to get his hands on Marsh's papers 20 years ago, when he'd spotted a passing mention in Margaret Lewis's biography of Dame Ngaio, Brawn tried again after publishing Sophie Hannah's first Hercule Poirot novel. A few months later he was sent photocopies of the early chapters, penned in 'very small and almost illegible handwriting', that had been found in the Alexander Turnbull Library in New Zealand. 'We realised that this was the start of what would have been a really interesting mystery for Inspector Alleyn, whom it was established from *Died in the Wool* was in New Zealand on wartime business.'

But who could they get to write the mystery? 'Because the story is set in New Zealand, I knew from the start that the ideal writer would have to be a New Zealander, someone who would be able to evoke the geography and mood of Ngaio Marsh,' says Brawn. 'Ideally, I wanted a female writer, someone with experience of plotting crime novels, but also someone with a literary flair, who might be able to match Ngaio's gift for description and characterisation. A knowledge of theatre, which was Ngaio's true passion, would also be really good if we were to do justice to the original, and a lively intellect and sense of humour, of course, as Ngaio excelled in creating grotesque and slightly theatrical characters which you can't achieve if you are a boring person. Frankly, it was an impossibly greedy list of attributes, and as I began researching possible writers, it was immediately clear that Stella Duffy was ideal in every respect.'

Talking later, Duffy admits she and Marsh shared quite a few traits, before revealing it was another connection that helped her find the necessary 'in' while wrestling with the novel. 'If I was to do the story justice, I had to find my own way into it – writing from and with her sensibilities and obvious motifs, but also writing for myself,' says Duffy. 'In a way, that it's set in New Zealand during World War Two is particularly useful. Because that's that past – another country – for all of us, and if I think of my Dad, my Nan, my aunts and uncles, I could begin to conjure up the rhythm of their voices, the tone of their speech (very different from now), also a sense of who these people are. My Dad being in the RNZAF, I do have a real feeling for some of the characters, some of the recuperating soldiers she introduces.'

Duffy's efforts paid off. She beautifully captures Marsh's style, delivering a continuation novel that feels both timeless and richly steeped in its wartime period. *Money in the Morgue* should please most long-time fans as well as mystery lovers who are new to Inspector Alleyn's adventures. Some of the world's best crime writers, including Sophie Hannah and Val McDermid, have sung the praises of what Duffy accomplished in *Money in the Morgue*, and the book went on to be shortlisted for major awards in both the United Kingdom and New Zealand.

While Duffy was conscious of the mystery's heritage – shifting her own style to blend seamlessly with Marsh's – she also brought touches less likely to be addressed by 1940s writers, such as characters suffering a range of emotions, trauma, and PTSD related to the conflict. She knew from her father's experience – he would have been about the same age as the soldiers in *Money in the Morgue* when he was a prisoner of war – that damage could lie beneath a tough exterior. 'These men that went to war had a hard time; it wasn't all glory,' she says. 'Many New Zealanders were killed, others came home damaged, and that's not so well known, so it was important for me to acknowledge that.'

Duffy also included a Māori soldier among the quarantined men at the hospital in *Money in the Morgue*, again reflecting realities of the time that aren't always recognised. While there was no conscription for Māori during the war, more than 20 per cent of the Māori population volunteered to serve, including as part of the famed 28th (Māori) Battalion. 'I didn't want to write a novel set in New Zealand and not have a Māori character,' says Duffy, whose upbringing in a forestry town in rural New Zealand might be surprising to those who think of New Zealand as historically a little island of Englishness at the bottom of the world. 'When I meet posh people at events in London, they think it must have been very hard growing up gay and an artist in a rural forestry town, but Tokoroa was a really multicultural community,' says Duffy. 'Very inclusive. There were 26 languages in my primary school in the 1970s. A big Polynesian community. You could see the hills from our house, and our neighbours were Scottish, Dutch, Māori, Samoan. Just loads of diversity.'

The hills. Many Kiwis feel a strong connection to our natural landscapes. It's something Duffy acknowledges, while living half a world away in London, and something she particularly enjoys about Dame Ngaio's own storytelling. Duffy read and re-read Marsh's novels in preparation for writing *Money in the Morgue*, particularly those set in New Zealand.

'She is a beautiful literary writer, with some astonishingly lovely phrases, most especially when she's talking about our land. Having lived away for so long, there's a great sense of knowing Aotearoa/ New Zealand from her writing, and while of course a nation and its people change over time, the land remains. So even though her work is inevitably dated in some ways, the understanding of place – *Papatūānuku* really – is vivid and strong.'

* * *

Author note: This chapter has been written specifically for this book, based on notes from interviews with Stella Duffy and David Brawn in 2016, and further discussions with Stella for a *New Zealand Herald* feature in 2017, at the Bloody Scotland festival in 2018, and for the 'Antipodean Noir' panel at the Theakston Old Peculier Crime Writing Festival in 2019.

FINDING PEACE – GARRY DISHER

Crime readers first met Wyatt in a taxi parked in an affluent suburb of Melbourne, watching a family drive away from their home in a silver BMW. The kind of home with valuable paintings on the wall, Rolex watches and Cartier bracelets in cases in the bedroom, and Krugerrands and rare coins in a desk drawer in the study. Wyatt's kind of house. Unfortunately for ultra-professional thief Wyatt, the wannabe Cowboy in the driver's seat that he was forced to bring along for the job isn't his kind of partner, and things go awry.

Kickback was published in 1991, the same year Sisters in Crime Australia was launched in Melbourne and a few years before the Ned Kelly Awards and the Australian Crime Writers Association were established. Local crime writers were comparatively rare on the ground.

So why did Garry Disher, who at that time had already published several books spanning literary novels, short story collections, and non-fiction about various periods in Australian history, turn to a life of crime? And why did he start not with a cop, but a criminal?

'There were two reasons,' says Disher, talking from his home on the Mornington Peninsula, a landscape of bushlands and beaches 90 minutes from downtown Melbourne. 'One is that I've always loved reading crime fiction. So, part of me wanted to see if I could do it myself. And associated with that was realising early on that, if I wanted to be a professional writer, I needed to have a broad range of interests. It seemed to me that if I tucked myself away for several years writing a serious literary novel that no one read, then I was not going to exist for long as a professional writer. I wanted a few branches to my career. But mainly I wanted to write a crime novel because I loved reading them so much.'

There's a calm thoughtfulness to Disher as we chat. He's open, without being gregarious. He's known as a man who likes his solitude but is generous with his time and his answers. Listening back to our interview later, I'm struck by the feeling that I was absorbing lessons from a true master. Like Wyatt, Disher is a consummate professional of his craft. His peers at the Australian Crime Writers Association (ACWA) recognised something similar when they named Disher the winner of the 2018 Ned Kelly Lifetime Achievement Award. Though with the passing of the two Peters, Corris and Temple, that same year, some may posit that Disher now has few if any true peers in Australian crime writing.

'This year, we are honouring a giant not only of crime fiction but of Australian letters,' said ACWA Vice-Chair Robert Goodman in the official Recognition Speech. For his own part, when I ask Disher now about the honour, he says he was very touched. 'Part of me joked that it's an old farts award and it's time to put up my pen. But by the same token it was nice to be appreciated like that. I value it for sure.'

In 2019, Disher underlined again why no one wants him to put up his pen. His latest novel, *Peace*, is a scorching tale that sees the return of exiled constable Paul 'Hirsch' Hirschhausen from the outstanding *Bitter Wash Road*, a standalone in 2013 that no longer stands alone. Set in a dusty and remote farming community, wheat and wool country a few hours north of Adelaide, *Peace* adds to the burgeoning reputation of Australian rural crime. It's a book with numerous plaudits attached from Australian crime writers who've followed in Disher's footsteps. 'Disher is the gold standard for rural noir,' says Chris Hammer, who has earned plenty of plaudits himself for his outstanding rural noir tales *Scrublands* and *Silver*.

Having now written 50 books, Disher says he's launched new series (for example, after six straight Wyatt books, he shelved the professional thief for more than a decade and began his popular series starring Mornington Peninsula detectives Hal Challis and Ellen Destry) and written standalones to keep pushing his own boundaries, to try something different. 'That's been the main impulse I think,' he says. 'To keep myself fresh as a writer. Because each different sort of book poses different problems, which I embrace if you like.'

Switching between his series and standalones over the past 30 years, not to mention the other types of books he's written, including young adult and children's fiction (though Disher has focused on crime the past decade), ensures he's not following the same pattern over and over. He says he has a different way of thinking for each book and character. 'As for choosing the setting of *Bitter Wash Road* and *Peace*, I don't know if you've heard the term Outback Noir – it's a big thing in Australia at the moment – but I set those novels in that part of South Australia because that's where I grew up, simply, I wasn't trying to get on a bandwagon. Though *Bitter Wash Road* predates a lot of it, like *The Dry* and *Scrublands*.'

A need to break patterns was what prompted the launch of his award-winning Peninsula series back in 1999. Disher says he wrote *The Dragon Man*, his first Challis and Destry novel, because he needed a break from Wyatt after writing a book a year for six years. 'The books were starting to become a bit formulaic, in that Wyatt identifies a place to rob, puts a gang together to help him, gets betrayed, then he has to get his revenge or get his money back or whatever it may be,' says Disher. 'I managed to keep them fresh and interesting in each book, I hope, but for me as a writer I wanted something different.'

That something different was a series set near where he lives – not that being so close to home was Disher's original intention. 'I thought I was going to write police procedurals set in Melbourne, but I'd recently moved down to the Mornington Peninsula and coincidentally three young women had been raped and murdered in Frankston, which is an outer suburb of Melbourne really and the top of the Mornington Peninsula. I was in the local milk bar about a month after I moved to the peninsula, and I heard a group of women talking about how their behaviour had changed because they couldn't let their daughters catch the bus to netball anymore. So, I had a powerful sense of community fear, and I realised this was going to be my setting, the Mornington Peninsula, which is quite a distinctive region geographically and socially. It was a perfect setting for this new type of writing for me.'

The Challis and Destry novels aren't necessarily whodunnits, says Disher, more whydunnits where he is interested in criminal personality, or what derails someone in life.

Having been in the Australian crime writing scene for almost 30 years – as well as finding some success internationally – Disher has witnessed the growing appetite for antipodean noir (or Southern Cross Crime, if you will). One of the reasons he thinks crime fiction is growing in popularity is because of what it has to offer. 'Good crime fiction I think tells us about the world we live in, and a lot of literary fiction doesn't do that. Literary fiction may be beautifully written and tackle interesting ideas and all the rest of it, but you don't learn a lot about the world we live in. The corruption in high places, or the effect of homophobia or sexism on society, social justice issues, all those sorts of things we find in crime novels.'

For those looking to join the antipodean crime wave, Disher has some advice. First, it should go without saying but too often he came across the opposite when he did manuscript assessments and taught creative writing: if you want to be a writer, be a reader. Then, once steeped in the type of storytelling you enjoy and want to write, aspiring novelists should write the book that only you can write, says Disher. 'At the moment there's this new popular trend in Australia in crime fiction for Outback Noir or rural noir, and I would hate for new crime writers to come along and think "well okay, I should write an Outback novel because it sells" and think they can choose a dusty little Outback town with a secret and there's a novel. Because if you don't know Outback towns and you don't know crime fiction it's not going to work. It has to be a book that's true to you and you are true to. A book that only you can write. It shouldn't be a cheap copy of something that's gone before.'

So forget the trends and look within. 'Yeah, that would be my strong advice to a new writer,' says Disher, 'write about material that you're strongly connected to.' Wise words from the master.

* * *

Author note: This chapter has been written specifically for this book and hasn't been published elsewhere. It is based on an interview with Garry Disher in October 2019.

Appendix

NED KELLY AWARDS WINNERS

Best Novel

2019: *The Lost Man* by Jane Harper

2018: *Crossing the Line* by Sulari Gentill

2017: *Police at the Station and They Don't Look Friendly* by Adrian McKinty

2016: *Before it Breaks* by Dave Warner

2015: *Eden* by Candice Fox

2014: *In the Morning I'll Be Gone* by Adrian McKinty

2013: *Blackwattle Creek* by Geoffrey McGeachin

2012: *Pig Boy* by JC Burke

2011: *The Diggers Rest Hotel* by Geoffrey McGeachin

2010: *Wyatt* by Garry Disher

2009: *Deep Water* by Peter Corris & *Smoke and Mirrors* by Kel Robertson

2008: *Shatter* by Michael Robotham

2007: *Chain of Evidence* by Garry Disher

2006: *Crook as Rookwood* by Chris Nyst & *The Broken Shore* by Peter Temple

2005: *Lost* by Michael Robotham

2004: *Degrees of Connection* by Jon Cleary

2003: *White Dog* by Peter Temple

2002: *Death Delights* by Gabrielle Lord

2001: *Dead Point* by Peter Temple & *The Second Coming* by Andrew Masterson

2000: *Shooting Star* by Peter Temple

1999: *Amaze Your Friends* by Peter Doyle

1998: no award given

1997: *The Brush-Off* by Shane Maloney

1996: *The Malcontenta* by Barry
Maitland & *Inside Dope* by
Paul Thomas

Best First Novel

2019: *The Ruin* by Dervla
McTiernan
2018: *The Dark Lake* by Sarah
Bailey
2017: *The Dry* by Jane Harper
2016: *Resurrection Bay* by
Emma Viskic
2015: *Quota* by Jock Serong
2014: *Hades* by Candice Fox
2013: *The Midnight Promise* by
Zane Lovitt
2012: *The Cartographer* by Peter
Twohig
2011: *Prime Cut* by Alan Carter
2010: *King of the Cross* by Mark
Dapin
2009: *Ghostlines* by Nick Gadd
2008: *The Low Road* by Chris
Womersley
2007: *Diamond Dove* by Adrian
Hyland
2006: *Out of the Silence* by
Wendy James

2005: *A Private Man* by Malcolm
Knox
2004: *The Walker* by Jane
Goodall & *Junkie Pilgrim*
by Wayne Grogan (tie)
2003: *Blood Redemption* by Alex
Palmer
2002: *Apartment 255* by Bunty
Avieson & *Who Killed
Angelique* by Emma Darcy
2001: *Last Drinks* by Andrew
McGahan
2000: *The Wooden Leg of
Inspector Anders* by
Marshall Browne
1999: *The Last Days* by Andrew
Masterson
1998: no award given
1997: *Bad Debts* by Peter
Temple & *Get Rich Quick*
by Peter Doyle (tie)
1996: *Dark Angel* by John Dale

Best Teenage/Young Adult

2002: *Blue Murder* by Ken Catran

NGAIO MARSH AWARDS WINNERS

Best Novel

2019: *This Mortal Boy* by Fiona Kidman

2018: *Marlborough Man* by Alan Carter

2017: *The Last Time We Spoke* by Fiona Sussman

2016: *Trust No One* by Paul Cleave

2015: *Five Minutes Alone* by Paul Cleave

2014: *Where the Dead Men Go* by Liam McIlvanney

2013: *Death on Demand* by Paul Thomas

2012: *Luther: The Calling* by Neil Cross

2011: *Blood Men* by Paul Cleave

2010: *Cut & Run* by Alix Bosco

Best First Novel

2019: *Call Me Evie* by JP Pomare

2018: *All Our Secrets* by Jennifer Lane

2017: *Dead Lemons* by Finn Bell

2016: *Inside the Black Horse* by Ray Berard

DAVITT AWARDS WINNERS

Best Adult Novel

2019: *The Ruin* by Dervla McTiernan

2018: *And Fire Came Down* by Emma Viskic

2017: *The Dry* by Jane Harper

2016: *Resurrection Bay* by Emma Viskic

2015: *Big Little Lies* by Liane Moriarty

2014: *Dark Horse* by Honey Brown

2013: *Mad Men, Bad Girls and the Guerrilla Knitters Institute* by Maggie Groff

2012: *A Decline in Prophets* by Sulari Gentill

2011: *Cold Justice* by Katherine Howell

2010: *Sharp Shooter* by Marianne Delacourt

2009: *A Beautiful Place to Die* by Malla Nunn

2008: *Frantic* by Katherine Howell

2007: *Undertow* by Sydney Bauer

2006: *The Butterfly Man* by Heather Rose

2005: *Malicious Intent* by Kathryn Fox
2004: *Due Preparations for the Plague* by Janet Turner Hospital
2003: *Baby Did a Bad, Bad Thing* by Gabrielle Lord & *Blood Redemption* by Alex Palmer
2002: *A Simple Death* by Carolyn Morwood
2001: *Eye to Eye* by Caroline Shaw

Debut Book

2019: *Eggshell Skull* by Bri Lee
2018: *The Dark Lake* by Sarah Bailey
2017: *Ghost Girls* by Cath Ferla
2016: *Resurrection Bay* by Emma Viskic & *Risk* by Fleur Ferris
2015: *Intruder* by Christine Bongers
2014: *Burial Rites* by Hannah Kent
2013: *Mad Men, Bad Girls and the Guerrilla Knitters Institute* by Maggie Groff
2012: *Beyond Fear* by Jaye Ford

Readers' Choice

2019: *The Lost Man* by Jane Harper
2018: *Force of Nature* by Jane Harper
2017: *The Dry* by Jane Harper
2016: *Resurrection Bay* by Emma Viskic
2015: *Tell Me Why* by Sandi Wallace
2014: *Burial Rites* by Hannah Kent
2013: *Taman Shud: The Somerton Man* by Kerry Greenwood
2012: *The Brotherhood* by YA Erskine & *Beyond Fear* by Jaye Ford
2011: *The Old School* by PM Newton
2010: *Forbidden Fruit* by Kerry Greenwood
2009: *The Darkest Hour* by Katherine Howell
2008: *Scarlet Stiletto – The First Cut* by Lindy Cameron
2007: *Devil's Food* by Kerry Greenwood & *Silent Death: The Killing of Julie Ramage* by Karen Kissane
2006: *Heavenly Pleasures* by Kerry Greenwood & *Rubdown* by Leigh Redhead

2005: *Peepshow* by Leigh Redhead

2004: *Thicker Than Water* by Lindy Cameron

2003: *Skin Deep* by Cathy Cole

2002: *Bleeding Hearts* by Lindy Cameron

Best Young Adult Novel

2019: *Small Spaces* by Sarah Epstein

2018: *Ballad for a Mad Girl* by Vikki Wakefield

2017: *Frankie* by Shivaun Plozza

2015: *Every Word* by Ellie Marney

2014: *The Midnight Dress* by Karen Foxlee

2013: *The Tunnels of Tarcoola* by Jennifer Walsh

2012: *Surface Tension* by Meg McKinlay

2011: *A Girl Like Me* by Penny Matthews

2010: *Liar* by Justine Larbalestier

2009: *Genius Squad* by Catherine Jinks

2008: *The Night Has a Thousand Eyes* by Mandy Sayer

2007: *The Betrayal of Bindy Mackenzie* by Jaclyn Moriarty

2006: *Evil Genius* by Catherine Jinks

2005: *Devastation Road* by Joanna Baker

2004: *Muck-Up Day* by Ruth Starke

2003: *Fireworks and Darkness* by Natalie Jane Prior

2002: *Three-Pronged Dagger* by Kerry Greenwood

Best Children's Novel

2019: *Wakestone Hall* by Judith Rossell

2018: *The Turnkey* by Alison Rushby

2017: *Wormwood Mire: A Stella Montgomery Intrigue* by Judith Rossell

2016: *Friday Barnes, Under Suspicion* by RA Spratt

2015: *Withering-By-Sea* by Judith Rossell

2014: *Truly Tan: Spooked!* by Jen Storer

Kia ora rawa atu

While, in the words of my Oscar-winning compatriot Taika Waititi, "I did all the typing ... and all the words came from my head", this book wouldn't exist without the influence and talents of many other people. A full list would be encyclopaedic; here are a few key *kia ora*.

Thank you Barry Forshaw, who not only paved the way with his excellent series of reader's guides to the genre we both love, but generously introduced me to his publisher and recommend that I be the one to cover Australian and New Zealand crime writing.

Many thanks to the team at Oldcastle Books, particularly Ion, Clare, Ellie, and Claire.

Back in 2008 I'd just started at *NZLawyer* when I wrote a fiction review near deadline to fill an empty page in the magazine. Thanks to Darise Bennington for letting me cover two crime novels – sheesh, neither of us had any clue about all the places that would lead. *Kia ora* Darise for all your guidance, support, and friendship. And hey, we got you reading crime.

Thanks to all the newspaper and magazine editors who've given me rein to write features and reviews on many subjects. In particular, *kia ora* to Linda and Dionne at the *Herald*, Guy, Mark and Russell at the *Listener,* Rowena at *Good Reading,* Mark and Eleanor at *Sunday Star-Times,* Jo at *Latitude,* Kate at *Mystery Scene,* Steve at *The Spinoff* and *Newsroom,* and Jon at *Crimespree* for letting me fill your pages with coverage of antipodean crime.

Cheers to my FriendFeed and Petrona crime & mystery pals from my early blogging years.

Kia ora and rest easy to Bernadette, Maxine, Lou, and Ken.

Thanks to everyone involved with the Ngaio Marsh Awards over the past decade – so many judges, authors, libraries, publishers, media, and supporters. A special *kia ora* to Rachael, Marianne, Morrin, and Ruth of WORD Christchurch for all your support, every year.

The international crime writing community, overall, is a wonderful group of people. This bloke from the bottom of the world has been welcomed by authors, publications, and festivals organisers all over the world. I'm grateful to be a wee part of this tribe. *Kia ora.*

My love of stories, reading, research, and writing was started by my parents and stoked by the librarians and teachers in my hometown at the top of the South Island of New Zealand.

Kia ora to Mrs Gately, Mr Joyce, Mrs Sivak, Mr Ledingham, and Mrs Hall.

A special *kia ora rawa atu* to Mrs Clouston.

I read long ago that you could judge a man's worth by his friends. Thank you to all my amazing, crazy, cool mates spread across the world who've made my life infinitely better.

Finally, to my family. There aren't enough words to do you justice. Mum, Dad, and Claire, for loving me, challenging me, and supporting me through everything, over all my decades. To Helen and Madi, the two girls who've changed my life in adulthood. *Arohanui ahau ki a koe.*

Index of storytellers & screen stories